THE
LITTLE BROWN
ENCYCLOPEDIA
OF
INSECTS
AND
INVERTEBRATES

THE
LITTLE BROWN
ENCYCLOPEDIA
— OF —
INSECTS
— AND —
INVERTEBRATES

MAURICE BURTON
& ROBERT BURTON

LITTLE, BROWN AND COMPANY

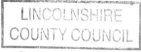

Contents

A LITTLE, BROWN BOOK

This edition first published 2002

This book is adapted from *The Little Brown Encyclopedia of Animals*
ISBN 0 316 86192 8

Production by Omnipress, Eastbourne
Printed in Singapore

Little, Brown
An imprint of Time Warner Books UK
Brettenham House, Lancaster Place
London WC2E 7EN

Introduction

It is usually stated that there are a million species of animals. More correctly, this should be at least a million known species. By 'known' is meant species that have been given a specific name and of which a description has been published in a recognised scientific journal. It is important to make this distinction because the truth is that there are not enough zoologists classifying animals to keep pace with the collection of new forms. In addition, there must be large numbers of species yet to be discovered, and estimates of the true number of animal species living today vary between three and ten million. The great majority of the million usually referred to are insects, of which there are at least 750,000. If we ever reach the point where all the species of insects have been described and named the total will probably be nearer three million.

The present day classification of animals emerged after a series of tentative attempts on the part of a number of authors to arrange the animals in orderly groups, but the real breakthrough came with the acceptance of Darwin's theory of natural selection and involved a long arrangement along evolutionary lines. The theory of evolution itself had been mooted long before Darwin's days, but his theory of how species arose gave the maximum publicity to an idea that had previously only been studied by a select few scholars.

Arrangement on an evolutionary basis meant that classification was based on the study of comparative anatomy. In practice, this meant putting the simplest, least organised animals at the top. The rest were arranged intermediately according to the degree of organisation in their bodily structures.

The most that can be done to represent the thousands of invertebrate animal species, and this is the purpose of this volume, is to give a skeletal representation in pictorial and textual form of the living members of this vast assemblage of organisms we refer to when we speak of insects and other invertebrates.

In the following pages, a selection of invertebrates known to be in existence today are detailed, comprising two main sections: the lower invertebrates and the higher invertebrates. A broad array of the phyla are illustrated and the effect is to provide within two covers a brief outline of the scope of the invertebrate world, its components arranged in their evolutionary sequence, so far as we know it.

The Lower Invertebrates

The invertebrates, or animals without backbones, include 21 phyla, all but one of which can be reasonably referred to as lower invertebrates, the exception being the phylum Arthropoda. The number of living species of lower invertebrates so far named and described is nearly a quarter of a million, but the actual number yet to be described must far exceed this. For example, the lower invertebrates include many small to minute parasitic worms and these have by no means been exhaustively studied. Probably every species in the animal kingdom is parasitized by several different kinds, and if this surmise is correct, it would mean that species of parasitic worms alone are numbered by the million instead of the 10,000 or so described to date.

The lower invertebrates are more diverse in form and structure than any other section of the animal kingdom. Their remains give us the earliest fossils known. These two facts taken together suggest that these animals represent early 'experimentation' in evolution, before the main pattern had emerged that would lead to the production of the higher animals. Looking at the various types they compromise it is as if attempts had been made to try this or that shape, this or that way of life, this or that type of nervous system and so forth.

Animal feeding and digestion is of various types, but in the main the digestive apparatus must follow fairly orthodox lines. The main differences between the various lower invertebrates lie in their shapes and in the development of the nervous system and the sense organs.

In the Protozoa, the single-celled animals, all the life processes take place within the confines of a single cell. The animals are sensitive but have no nerves, therefore no brain, and the special sense-organs do not go much beyond an eye-spot, a granule of pigment reacting to light, the simplest fore-runner of an eye.

In the next group, the Parazoa or sponges, there is a slight sensitivity but at best only scattered and very simple nerve-cells, and no sense organs. In the Cnideria, the anemones, jellyfishes and corals, the body is controlled by a simple network of nerve-cells and there may be, in rare instances, eye-spots and organs of balance, known as statocysts, although these are found only in those Cnideria, for example jellyfishes, that move about.

The remaining lower invertebrates have nerves. In some there is even a ganglion, a knot of nerve cells fore-shadowing the brain, and more or less of special sense-organs. In a few, such as the squid and octopuses the brain is of a fairly high order and the eyes are well developed, quite unlike anything found in other molluscs. Taken as a whole, however, the lower invertebrates are somewhat senseless animals – in more than one meaning of the term.

Most animals are what is known as bi-laterally symmetrical. That is, if a line is drawn down the long axis of the body the half on one side is the mirror image of the other half. Many of the lower invertebrates are radially symmetrical the body plan being apparently based on the spokes of a wheel, as in sea anemones, jellyfishes and starfishes. The bilateral symmetry is the only shape permitting segmentation leading to higher organisation of structure. Segmentation can readily be seen in the earthworm. Its body is divided into rings, or segments. This permits the elaboration of an efficient muscle system, and thus more controlled and co-ordinated movements, especially for locomotion. The classification of the lower invertebrates is as follows:

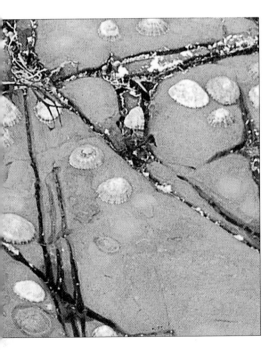

THE CLASSIFICATION OF THE LOWER INVERTEBRATES	
Phylum Protozoa	50,000 species
Phylum Mesozoa	50 species
Phylum Parazoa	2,500 species
Phylum Cnidaria	9,600 species
Phylum Ctenophora	80 species
Phylum Platyhelminthes	13,000 species
Phylum Nemertina	750 species
Phylum Aschelminthes	12,500 species
Phylum Acanthocephala	650 species
Phylum Entoprocta	60 species
Phylum Bryozoa or Polyzoa	4,000 species
Phylum Phoronida	15 species
Phylum Brachiopoda	260 species
Phylum Mollusca	128,000 species
Phylum Sipunculoidea	250 species
Phylum Echiuroidea	150 species
Phylum Annelida	8,700 species
Phylum Chaetognatha	50 species
Phylum Pogonophora	100 species
Phylum Echinodermata	44,066 species

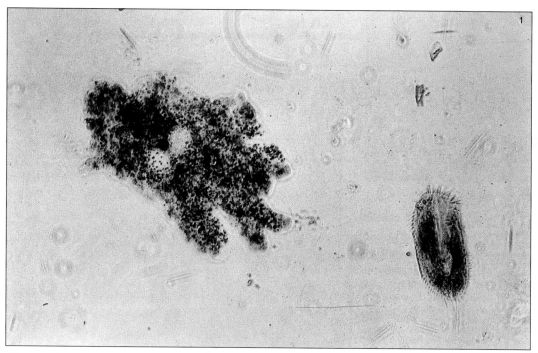

Amoeba

Amoebae form a group of the single-celled organisms called Protozoa. Protozoa means 'first animals'. These organisms have affinities with plants – some of them photosynthesise.

Like any cell the amoeba consists basically of an envelope containing the substance protoplasm. In the middle of the cell, surrounded by the protoplasm, is the nucleus, a body which can be thought of as a blueprint for the organisation of the cell's activities. If an amoeba is cut in two the half with the nucleus may survive and reproduce; the other moves around for a while but cannot digest its food, and when its reserves are gone it dies.

The protoplasm is not, as was once thought, a jelly; it has a very complicated structure, and consists of a cytoplasm divided into a granular endoplasm and at the ends of the pseudopodia, and elsewhere under the surface, a clearer layer known as ectoplasm.

Many amoebae

The name amoeba is applied not only to members of the genus *Amoeba* but to a range of different types of Protozoa with pseudopodia (see below) living in the sea, in fresh water, in damp soil and in the bodies of larger animals. They include some with shells, like *Arcella*, and also the half-dozen species that live in the human mouth and digestive system, one of which is the cause of amoebic dysentery (*Entamoeba*). Some

amoebae contain many nuclei, among them the giant *Chaos carolinensis*, which may measure up to $\frac{1}{5}$ in.

Amoeba proteus, the textbook amoeba, measuring about $\frac{1}{50}$ in., is just visible to the naked eye and may be found in fairly still fresh water. It moves about by extending a finger of protoplasm, called a pseudopodium ('false foot'). As the pseudopodium enlarges, the cell contents – protoplasm and nucleus – flow into it, while the rest of the cell contracts behind. Though it has no definite shape, the amoeba is not a shapeless sac of protoplasm, for it has a permanent hind end and forms its pseudopodium in a characteristic pattern according to the species.

Feeding

The amoeba feeds mainly on other Protozoa and also small rotifers. It does so by 'flowing' around them, the protoplasm completely surrounding the food to enclose it in a 'food vacuole' containing fluid in which the prey was swimming. Digestion is a similar process to that occurring in many other organisms: digestive juices are secreted into the food vacuole and the digestible parts are broken down and absorbed. The rest is merely left behind as the amoeba moves along.

This process is known as phagocytosis, from the Greek 'eating by cells'. In a similar process called pinocytosis, or 'drinking by cells', channels are formed from the cell surface, leading into the cell. Fluid is drawn into the channels and from their tips vacuoles are pinched off. The fluid is then absorbed into the protoplasm in the same way as the digested contents of the food vacuoles. This is a method of absorbing fluids in bulk into the cell.

1 *The well known one-celled animal, amoeba, showing large water excreting vacuoles. This picture includes a Stylonychian which belongs to another, ciliated, group of protozoans. (Magnified 150 times.)*

Water is continually passing in through the cell membrane as well as being brought in by phagocytosis and pinocytosis. Excess is pumped out by contractile vacuoles which fill with water and then collapse, discharging the water to the outside.

Reproduction

The amoeba reproduces itself by dividing into two equal parts, a process known as binary fission and taking less than an hour. It begins with the amoeba becoming spherical. The nucleus divides into two. The two halves move apart and the cell then splits down the middle.

Some species of amoebae can reproduce in a different manner. The nucleus divides into hundreds of small ones and each becomes surrounded by a little cytoplasm and a tough wall – all within the original cell. The resulting 'cysts' can survive if the water dries up and can be dispersed to found new populations. Larger cysts may be formed without reproduction taking place, when the whole cell surrounds itself with a thick wall. Though some amoebae reproduce sexually, *Amoeba proteus* has never been seen to do so.

Pushing or pulling?

The story of the amoeba illustrates not only the advances made in the last few decades in the techniques of microscopy but also

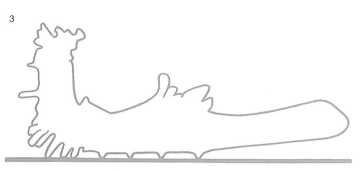

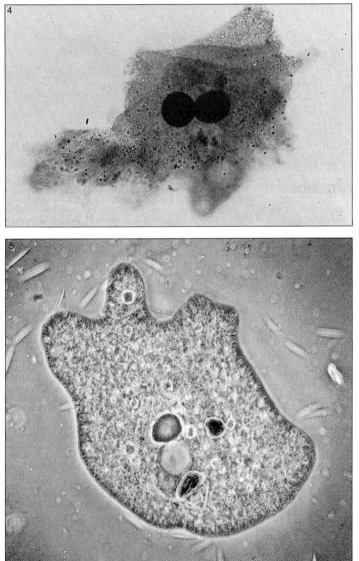

2 *Amoeboid movement – showing pseudopodia in action, from above.*
3 *Diagram of modern microscope's side view of amoeba moving to the right on small protoplasmic pegs with pseudopodium, or false-foot, extended.*
4 *Amoeba with nucleus, which controls cell, divided, prior to cell splitting into two.*
5 *Special light phase contrast microscope gives this beautiful view of amoeba showing food in vacuoles.*

the difficulties involved in research.

Years ago microscopists could watch amoeba only from above in the usual manner of looking at very small objects. From this angle one could see the pseudopodia advancing over the surface of the microscope slide and apparently in contact with it. In recent times a technique has been devised for watching it from the side and a new detail has come to light. In fact, when each pseudopodium moves forward it is supported by an extremely small peg of protoplasm which remains attached to the ground at one spot while the rest of the animal, raised just above the ground, advances over it. Finally, the pseudopodium is withdrawn and reincorporated into the body of the amoeba.

A number of theories of 'amoeboid movement' have been proposed over the last 20 years but its mechanism is still not thoroughly understood. One can see, under the higher powers of the microscope, the protoplasm streaming forwards along the centre of the pseudopodium and moving out to the sides at the tip in what has been descriptively named the 'fountain zone', and there acquiring a firmer consistency. At the same time the reverse change occurs at the 'tail', where the protoplasm resumes its forward flow.

What is still in doubt is whether the advancing protoplasm is being pushed forward from behind, like toothpaste in its tube, or pulled by changes in the proteins in the fountain zone. The problem is by no means trivial, for some of our own cells move in an amoeboid manner and its solution in terms of the behaviour of protein molecules could cast light on one of the basic properties of protoplasm.

phylum	**Protozoa**
class	**Sarcodina**
order	**Amoebida**

9

Bath sponge

The sponge seen in the bathroom is the fibrous skeleton of one of the lower forms of animal life. In life the gaps in the skeleton are filled with a yellowish flesh, the whole being covered with a dark purple skin. A sponge has no sense-organs and few specialized organs apart from chambers containing collared cells. At best there are a few scattered muscle cells and very simple nerve cells.

Although there are nearly 3,000 species of sponges, the most familiar is the group of half a dozen species of horny sponges known scientifically as

Spongia. On the market, bath sponges are given common names, such as fine turkey, brown turkey, honeycomb for Mediterranean sponges, and wool, velvet, reef, yellow and grass for Bahamas sponges. These names express mainly the varying textures of the fibres. There are many other names, but the fine turkey and the honeycomb are those most often seen for sale. They are found in warm seas only, at depths down to 600 ft. They are most numerous in the Mediterranean, particularly the eastern half, and in the Bahamas and Florida. Elsewhere, in tropical and sub-tropical waters, sponges are found of similar type but less durable or

pleasing texture, although in places, as in south-east Asia, there may be limited fisheries supplying a local market.

Sedentary habit
A sponge normally draws all it needs from the sea without departing from the spot on which the larva settled. The beating of the protoplasmic whips, or flagella, of its collared cells, which are grouped in rounded chambers in the network of canals running through the body, draws in currents of water. These enter through many minute pores in the skin. Having passed through these chambers the water is driven towards the surface and expelled with moderate force, through crater-like vents. In its course

▽ *Bath sponge growing in natural surroundings. They are found only in warm seas at depths down to 600 ft.*

△ *Curing sponges on Kalimnos, Greece. Greek islands are the centre of the sponge industry.*

▽ *The finished article which gives good service on bath night. Largely replaced by synthetic ones.*

and, when ripe, they burst from their capsule into the water canals and escape by the vents into the sea. They swim around until near another sponge and are drawn in by the water current entering through its pores. Inside, they travel through the canals until they meet an ovum, which one of them fertilises.

The ovum, once fertilised, begins to divide repeatedly to form an oval mass of cells, the embryo. Some of these put out flagella, and as they beat together, they cause the embryo to rotate. This breaks its capsule, and the embryo, now a free-swimming larva, swims out through one of the vents. For the next 24 hours it continues swimming in a spiral motion, with its flagella. Then the flagella begin to weaken, the larva sinks to the sea-bed, and is transformed into a small platelet of tissue, the size of a pin head. This is a new sponge.

Enemies

Sponges are virtually without enemies and subject to only one known disease. This is a fungal disease which was unknown until 1938, when it attacked sponges in the Bahamas and adjacent seas, almost wiping them out.

Sponge farming by cuttings

From the moment that the larva changes into the pinhead-sized sponge to the time this has grown large enough to be put on the market, 7 years must elapse. Then the pinhead would have grown to a purple-skinned sponge the size of a man's two fists. This gives us an idea of how long a sponge could live assuming no diver comes down to cut it from the rock and take it to the surface to be cured for market. Bath sponges 20 in. in diameter have been brought up. These were probably 20 or more years old.

You can cut a bath sponge into two and each half will heal the cut and grow into a new sponge. The same will happen if you cut it into 4, 6, 12, or even more pieces. A century ago Oscar Schmidt, the Austrian zoologist, suggested that sponges might be grown as one does plants, from cuttings. Fifty years later the idea was adopted by the British Colonial Office. Experiments were carried out in the Bahamas and elsewhere in the Gulf of Mexico, in growing sponges by cuttings, each fastened to a concrete disc, and all laid out in rows on the sea-bed. One misfortune after another dogged the experiments. But by 1938, sponge-farming was seen to be a practical proposition when some 600,000 tons of sponges were harvested from the Gulf of Mexico alone. That was the year the fungal disease struck, causing 90% mortality among bath sponges in the Bahamas and Florida.

through the sponge the water yields food-particles and oxygen and it leaves bearing waste products of digestion and respiration.

Sponges are almost completely still once the free-swimming larva has settled on a solid substratum — usually a rock or a large stone. There is, however, some evidence of limited movement, particularly in the young sponges, their speed being 1 in. in a fortnight. Some movement may be in response to adverse conditions.

Particulate feeders

We know more by inference than direct observation that sponges feed on bacteria and minute particles from the breakdown of plant and animal bodies. They are therefore particulate feeders, and scavengers.

Having no separate digestive system, food particles are taken into the collared cells which digest them and reject any inedible scraps. The food is then passed into the body by specialised migrating amoeba-like cells.

Ciliated larva

There are no males and females, ova and sperm being found in the same individual, but not in specialized reproductive organs. At various points in the body of the bath sponge, one of the body cells will be fed by neighbouring cells so that it grows noticeably large. Of the many thousands that do this, some are destined to become egg cells or ova. The others have a different fate. They subdivide repeatedly until masses of tiny cells are formed. These are the sperms,

phylum	**Parazoa**
class	**Gelatinosa**
order	**Keratosa**
family	**Spongidae**
genus & species	***Spongia officinalis*** bath sponge others

Anemone

'Anemone', from the Greek for wind, was first used for a flower in 1551. At first the marine animals that look like flowers were called plant-animals. The name 'sea-anemone' was not used until 1773. Today, marine zoologists almost invariably speak of the animals as anemones. That they are truly animals is no longer in doubt although the order to which they were assigned is still called the Anthozoa, that is, plant-animals. The basic differences between plants and animals are:

1 A plant manufactures its own food, by photosynthesis, using the green chlorophyll in its leaves; an animal takes solid food.

2 A plant is incapable of locomotion; an animal can move about.

3 A plant has no obvious sensitivity; an animal usually has recognisable sense-organs

There are exceptions to all three principles, especially among the lower plants and the lower animals, but these are good working guides.

A sea-anemone has simple sense-organs, takes solid food and, surprisingly, is capable of locomotion.

The most outstanding feature of sea-anemones is the variety of their colours and, in many species, the beauty of the patterns these make. Colours and patterns in higher animals are known to serve as camouflage, warning coloration, recognition marks and other utilitarian purposes. Sea-anemones neither need nor could use any of these; their colours and patterns consequently appear as pure art-form.

Long-lived and motile

Anemones are found only in the seas but there they are world-wide, from between tide-marks to the great depths of the ocean. They are most abundant in warm seas where they can reach up to 3 ft across. The smallest are little more than a pin's head, but this requires some explanation. Voracious feeders, anemones will eat any animal flesh they can catch and swallow, and they may swallow prey of large size relative to their own bulk. It is not unknown for one anemone to swallow another and they are not immune to each other's poison. They can, however, survive for a long time without food, gradually dwindling in size until quite minute. This may be one of the secrets of their long life—anemones have been kept in aquaria for as much as 100 years.

Sea-anemones are by no means 'rooted to the spot'. There are even burrowing anemones. Those that are normally seen fixed to a rock move by gliding on their base. Others somersault, bending over to take hold of the substratum with their tentacles, then letting go by the base and slipping this over to take hold beyond. A few species lie on their side to glide along, or blow themselves up, let go with their foot, and float away.

Stinging tentacle feeders

An anemone is a cylindrical bag with a ring

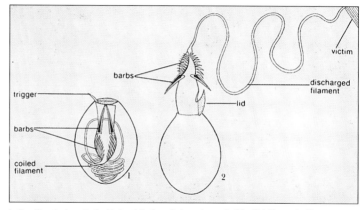

1. *Bag-like stinging cell of cnidarian full of paralysing poison and with coiled filament inside.*
2. *When the cell is activated by having its trigger touched or by food chemicals, the lid flies open and the coiled contents turn inside out, shooting the poison-filled filament into the body of its victim, which is also retained by the barbs.*

Plumose anemone, **Metridium senile**, *can be quite large, up to 9 in. high and 6 in. across the head.*

of tentacles surrounding the mouth on the upper surface. The opposite end is flattened and forms a basal disc, or foot, by which the animal sticks to a solid support. The interior of the bag is one large stomach, subdivided by curtains of tissue, or mesenteries, which hang down, partially dividing the stomach into eight compartments. Food is caught by the tentacles, which are armed with stinging cells. When a small animal, such as a shrimp or a fish, touches a tentacle the stinging cells come into action, paralysing and holding it. Adjacent tentacles also bend over to continue the stinging and holding until all begin to move towards the mouth, where the prey is engulfed. Indigestible remains from a meal are later voided through the mouth.

Stinging cells are a characteristic of the phylum Cnidaria to which sea-anemones belong, and included in the phylum are jellyfishes, the stinging cells of which are more familiar to most people. The Cnidaria are accordingly spoken of as stinging animals or, better still, nettle animals. Sting-cells, or nematocysts, are double-walled capsules, filled with poison, set in the outer surface of the tentacles. Each contains a coiled hollow thread, sometimes barbed at the base. At the outer end of the capsule is a thorn-like trigger. When this is touched the coiled thread is shot out. It turns inside-out as it is ejected, its fine point pierces the skin of the prey, and the paralysing poison flows down the hollow thread. Some kinds of nematocysts stick to the prey instead of piercing the skin, and in a third type the thread wraps itself around the victim. In addition to being triggered off by touch some nematocysts come into action as a result of

Left: Anemones can have little use for warning coloration or camouflage, so their colours appear as nature's art. This red anemone is **Tealia crassicornis.**
Right: **Anthopleura xanthogrammica**, the giant green anemone, is one of the few anemones to live in direct sunlight. Its green colour is due to minute one-celled green algae living in its cells and photosynthesising.

the presence of certain chemicals.

The body-wall of an anemone is made up of two layers of cells. There is, however, a good series of muscles. One set is longitudinal, running from the foot to the bases of the tentacles. The other is circular, running round the body. By the lengthening and contraction of these muscles the body can be drawn out or pulled in. There is also a series of retractor muscles which assist in the sudden withdrawal of body and tentacles. There are only very simple sense-organs and there is only a simple nerve system, a mere network of nerve-cells.

The action of the nematocysts is automatic, the result of the trigger being touched – it is a reflex action. A nerve strand also runs to the base of each nematocyst and it is these nerve strands that control the concerted action of the tentacles once a nematocyst has been discharged. The nerve network comes into action to cause the contraction of an anemone when it is touched. It can be made to expand again by adding a nutrient solution to the water. The slime from a mussel, for example, in the proportions of one part in a million, will make the body expand, and the tentacles extend, very slowly, perhaps taking an hour to come full out. Then the body sways slightly and the tentacles wave as if groping for food.

Sexual and asexual reproduction

Most anemones are either male or female, but some are hermaphrodite. In some, eggs and sperm are shed into the surrounding water, in others the larvae develop inside the parent body. The eggs vary in size, the largest, only $\frac{1}{25}$ in. wide, being a thousand times larger than the smallest. The fertilised eggs sink to the bottom and divide, or segment, to form oval larvae. These move about the seabed but finally each comes to rest, fastens itself to the bottom of the seabed,

grows tentacles and begins to feed.

An anemone can reproduce in other ways. It may split longitudinally to form separate individuals, or grow a ring of tentacles halfway down the body, after which the top half breaks away to give two anemones where there was one before. Young anemones may be formed, in some species, by fragmentation, or laceration. In fragmentation small anemones, complete with tentacles, arise from the base of a parent, become separated and move away. Laceration occurs in some species with a roving disposition. As the anemone glides over the rocks pieces of the base are ripped away and, being left behind, regenerate to form very minute but otherwise perfect anemones.

Enemies

Enemies are large sea-slugs, sea-spiders, fishes and sometimes starfishes and crabs.

Restless anemones

Aside from their diverse methods of locomotion, which are used but sparingly, anemones are always on the move, in a kind of slow-motion ballet. This led to an important discovery, the subject of which was the plumose anemone, 3–4 in. high, with a feathery crown of numerous small tentacles. When several scores of these are living in a large aquarium they are seen, at any given moment, to be in different attitudes. The body of some may be stretched up, others shortened and thickened; perhaps it is shortened and slender, its surface thrown into wrinkles, or it may be bent over to one side. The tentacles also will be in various stages of extension and retraction. Sometimes one or more anemones will be dilated and their tentacles withdrawn, so that they look like balloons anchored to the rock. Others may be so withdrawn that they look like buttons on

the rock. They may be watched for some minutes and no movement seen; but when anemones are watched closely and continuously against a black background, and their shapes drawn at intervals, they can be seen to be in continuous movement. This has been confirmed by other experimental methods, including a speeded-up film. Even when anemones are kept under conditions of constant temperature, in water free of food or undisturbed by vibrations the rhythm of activity continues. It can be interrupted by the presence of food or other disturbing factors, when the anemones react by more purposeful movements. One effect of this inherent rhythm of activity is to keep the animal in a state of constant preparedness for feeding, defence and other activities essential to the maintenance of life.

This movement is called the inherent rhythm of activity because it is self-starting and self-maintaining. It is common to all living organisms, as we now know. Obvious manifestations of it are seen in such processes as the beating of the heart, as well as in less obvious ways. When we sleep, for example, we do not simply lie still. Our bodies are in constant, if slow movement, in much the same way as the bodies of plumose anemones were shown to be.

phylum	**Cnidaria**
class	**Anthozoa**
order	**Actiniaria**
genera	***Actinia*** ***Anemonia*** ***Metridium*** *and others*

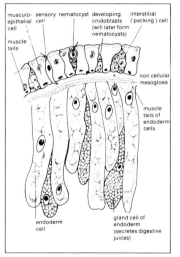

musculo-epithelial cell
sensory cell
nematocyst
developing cnidoblasts (will later form nematocysts)
interstitial ('packing') cell
muscle tails
non cellular mesogloea
muscle tails of endoderm cells
endoderm cell
gland cell of endoderm (secretes digestive juices)

△ Cross-section through body wall of hydra. It has only two layers of cells. The inner (endoderm) cells are for food breakdown. The outer (ectoderm) cells perform all other functions.

Hydra

The hydra's simple tubular body with its crown of tentacles has earned it a place in every elementary textbook of zoology and made it the object of many detailed studies. It is one of the few freshwater cnidarians, the bulk of which are marine. The body of a hydra is a bag whose wall is made up of two layers of cells separated only by a very thin layer of non-cellular material. The tentacles, which usually number 5 or 6 but may be as few as 4 or as many as 12, are hollow. They surround the mouth, while the other end of the body is a basal disc which normally anchors the hydra by a sticky secretion. Though often abundant in ponds, hydras frequently escape notice because of their habit of retracting into a tiny blob when disturbed.

Both tentacles and body are very extensible, for the bases of many of the cells are drawn out as muscle fibres—those of the outer layer of cells running lengthwise and those of the inner layer running around the body. The nervous system co-ordinating the movements is extremely simple, consisting of only a network of nerve cells. There is no brain of any sort.

There are three species of hydra in Britain. The green hydra **Chlorohydra viridissima**, which used to be called **Hydra viridis**, has short tentacles that are never as long as the body. The brown hydra, **Hydra (Pelmatohydra) oligactis**, has tentacles 4—5 times the length of the body, which is usually clearly divided into a stomach region and a narrower stalk. These two species are found throughout the world and their colours are caused by single-celled algae living within their cells. When animal prey is scarce the hydra draws nourishment from these algae. In both species the body may be as much as $1\frac{1}{5}$ in. long but it is usually much shorter. The third species found in Britain is the slender hydra **Hydra attenuata**. Its body is never much more than $\frac{1}{2}$ in. in length when fully extended, it lacks a stalk, and its tentacles never measure any more than 3 times the length of the body.

▽ Stuck to a water plant by special cells in their basal discs, five brown hydras hang in wait for the touch or taste of prey (7 × life size).

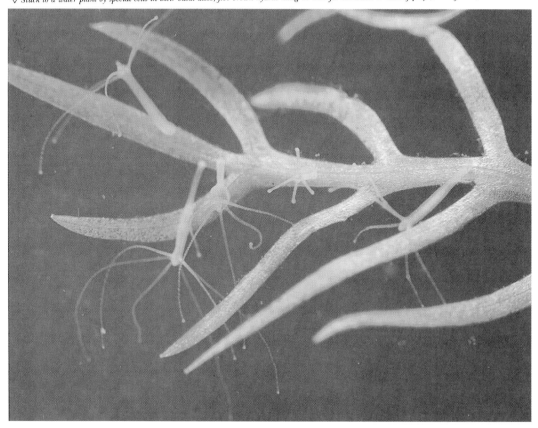

The stinging cells

Hydras, like their relatives the sea anemones and jellyfishes, have stinging cells with which they capture their prey. Each stinging cell or nematocyst is a rounded cell with a hollow coiled thread inside that can be shot out at great speed (see anemone, page 12). Hydra has four kinds. In one kind the thread is shot into the prey, injecting a poison. In a second kind the thread coils after it is shot out, and if the prey has bristles of any kind these tend to become entangled in it. The third type of nematocyst is probably truly defensive. It is shot out at animals not normally eaten by the hydra. The fourth kind of nematocyst is used to fasten the tentacles when the hydra is walking. This is not strictly a stinging cell, and is best referred to as a thread capsule. Some people prefer to use the term 'thread capsule' for all of them, because some do not sting.

When a nematocyst is discharged, its thread is forced inside out like a stocking, except that forces inside the thread itself are responsible for driving it out. The nematocysts used in capturing prey are discharged when the prey touches a little trigger on the side of the cell. Touch, however, is not enough, for the stinging cell must also be stimulated by chemicals in the water that are given out by the prey.

In all types, the stinging cells cannot be used again but are replaced by new ones migrating in from other parts of the body.

Progressing by somersaults

Although normally anchored, hydra can move about by creeping slowly on its basal disc in a sort of sliding movement. It can move more rapidly by a looping movement or a series of somersaults. To do this, a hydra bends over and gets a grip with special thread capsules on the tentacles. It lets go with its basal disc and brings this over in turn, very much like somebody doing 'cartwheels'. Hydras can also float at the surface of the water buoyed up by gas bubbles given out by the basal disc. The characteristic feature of the behaviour of hydras is that they suddenly contract into a tight ball every 5 or 10 minutes, for no obvious reason. This happens less often at night than by day.

Snagging its prey

The diet includes insect larvae, water fleas, worms, even newly-hatched fishes and tadpoles. Between meals the tentacles are held outstretched and more or less still, but at the approach of prey they start to writhe and later they bend in towards the open mouth. They will do these things if offered only extracts from other animals without

△ *Murder in miniature: after paralysing a water flea with stinging cells and drawing it in with sticky threads and tentacles, a hydra stretches its mouth round an outsize victim.*

▽ *Coelenterate mealtime: the green hydra at left is stinging a water flea into submission, the one at right is swollen with similar repast (9 × life size).*

△ Chips off the old block: a parent hydra with two buds, one advanced, one very very young.

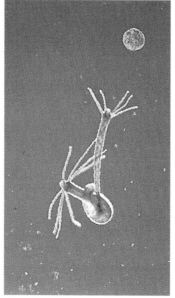

△ Budded hydra almost ready to break free while a **Volvox**-like 'plant animal' just escapes.

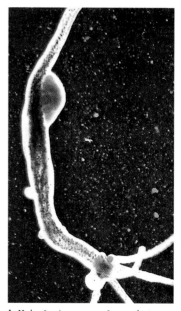

△ Hydra forming an ovary for sexual reproduction. It does this in harsh conditions.

any solids. For example, the juice from crushed water fleas alone will make a hydra go through the motions of putting food into its mouth. In fact a single chemical – glutathione – is responsible. If, however, the prey touches the tentacle the threads of the nematocysts are shot out, it is caught, held and paralysed, then carried to the mouth and swallowed. The mouth can open wide enough to take in animals that are themselves wider than the body of the hydra, which will stretch to accommodate them. Once inside the baglike body of the hydra, the prey is partially digested by enzymes given out by the inner layer of cells. Small particles breaking off are engulfed by individual cells for the final stages of digestion and indigestible particles are rejected through the mouth.

While food is in the body whiplike flagella on the cells of the inner layer are stirring the food around the inside of the body, a churning which aids digestion.

Multiplying in two ways

Hydra reproduce both sexually and by budding. Most species of hydra reproduce sexually in autumn or early winter although some do so in spring or early summer. One thing that can cause sexual reproduction, even out of season, is an accumulation of carbon dioxide in the water – as happens when a number of hydras are overcrowded. There are no special reproductive organs but small cells appear as bulges on the body in the upper half. Ovaries which are borne on different individuals in most species appear lower down on the body, also as bulges, each containing a single large eggcell, or ovum. The ripe ovum pushes through the outer layer of the hydra's body and the cells around it form a little cup or

cushion for the ovum. The male cells or sperms are shed into the water where they swim about and eventually reach the ova and fertilise them. The embryo which results from the division of the fertilised ovum secretes around itself a hard, sticky yellow shell $\frac{1}{50}$ to $\frac{1}{25}$ in. across. The shell may be smooth on the outside or spiny, according to the species. Thus enclosed, the embryo can survive drying and freezing. After lying dormant for 3–10 weeks it breaks out of its capsule, grows tentacles and becomes a new hydra, a perfect miniature of the adult.

Budding technique

New hydras can also be formed by buds. Each bud begins as a little bump on the side of the body. This grows out, and an opening appears at its free end. Tentacles are pushed out all round the mouth and finally the bud breaks away from the parent, settles down and grows into a new hydra, the whole process occupying 2 days, and a single hydra may bear several buds at once.

Inside-out hydras

In Greek mythology Hercules found himself trying to kill a monster called Hydra which had many heads. As fast as Hercules cut off one head another grew in its place. In 1744, Abraham Trembley, Swiss tutor to the children of the Comte de Bentinck, published his story of another hydra – the animal we are concerned with here. Trembley had found that a complete hydra would be regenerated from only ¼th of the parent body. He also succeeded in turning these animals inside out, a remarkably delicate operation which he performed by threading them on horse hairs. Trembley showed that the hydras would survive even this drastic operation. These experiments caught on

and for a while became very popular among certain scientists. More recently, they have been pursued in much greater detail. We now know that even tinier pieces of hydra, even a piece only $\frac{6}{1000}$ in. long, will grow into a new hydra provided that cells from both layers of the wall of the parent body are present. Even if the cells are separated into a mush of independent cells, these will come together to form a new hydra. The experiments are called 'Dissociation and Regeneration'.

We also know now that when a hydra is turned inside out it gets back to normal because the cells of the two layers migrate past each other to get into their proper positions. In fact, hydras are continually remodelling themselves and replacing old cells with new. If the tissues just below the tentacles of a hydra are marked with dye, they can be seen to move gradually down to the basal disc, eventually being lost and replaced by growth of new cells in the region from which they started.

phylum	**Cnidaria**
class	**Hydrozoa**
order	**Hydrida**
family	**Hydridae**
genera & species	***Chlorohydra viridissima*** green hydra ***Hydra attenuata*** slender hydra ***H. oligactis*** brown hydra others

Coral

Corals are polyps similar to anemones (see page 12) except that they are supported by a hard chalky skeleton. This, often white when dead, is covered in life with a continuous layer of flesh from which the polyps spring, and the whole is often beautifully coloured. The true corals, or stony corals as they are often called, may be either solitary or colonial. In the first a single polyp lives on its own, seated in a chalky cup or on a mushroom-shaped chalky skeleton. The colonial corals are made up of a sheet of tissue, formed by hundreds or thousands of polyps, covering the chalky skeleton. They may be tree-, cup- or dome-shaped, made up of flattened plates or branching like stag's horns.

There are also soft corals, some of which are precious. They are not true corals. One important difference is that their tentacles, instead of being simple as in the true corals and sea-anemones, are fringed, and each polyp has eight tentacles instead of, as in true corals, six or some multiple of six. Soft corals are usually tree-like and the centres of the stems and branches are strengthened by a chalky material, coloured red or black, and this, stripped of its flesh, gives the precious corals of commerce. Related to the precious corals are the sea-fans, the stems and branches of which are strengthened by a flexible horny material. Another relative is the beautiful organ-pipe coral, a mass of vertical tubes joined at intervals throughout their length by thin horizontal plates. The skeleton is reddish-purple and the polyps a pale lilac. When expanded these look like delicate flowers.

Tropical reef builders

Corals live in all seas, but few are found in temperate and polar regions compared with those found in the tropics—and in particular the reef-builders. Thousands of miles of tropical shores, especially in the Indian Ocean, are edged with reefs. In places, barrier reefs are formed, many miles offshore, like the Great Barrier Reef, which runs for 1 200 miles parallel with the northeast coast of Australia. In mid-ocean, especially in the Pacific, are ring-shaped atolls made of living coral, topping accumulations of dead coral skeletons, which in places go down to about a mile deep.

Birth of a reef

Reef-building corals are found north and south of the equator about as far as the 25th line of latitude, where the temperature of the sea does not fall much below 18°C/65°F. Each begins as a larva which, after swimming about for a while, settles on the bottom and changes into a polyp. A small lump appears on its side. This is a bud. It gets bigger, a mouth appears at its free end and a crown of tentacles grows around the mouth. The bud then continues to grow until it is the same size and shape as the parent, but without becoming separated from it. By repeated budding of the parent stock, and of the new growths formed from it, a colony numbering sometimes hundreds of thousands is formed. Between them they build a common skeleton, which in the end may be several feet high and the same across. Since all the polyps are in close connection with each other they are fed communally by their many mouths and stomachs.

Living animal traps

Corals, whether solitary, reef or soft, feed like sea-anemones. The tentacles are armed with stinging cells by which small swimming animals are paralysed and then pushed into the mouth at the centre of the ring of tentacles. In reef corals the polyps are withdrawn during the day, so the surface of each coral mass is more or less smooth. As night falls and the plankton animals rise into the surface waters, the polyps and their tentacles become swollen with water drawn in through the mouth by currents set up by cilia on the skin. The polyps now stand out on the surface, their delicate tentacles forming a semi-transparent pile in which are many mouths waiting to receive prey. The seemingly inert coral has been converted into a huge trap for any small animals which pass nearby—underlining the relationship with anemones.

The polyps of some corals have short tentacles, which do not carry food to the mouth. Instead, it is passed to the mouth by the cilia coating the tentacles.

There has always been some doubt, however, whether this was their only method of feeding. In coral tissues live microscopic single-celled plants known as zooxanthellae. It has been supposed that these two, the polyps and the zooxanthellae, were living in symbiosis: that the zooxanthellae received shelter and used the waste products from the coral, while the coral benefited from oxygen given off by its plant guests. Some scientists maintained that in addition the coral fed on the surplus populations of the plants.

This has been disputed, and one reason why it was hard to reach the truth is that digestion is very rapid. Consequently no animal food is found in the coral stomachs by day, therefore it has been assumed that they must be feeding on something else and, so it was argued, they must be eating the zooxanthellae. On the other hand, the tentacles react to animal food only, suggesting that corals are wholly carnivorous. Moreover, if coral polyps are deprived of animal food they soon shrink, showing signs of malnutrition. These are only a few of the arguments and they are enough to indicate the causes of disagreement.

From investigations carried out about 1960 by TF Goreau in the West Indies it seems that the zooxanthellae help the corals to grow by removing carbon dioxide from their tissues. Corals grow best in bright light, less well in dull light when zooxanthellae are fewer, and least of all in darkness when their zooxanthellae have been killed off by lack of sunlight. This alone suggests that there is a close link between the rate of growth of the coral and the presence of tiny plants in its tissues.

Walking corals

The majority of corals are sedentary. The original meaning of this word is 'to sit for long periods', but in zoology it is used more to indicate animals that are permanently fixed to the substratum. There is, however, at least one coral that moves about, but it does not travel under its own steam. It represents a very picturesque example of symbiosis, or living together for mutual benefit.

In October 1967, TF Goreau and Sir Maurice Yonge were exploring the Great Barrier Reef of Australia when they discovered on the lee side of the reef, on a muddy bottom, small corals, less than an inch across, which moved about over the mud. They were able to take some to the laboratory and watch them in an aquarium.

The coral *Heteropsammia michelinii* is solitary, with usually one polyp seated on the limy base, although sometimes there may be two or even three polyps on the same base. This coral belongs to the same kind as those that form the reefs, but its limy skeleton contains a cavity and in the cavity lives a marine worm. The worm drives its head into the mud to extract edible particles from it, in the usual manner of a worm, but as it feeds it travels along dragging the coral with it.

phylum	Coelenterata
class	Anthozoa
order	Scleractinia
genera	*Fungia, Porites, Heteropsammia* others

▽ *Diagram of the basic colony of the **Heliopora** blue coral shows the shape of the hard, chalky skeleton (in red) and the polyps which grow from it (top).*

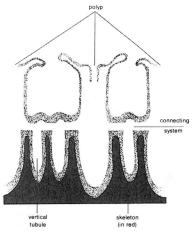

polyp

connecting system

vertical tubule

skeleton (in red)

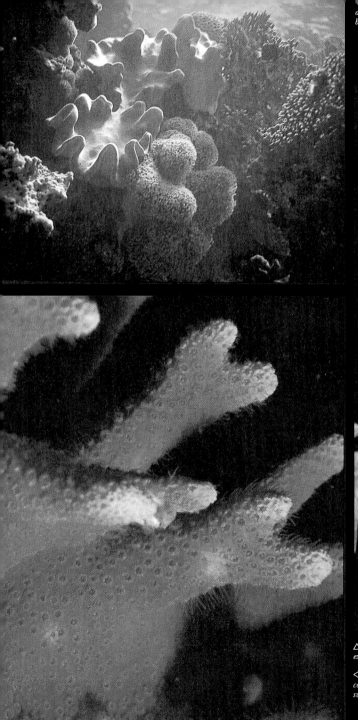

◁ This assortment gives a good idea of the different types of coral which will grow side by side to form a coral reef.

△ All systems 'go': the polyps of a coral, fully extended while feeding at night.

◁ A closer view of feeding polyps of a hard coral show the fine, whiskery tentacles that sweep the surrounding water for food.

▷ *Living polyps protrude from branches of staghorn coral off Mauritius.*

▷▷ *Unidentified shallow-water coral in the Seychelles has a squat, bunched structure.*

▷ *Fish swarm around a coral reef precipice in the Red Sea.*

Jellyfish

Jellyfish are free-swimming relatives of sea anemones, corals and hydroids, all belonging to the phylum Cnidaria. In the life cycles of many cnidarians there are two distinct phases. One is a free-living jellyfish, or medusa, that reproduces sexually, while the other develops from an embryo and is an anchored, or sessile, polyp, or colony of polyps, that in turn buds off jellyfish. One or other phase may be dominant and the other less important or even non-existent. The large jellyfishes make up one class, the Scyphozoa (or Scyphomedusae), in which the polyp stage is very small. Attention will be concentrated here on this group.

Upside-down hydra

The typical jellyfish is umbrella-shaped, globular or conical with 4 or 8 tentacles around the margin, or many tentacles may form a ring around the margin. Under the umbrella, and like a handle to it, is the mouth, leading into the digestive cavity. The mouth is drawn out at the corners into four long lips. The basic form of the body of the jellyfish can best be understood by comparison with that of hydra. The body of hydra consists essentially of two layers of cells forming a sac and separated by a very thin layer of non-cellular material, mesogloea. In the jellyfish the mesogloea is very thick. Although the body of a jellyfish is more elaborate than that of hydra it still has the same two-layered structure and ring of tentacles around the mouth.

Some common jellyfish

A jellyfish found in seas throughout the world and which is common off the coasts of Europe is *Aurelia aurita*. It grows to nearly 1½ ft across, with many very short tentacles. The blue, yellowish, reddish or brown jellyfish *Cyanea*, also known as sea blubber, can reach 6 ft across in Arctic waters but is usually less than half that. The jellyfish *Chrysaora* has 24 tentacles, and these may be 20 yd long in one species. Around the centre of its white or yellowish disc there is often a brownish ring from which streaks of the same colour radiate. Another common jellyfish is *Rhizostoma*, or 'the root-mouthed', named for the shape of its lips. It is a whitish dome, about a foot across, with a deep purple rim. It has no tentacles but is easily recognized by the cauliflower-like oral lips. In the United States it is called 'cabbage blebs'. Some jellyfish are luminescent and one of the most intense, which is occasionally found in north European waters, is *Pelagia noctiluca*.

Different ways of feeding

Jellyfish swim by rhythmic pulsations of the umbrella or bell. The movement is very like an umbrella being opened and shut slowly. It is co-ordinated by a very simple nervous system and by sense organs around the edge that are sensitive to light, gravity and chemicals in the water. Jellyfish are carnivorous and many of them capture fish, shrimps and other animals on their trailing

*The polyp generation of **Aurelia aurita**, like all other jellyfish, is a small sedentary phase passing the winter hanging from a rock. In spring the polyp becomes divided by transverse grooves, a process known as strobilisation, until it looks like a pile of saucers.*

tentacles, paralyse them with their stinging cells and transfer them to the mouth. *Aurelia* catches fish when young, but once grown to about 1 in. across feeds in quite a different way on small planktonic animals. These are trapped in sticky mucus all over the surface of the body and are driven by cilia to the rim. There the accumulating blobs are licked off by the 4 long oral lips. Further cilia propel the food in currents of water into the digestive cavity, from which a system of branching, cilia-lined canals radiate out to the rim, carrying food to all parts of the body. *Rhizostoma* feeds in the manner of a sponge, drawing in small planktonic animals by means of ciliary currents through thousands of separate mouths on the greatly elaborated oral lips. It is these mouths and the many little sensory palps on the oral lips that give the

jellyfish its characteristic cauliflower appearance. Another plankton feeder is a tropical jellyfish *Cassiopeia* which lies mouth upwards on the sea bottom in shallow water, pulsating its bell gently and capturing plankton with its lips as it is wafted by. It has symbiotic algae in its oral lips which benefit from the sunlight falling on them (see also anemone *Anthopleura*, page 13).

Piles of saucers

The common *Aurelia* is readily recognised by the four nearly oval purple or lilac reproductive organs, ovaries in the females, testes in the males. These lie in pouches in the digestive cavity but show through the transparent bell. The male sheds his sperm into the sea and these are wafted to the female and taken in along with her food. The eggs are fertilised and develop for a

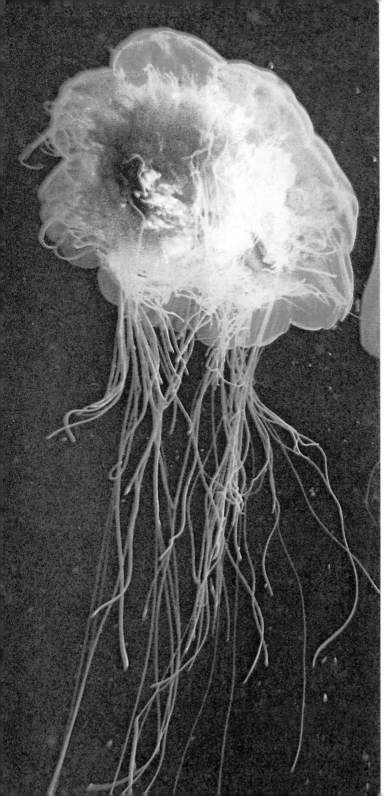

while in pouches on the oral lips. They are eventually set free as tiny planula larvae which soon attach themselves to seaweed or stone and develop into small polyps, known as scyphistomas or hydratubas, each with 16 tentacles. From the base of each, stolons, like runners of strawberry plants, grow out and new polyps develop on them. Each polyp eventually gives rise in the following winter to a number of young jellyfish called ephyra larvae, not round like the adult, but with the edge of the bell drawn out into 8 arms, notched at the tips. To do this, the polyp becomes pinched off into segments so it resembles a pile of lobed saucers. Then the tissue connecting these saucers contracts and snaps and each one swims off as a little ephyra. The growing ephyras transform gradually into adults by filling in the spaces between the arms.

An alternation of forms like this is typical of these jellyfish, though, in *Pelagia*, the egg develops directly into ephyras.

Sea wasps

Jellyfishes are practically all water. A jelly-fish stranded on the shore will soon vanish under the hot rays of the sun leaving little more than a patch of water in the sand. Their bodies are nearly 99% jelly and the whole body contains less than 5% organic matter. Yet jellyfishes can be extremely venomous as anyone knows who has hauled on a rope covered in long trailing tentacles. The stings of jellyfishes come from the many stinging cells or nematocysts which shoot out a poisonous thread when touched. The severity of the sting depends very much on the number of nematocysts discharged and also on the type of jellyfish. The most venomous jellyfishes are those living in the coral seas and the least trouble-some are those in temperate seas, but even these, if enough tentacles are allowed to touch our bodies, can sometimes lead to a loss of consciousness and, in the case of one bather, to drowning. This kind of accident is happily very rare. The most venomous jellyfishes belong to what are known as the Cubomedusae, so called because of their somewhat squarish shape. They range in size from as small as grapes to as large as pears and have four tentacles or four groups of tentacles. Some of these, like bathers, seem to prefer quiet shallow waters in the warmer seas, and are par-ticularly troublesome around the northern Australian coasts, the Philippines and Japan. They have been called sea wasps and they can kill in as short a time as half a minute, usually in a quarter of an hour, the victim dying in excruciating pain.

| phylum | **Cnidaria** |
| class | **Scyphozoa** |

◁ *Young* **Cyanea** *or sea blubber. This is the giant among jellyfish, sometimes 6 ft across with trailing tentacles 200 ft long.*

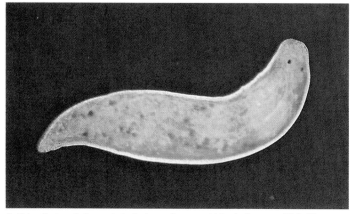

△ Not a sliced unripe banana but a freshwater flatworm rejoicing in the name of **Dalyellia**, enlarged 110 × natural size. These flatworms normally get about by crawling on a track of slime.

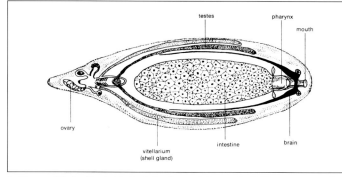

△ Diagram of the 'working parts' of a similar flatworm (after von Graff). The nervous system is simple and very primitive; a flatworm does not die if it loses its brain in an injury.

△ Land planarian on a Malayan forest floor. These tropical land-living species grow large.

Flatworm

Free-living flatworms are of great interest to scientists because of the light they shed on animal behaviour at a low level. There are three classes of flatworms: a variety of free-living forms and also the parasitic flukes and the tapeworms. Only the free-living Turbellaria will be considered here. They are soft-bodied, unsegmented and generally flattened worms. The planarians of our rivers and ponds are the best known. They range in size from microscopic to, exceptionally, well over a foot long in the case of certain terrestrial species in humid tropical forests.

Living without a brain

Turbellarians live mainly in fresh or salt water. Those living on land are restricted to moist places and are mainly tropical, although there is one, *Rhynchodermus terrestris*, like a small slug, ¼ in. long, sometimes as much as 1 in., dark slate grey, found under the bark of decaying trees in Britain. Turbellarians usually move about in two ways. Most of the time they crawl on a track of slime laid down by their undersurface, movement being due to cilia beating against the track. At other times they move more rapidly, by means of muscular contractions. Certain freshwater species move about over the surfaces of such animals as crustaceans and snails by alternately attaching themselves by a sucker at the hind end and by tentacles at the other.

The nervous system is primitive and extremely simple, and ill-defined. There is a simple 'brain' at the front end where the eyes, if any, and other sense organs are located. The brain is in some respects relatively unimportant. For example, the animal can feed almost normally even when the brain has been lost by injury. Nevertheless, turbellarians do show well-defined reactions to light, gravity, water currents and chemical stimuli, and these reactions have interested biologists because of the lowly state of the nervous system which produces them. Moreover, flatworms also show an ability to learn, for example, to turn right or left in particular laboratory situations. They have attracted special attention because of experiments carried out in the hope of showing that 'memory' can be transferred from one animal to another in chemical form. As we shall see later, a flatworm can be cut into several pieces and each

will reform to make a new, very small flatworm. In an experiment a flatworm was 'trained'. Then it was cut up, the separate pieces regenerated and each new flatworm was tested to see if it 'remembered' the training. The scientists carrying out the experiment claimed that each new flatworm remembered. Were this so it would mean that memory, contrary to what we normally suppose, could have a chemical basis independent of the nervous system. There is, however, some doubt about the validity of these experiments.

Secondhand defence

The digestive system has only one opening, the mouth, and the form of the mouth serves to distinguish the four different kinds of flatworms. In the Rhabdocoelida the intestine is straight and the mouth is at the front of the body. In the Tricladida, or planarians, the mouth with a protrusible proboscis is near the centre of the body and the digestive system has three main branches, each of which branches extensively through the body. In the marine Polyclads, there are many branches of the gut leading from a mouth at the posterior end of the animal and in the Acoela there is a simple gut that is not even hollow. This last is less mystifying than it appears when we realise

In the diagram, the following parts are labelled: testes, pharynx, mouth, ovary, vitellarium (shell gland), intestine, brain.

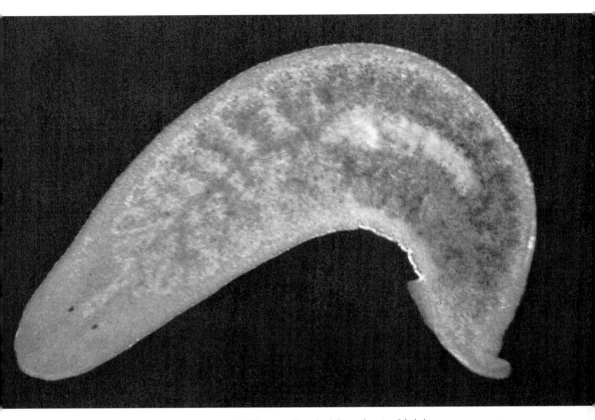

△ Planarian flatworm **Dendrocoelum lacteum**. *The mouth with a protrusible proboscis is near the centre of the body.*

that digestion in all these animals is largely carried on, not inside the intestine but in the cells of the wall of the intestine.

The turbellarians are carnivorous, feeding on a variety of small animals. Some of them can be caught by lowering a piece of meat on a string into a pond. The typical planarian catches its prey with the help of sticky secretions from glands in the head region. When the prey gets caught in these the planarian wraps its body around it. The proboscis is then protruded from the mouth and small particles of the prey are sucked up. One of the Rhabdocoelida *Microstomum* has the remarkable habit of feeding on hydra, a freshwater relative of anemones. It eats portions of the hydra, including its stinging-cells and these find their way into the skin of the *Microstomum* and are used in defence by their new owner. In fact, *Microstomum* is believed to eat only hydra when it needs to replenish its armoury.

On the sandy shores of Normandy and Brittany live two species of flatworm Acoela that may be so abundant as to colour the sand green. The colour is due not to the worm itself but to single-celled algae living in its tissues. One of them, *Convoluta roscoffensis*, gets all its food from these plant cells once it is mature, but the other, *C. paradoxa*, like the young of *C. roscoffensis*, takes in solid food as well.

Cannibalism is common in Turbellaria. Even *Convoluta* when kept in the dark will eat their fellows. By contrast not many other things eat them.

If starved, flatworms get smaller and smaller, their internal organs disappearing in an orderly sequence, the reproductive organs first and the nervous system last.

Elaborate reproductive organs

The reproductive organs of Turbellaria are most complicated. Each individual has elaborate sets of both male and female organs. Propagation is, however, not always sexual. A number of freshwater planarians reproduce by tearing themselves in half, the front end of the body advancing while the rear attaches itself firmly to the substratum by sticky secretions. The body gives way along a predetermined line of weakness. The two halves subsequently reconstitute themselves as whole worms. The common American *Dugesia tigrina* does this, and in some localities there is, apparently, no sexual reproduction at all. In some rhabdocoels a chain of individuals is formed, each with its own brain and other organs, and after that they separate. Other turbellarians propagate by fragmentation. An interesting example is provided by the large *Bipalium kewense*,

discovered in 1878 in the greenhouses of Kew Gardens and now occasionally turning up in others elsewhere. It is also established in gardens in the West Indies and the warmer parts of North America although its relatives are mainly native to the forests of southeast Asia. It sometimes reaches 1 ft long and has five dark stripes on a lighter background. This species cannot reproduce sexually in temperate regions so for its survival there it depends on multiplication by fragmentation.

Regeneration

Turbellarians also have very good powers of regeneration following injury. Indeed, they have been favourite animals for studies on this subject and zoology textbooks often contain pictures of monstrous flatworms with several heads or with a head at each end. In some species, new individuals may be regenerated from as little as a thousandth part of the whole.

| phylum | **Platyhelminthes** |
| class | **Turbellaria** |

Ribbon worm

'Ribbon worm' aptly describes many of these long, thin, often flattened animals. Many are gaily coloured, especially on the upper surface, in various shades of orange, red, green or brown, often with contrasting stripes or bands. A few are transparent and one Japanese species is luminescent. There are nearly 600 named species—and probably many more yet to be discovered— varying in length from a fraction of an inch to yards. About 60 yd is the extreme, although the majority are less than 8 in. A characteristic feature of all ribbon worms is a long muscular proboscis which can be shot out at prey from its sheath down the middle of the body, becoming turned inside out in the process. The proboscis may be two or more times the body length, sticky or armed with one or more stylets. In **Gorgonorhynchus** *it is divided into as many as 32 branches and looks like a bunch of writhing worms when shot out. At the front end of the unsegmented body there may be a lobe bearing from two to several hundred eyes and other sense organs, but this area is not called the head since the brain may be further back. The pore by which the proboscis emerges is just below the tip of the body, or just behind that, on the lower surface. The digestive tract may share this opening, but usually there is a separate mouth farther back. The body sometimes ends in a short slender tail.*

Ribbon worms are known also as nemertines or nemerteans—after Nemertes, one of the sea-nymph daughters of Nereus and Doris. Nemertine worms are not to be confused with nematode worms (Nema= thread), for example the hookworm and the threadworm.

Mainly in shallow seas

Most ribbon worms live in the sea, mainly on temperate coasts among seaweed or in mud or sand. Some inhabit mucus-lined cavities or parchment-like tubes while a few live in association with other animals, like *Carcinonemertes* on the gills and egg masses of crabs. Nemertines living in deep water are usually either swimmers, with fins on the sides or at the hindend, or more gelatinous floating forms. There are some freshwater ribbon worms, especially in the northern hemisphere, and also a genus of terrestrial worms, *Geonemertes*, found along shores, under logs or in soil in warm regions such as Bermuda, New Zealand, Australia and many of the islands of the Pacific. One species lives, often high off the ground, in the leaf bases of screw pines which grow in the Seychelle islands in the Indian Ocean.

Ribbon worms typically glide along on a trail of mucus using the cilia that cover their bodies, but sometimes the muscles are brought into play. The proboscis is sometimes used as an aid to locomotion, the worm throwing it out and pulling itself along, and also in burrowing, but it is more important in feeding. Ribbon worms feed mainly at night, principally on annelid worms, but also on crustaceans, molluscs and fish. These are caught by the proboscis as it is shot violently out and wrapped around them. The prey may be swallowed whole or, if large, its tissues sucked out of its body. Prolonged starvation is tolerated by ribbon worms in captivity but with great reduction in size. In an extreme case of starvation, lasting more than 2 years, some regenerating pieces of ribbon worm ended up as masses of large round cells.

Three kinds of larvae

Though some species are hermaphrodite, particularly among those living on land or in freshwater, the sexes are usually separate and look alike, although the male of one swimming species *Nectonemertes mirabilis* differs from the female in having a tentacle on each side in the position of arms. The reproductive organs are generally arranged in a row on each side of the body and each discharges by a separate hole. In *Carcinonemertes*, they all discharge into the rear end of the intestine. Males and females may spawn without touching or a male may crawl over a female releasing his sperm; or two or more worms may spawn enclosed together in a sheath of mucus. Fertilisation can be internal or external and the eggs may be laid in strings or in masses of jelly, or, less often, develop into young worms while still inside the mother.

Some ribbon worms leave their eggs as small worms, while others hatch as ciliated pilidium larvae, usually described as 'helmet-shaped' because of the two lobes directed downwards like ear-pieces either side of the mouth. The pilidium larvae swim around, feeding on minute plants and animals, and eventually a worm emerges from each one, casting aside the outer skin. In addition to these distinct types of development, there is a third involving the so-called Desor's larva. This is an oval ciliated larva named after E Desor who observed

▽ *Turning over stones often reveals the unexpected such as this 'boot-lace worm'* **L. longissimus** *found on the shore at low tide.*

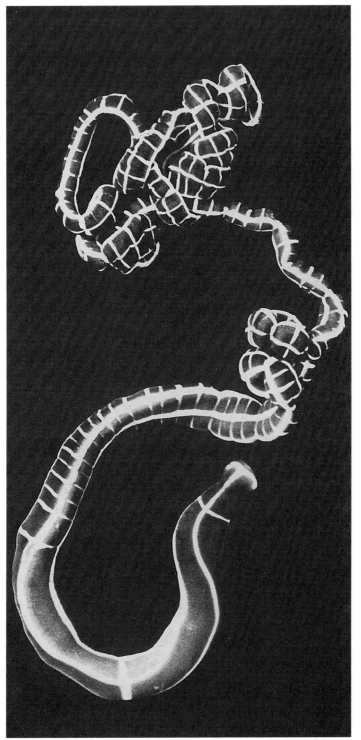

it in the eggs of *Lineus* in 1848. It develops in much the same way as a pilidium larva but remains inside its egg membranes. This larva is thought to be an adaptation to shallow water where conditions are more variable than those in the open sea.

Some ribbon worms, such as *Lineus*, propagate asexually by fragmentation. The hind end of the body breaks up by strong muscular contractions into a number of pieces, perhaps 20 or more, and each one grows into a new worm. Longer fragments may in turn break up into shorter lengths before becoming fully regenerated. Worms that can reproduce in this way are also those with good general powers of regeneration and, in some, even tiny pieces suffice to produce new worms provided they contain part of the nerve cord. Ribbon worms are apt to break up when handled or otherwise disturbed and the proboscis may be thrown out with such force as to tear itself loose from the body.

Yards of ribbon

The maximum length of a ribbon worm is given above as 'about 60 yd' and it is perhaps as well to reassure the reader now that this is no misprint. Some books quote a more hesitant 'several yards', but there is little need for such scepticism. It was Professor WC McIntosh who described, in a monograph on these worms, a giant specimen of the bootlace worm *Lineus longissimus* he had found at St Andrews after a severe storm in 1864. It half filled a jar 8 in. wide and 5 in. deep and McIntosh was able to measure 30 yd of it before it ruptured. Apparently he gave up at that point, 'yet the mass was not half uncoiled'. Just how long it was we will never know, but in any case an individual worm can vary its length very considerably, perhaps contracting from a length of several yards to several inches. An even more extreme shrinkage can occur on contact with alcohol with one part of the body becoming turned inside out on another and it has been known for specimens of *Lineus gesserensis* to turn completely inside out as a result of the influence of certain irritants in the water.

phylum	**Nemertina**
class	**Anopla**
order	**Palaeonemertina**
order	**Heteronemertina**
family	**Lineidae**
genera	*Lineus* *Gorgonorhynchus*
class	**Enopla**
order	**Bdellonemertina**
order	**Hoplonemertina**
family	**Prosorhochmidae**
genus	*Geonemertes*
family	**Emplectonematidae**
genus	*Carcinonemertes*

◁ *Its body thrown into coils,* **Tubulanus annulatus** *is a strikingly marked ribbon worm.*

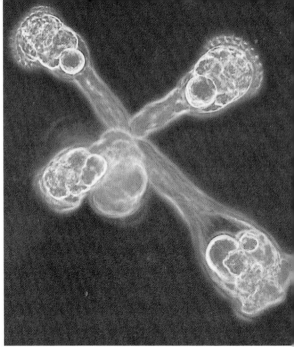

Rotifer

Rotifers have long been a delight to microscopists. They are very numerous, easily obtained from almost any pond and are of endless variety. Wheel animalcules, as they are also called, are among the most abundant of freshwater animals. Only a few live in the sea. In the British Isles alone, there are more than 500 species. They range in length from 0·04 to 2 mm., and most are shorter than ½ mm. They are therefore about the size of Protozoa and were once confused with them, but they are nevertheless multicellular. They are unusual in that, within a species, every individual and each of its organs is made up of a definite number of cells. The adult female of **Epiphanes senta***, for instance, is made up of 959 cells. There is even a parasitic rotifer with all its minute organ systems living within the confines of a single protozoan. This is* **Proales latrunculus***, which lives in a heliozoan* **Acanthocystis***. Rotifers are named for the arrangement of cilia on the front end which often look like rotating wheels for which they were mistaken by some early microscopists, including Leeuwenhoek, the inventor of the microscope.*

Endless variety

The body of a rotifer may be worm-like, flattened, bag-like or spherical, symmetrical or skewed, soft-skinned or armoured. It is generally divisible into what may be called for convenience a head, a trunk and a 'foot' ending usually in one to four 'toes'. Covering the body is a yellowish cuticle, often ringed so it looks as if the body is segmented. This cuticle is thickened, especially on the trunk, to form one or more hard, and sometimes ornamented, plates. It is usually transparent enough for all the internal organs to be seen. There are endless variations on the basic body plan: there are species with dumpy trunks and feet like the stems of wineglasses, species with long thin bodies and even longer feet and a spherical species *Trochosphaera* with no feet. The trunk may have projections of various kinds including long fixed spines and moveable spines which enable the rotifer to skip through the water. The head bears a mouth, a variety of projections, often sensory, single or paired eyes seen as red flecks, and the cilia of the wheel organ or corona. The latter varies greatly in form and function.

Several ways of feeding

When we say rotifers occur mainly in fresh water, this includes even the thin films and drops of water in such places as the surface layers of the soil and the moss on walls. Some propel themselves through the water by the cilia of their wheel organs or by special appendages. Those of the order Bdelloidea are typically bottom dwellers and loop about like leeches (*bdella* = leech), alternately attaching the toe and head ends to the substrate. Yet other rotifers live anchored by their often elongated feet, and secrete around themselves tubes or cases of jelly. The 'floscule' *Floscularia* — formerly known to thousands of microscopists as *Melicerta* — is famed for its tube of neatly arranged little pellets. These are made by concentrating particles in a special ciliated pit on the head before being cemented to the rim of the

◁△ *The 'floscule'* **Floscularia ringens** *a freshwater, sessile rotifer which makes a case of neatly arranged little pellets from particles in the water and its own excrement (× 60).*
△ **Conochilus hippocrepis** *a colonial rotifer (× 800), individuals attached in a common ball of mucus. The wheel organ is the crown of cilia.*
▽ *Rotifer of the order Monogononta (× 500).*

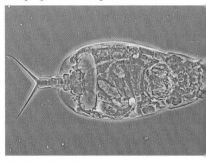

tube. If particles of carmine dye are added to the water, this rotifer will use these producing a gay red tube. The wheel organ of *Floscularia* has four large ciliated lobes which set up currents of water bringing in food particles. Rotifers feed in one of three ways: by extracting small organisms and particles from water currents set up by the wheel organs, grasping large prey, and trapping it. Rotifers are peculiar in having a masticating pharynx, called the mastax. This is muscular with several hard pieces. It takes several forms and may be used in chewing, sucking or grasping prey. Among the trapping carnivores are species of *Collotheca* that catch their victims with a widely spread funnel on top of the body. This bears long

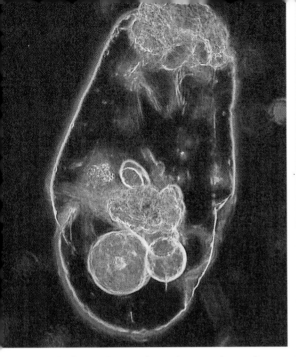

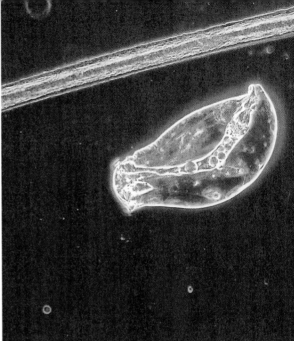

△ *Asplanchna priodonta* — *predatory rotifer able to swallow whole crustaceans and other rotifers as well as colonial algae after chewing them in its masticating pharynx, called the mastax. The less frequent male (right) with human hair to show size is much smaller than the female (left) (× 625).*
▽ *Fimbriatus stephanoceros on plant (× 75).*

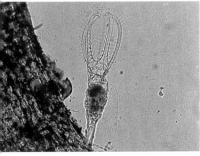

motionless bristles instead of the usual cilia and, should a small animal blunder into it, the lobes or arms bearing the bristles close over it and the mastax is soon at work.

Males adult at birth

What has been said so far applies particularly to the females, for in most species the males are much smaller, being perhaps only one half or a tenth the size of the females. The males sometimes have a degenerate gut. In any case, females are more often seen, since the males usually appear only at certain times of the year, though they may then be very abundant. The small size of the typical male is due to the fact that he hatches from a smaller egg and does not

subsequently grow. He is often sexually mature at birth and so large numbers of mature males can be produced in a short time. In the order Bdelloidea, there are no males and the eggs develop without fertilisation. In some other rotifers males deposit their sperm in the cloacas of the females, but it is more usual for them to inject it through the cuticles and into their general body cavities.

Each female can produce only as many eggs as she has nuclei in her ovary to begin with — less than fifty, and often only ten in some species. The oval eggs are laid on the bottom or stuck to the body of either the mother or another animal. They have shells and in some cases these have gelatinous envelopes or thin membranes which enable them to float. In some species the egg has no shell, but develops inside the mother.

Females of free-swimming species usually hatch with the adult form and are mature in a few days, but in sessile species the females emerge as free-swimming juveniles. These eventually attach themselves and undergo changes necessary for their sedentary mode of life such as loss of eyes, elongation of the foot into a stalk and changes in the wheel organ.

Three kinds of egg

In most rotifers, three kinds of egg are laid, though not by the same individual: thin-shelled eggs that produce females without being fertilised; smaller thin-shelled eggs that can be fertilised but produce males if they are not; and thick-shelled eggs that are always fertilised and always give rise to females. These thick-shelled eggs often bear spines, bristles or other ornaments. While the first two kinds hatch in a day or so, the last may remain dormant for months and

survive drying and low temperature. When they do hatch, the females that emerge soon start to lay eggs of the first kind and the population is built up by successive generations of females. Eventually a new kind of female appears, laying only the second, smaller, kind of egg. These are necessarily unfertilised at first and give rise to males. Then, to complete the cycle, thick-shelled, resting, fertilised eggs are produced again and the population perhaps dies off.

The thick-shelled dormant egg is clearly most helpful for the survival of the species, but most of the rotifers of soil and moss belong to the Bdelloidea which do not lay them. The bdelloids, the types most subject to drying, can, however, survive extreme desiccation lasting for periods even up to 4 years, during which time they may be blown about by the wind to seed new habitats. The longest dormancy on record is of one recovered from moss kept 59 years in an herbarium but it cannot be ruled out that dust from other specimens may have contaminated it. While dry, some have withstood temperatures up to 200°C/392°F for 5 minutes in an electric oven, and down to minus 272°C/457°F. In Antarctic lakes some rotifers are inevitably frozen in ice for most of the year but can make do with occasional periods of activity of a few days or weeks. At the other extreme, some bdelloids spend their lives in springs at 46°C/115°F.

phylum	**Aschelminthes**
class	**Rotifera**
orders	**Bdelloidea**
	Monogononta
	Seisonidea

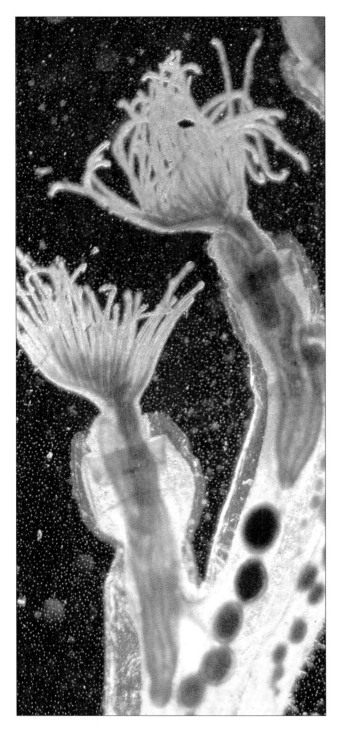

Moss animal

There are 400 living species of moss animals. Most of them live in the sea, but a few live in freshwater. In the sea they coat almost every object, from the surfaces of rocks and seaweeds to the hulls of ships and shipwrecks. In spite of their numbers, moss animals are unknown to most people. As a rule they form colonies, encrusting stones, shells and seaweeds, but some of them grow up into fan-shaped colonies, looking like corals or millepores. Many are white or pale in colour and those encrusting pebbles and seaweeds are usually small and lacelike, although sometimes they cover several square feet of rock surfaces. Some moss animals are often mistaken for seaweeds, such as the seamat **Flustra**. It can often be seen on the shore when the tide is out or cast up with seaweed along the driftline.

In Britain moss animals are usually called Polyzoa, which means many animals, but in other parts of the world they are given the collective name of Bryzoa, meaning moss animals. Moss animals are colony builders; each colony is made up of a number of tiny chambers like boxes, in each of which lives a polypide, a sort of polyp. Small colonies are made up of scores of polypides, large ones of hundreds or even thousands of polypides, and sometimes a single colony may contain millions of polypides. At first sight the polypides look like the polyps of small corals, but they differ considerably in structure, which is why they are called polypides, to distinguish them from the true polyps. Each has a crown of 8-100 or more ciliated tentacles around the mouth for capturing the microscopic plants and animals on which the polypides feed. The anatomy of each polypide is very simple because there are no special organs for breathing and excretion and there are no blood vessels. The mouth leads into a simple U-shaped digestive tube. There are a few simple muscles and a simple nervous system.

Until the last few years all moss animals were put into one phylum divided into two distinct classes, the Ectoprocta and the Entoprocta. Although superficially alike, the two groups are now thought not to be related and are no longer classed together. The ectoprosts, or true moss animals, are generally regarded as constituting a phylum of their own. The unsolved controversy as to whether they should be called Polyzoa or Bryzoa is also coming to an end as the phylum is now called Ectoprocta.

◄ Freshwater moss animal Plumatella (x25)

Rose coral **Pentapora foliacea**. This brittle moss animal, about 3 – 4 in. across, is found in the Mediterranean living on underwater rocks. The small crabs are **Porcellana longicornis**.

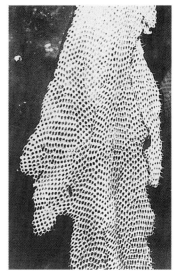

Flustra, seamat, is often mistaken for the seaweeds it encrusts (about × 3).

From the depths to freshwater

The walls of the chambers of some of the marine moss animals are decorated along the sides or around the opening, with long or short spines. The chamber or box is rarely more than $\frac{1}{50}$ in. across and it may be tubular, oval, squarish or even vase-shaped. The walls of the chamber are generally horny, but they often have a thick inner layer of calcium carbonate. At one end of each chamber is an opening through which the tentacles and the front part of the body can be pushed out. In one group, the opening has a hinged lid worked by muscles. Variations occur between the species and between individuals in the same colony who may do different work, as in a colony of termites. Some polypides are reduced to nothing more than the body wall and a few strands of tissue inside the chamber. These degenerate individuals make up the stalks, roots, stolons and attachment plates, or the margins of the colony.

Moss animals live in all seas and fresh waters, both warm and cold. Some live at great depths in the sea, but most live in shallow water or on the shore and they are among the most important fouling organisms on ships' hulls. Only a few species inhabit freshwater, and most of these, about fifty, belong to a distinct class in which, except in one genus, the crown of tentacles has a horseshoe arrangement. These freshwater forms sometimes block water pipes, as some of them such as *Pectinatella magnifica* form gelatinous masses which are occasionally up to several feet across. One of the gelatinous forms *Cristatella* moves by forming elongated colonies up to several inches long, which creep about on their flat undersurfaces at rates of up to 1 in. a day. Other freshwater species form branching or bushy colonies.

On the surface of the colony in some species are what look like very tiny birds' heads continually swaying to and fro and snapping their beaks. These 'avicularia', as they are called, are highly modified individuals in which the operculum, or lid, has become the 'lower jaw'. The avicularia may be either stalked or immobile, sometimes both types occurring in the same colony. The function of these structures seems to be much the same as the little jawed 'pedicellariae' of echinoderms – that is, capturing small organisms as they roam over the surface and, more important, preventing larvae of other encrusting animals from settling. Related to avicularia, and having probably a similar function, are the 'vibracula' in which the operculum is changed, not into a jaw, but into a long bristle that sweeps back and forth over the colony, keeping the surface clean.

Brooding the young

Some moss animals shed their eggs directly into the sea but the majority brood them. In freshwater species the embryos are nourished, until their release as ciliated larvae or juvenile colonies, in sacs attached to the body wall of the parent. In the marine species there is great variety in the method of brooding, which may be internal or external. Thus, the embryos may be sheltered outside in a space roofed over with arched spines or in a hood-like brood chamber, or they may be retained inside the body cavity, either free or in special sacs. Often each individual only nurtures a single embryo. The ciliated larvae vary in shape, some having a bivalve shell.

The freshwater moss animals also reproduce by an asexual method. They produce what are called statoblasts that can survive being dried up as well as extremes of temperature. Each statoblast, less than $\frac{1}{20}$ in., consists of a mass of cells enclosed in a pair of shells. Some kinds sink or are cemented to the parent colony but others have a ring of air-filled cells around them which act as a float. Other statoblasts have circlets of hooked spines by which they cling to a support. In due course a new polypide is formed from the cells in a statoblast, and hence a new colony is formed.

The shell of the statoblast breaks in two to release a mass of cells inside. These half shells are extremely small and they float. Quite astonishingly, drifts 1 – 4 ft across of millions of statoblast shells were reported along lake shores in Michigan, USA.

Moss animals' vital clue

Moss animals are relatively insignificant, and apart from the fact that they foul the bottoms of ships or choke water pipes they really have little value or interest to anybody but a scientist. People sometimes ask why is it necessary to spend so much time studying animals of this kind? Perhaps an incident that took place during the First World War may show how the unexpected can happen. A piece of metal from a sunken submarine was fished up by the Royal Navy and it was important to know how long it had lain on the sea bottom. The only possible clue lay in the marine animals such as the barnacles, the worm tubes and above all the moss animals encrusting it. The piece of metal was handed to a marine zoologist who was able, because of his knowledge of the moss animals, to say to within a few days how long the metal had been there. This represents the yardstick one must always use in assessing the value of a piece of research: you never know when it may be of use.

phylum	**Ectoprocta**
class	**Gymnolaemata**
genera	***Bugula, Flustra, Membranipora***
class	**Phylactolaemata**
genera	***Cristatella, Fredericella, Pectinatella, Plumatella***

Lampshell

Lampshells, which are all marine, look like clams and until the middle of last century were classified as molluscs. They are all small, at most 2 in. long, although some extinct forms were nearly a foot long. The shell is made up of two unequal parts or valves, which may be circular, oval or triangular. Sometimes it is made of carbonate of lime, sometimes of calcium phosphate with a horny covering. The shell is usually a dull grey or yellow, but it may be red or orange. Although so like a bivalve mollusc there is a basic difference between it and a lampshell. In the bivalve the valves can be regarded as left and right even though one lies uppermost. In a lampshell one shell is dorsal, or uppermost, and the other is ventral.

Lampshells are divided into two kinds depending on whether the two valves are hinged on each other or not. Usually a short fleshy stalk sticks out at the rear of the shell, anchoring the animal permanently to a solid surface, such as a rock or a branching coral, but in one kind it is used in burrowing in mud. The stalk may come out between the valves or through a special notch or hole. It is the presence of such a hole at the end of a sort of beak at the hind end of the larger ventral valve that makes some of the lampshells look like a Roman oil lamp, and so suggested the common name of these animals.

Inside the shell the greater part of the animal's body lies in the rear third, leaving a large space between the valves and the mantle or layer of tissue lining them. Within this mantle cavity lies a complex feeding organ known as the lophophore. It is covered with cilia and although its shape varies, most commonly it consists of coiled arms looking like huge moustachios on either side of the mouth. Along the arms are grooves and one or two rows of tentacles. The lophophore is stiffened by a skeleton of chalky rods.

There are about 260 living species, in almost all latitudes and at most depths although lampshells are most common in warm seas and the majority live on the continental slope. In some parts of the world they may occasionally be found on the shore.

Living food-pumps

Most lampshells remain permanently fixed after the larval stage. They can, however, move up and down and from side to side on the stalk. In a few species only, lacking a stalk, the shell itself is cemented to the rock. They have little need to move about since they feed on tiny particles, especially diatoms, that abound in the water around them. These are drawn in between the edges of the gaping valves in water currents set up by the concerted thrashing of the cilia on the lophophore. Edible particles are caught on the lophophore and driven along

the grooves to the mouth. Unsuitable particles such as sand grains are rejected and carried out again in the outgoing current. If too much silt is accumulating within the shell, some species can reverse the flow of the current to flush out the mantle cavity.

Mud-burrowing lampshells

One group of lampshells of the genus *Lingula* have a muscular stalk which can be shortened or lengthened and used for burrowing. There are a dozen species of these in the Indo-Pacific region, especially off Japan, southern Australia and New Zealand. In some places they are used for food. Their burrows, in the black and smelly mudflats, are vertical, 2 – 10 in. deep and with a slit-like opening at the top to match the animal's flattened shell. The advantage *Lingula* gains in such a habitat is that few other animals can live there. *Lingula* lies with its shell near the top of the burrow, filtering water in the usual way. Bristles around the edges of its mantle can be bent over the opening as the shell gapes, to keep out the larger grains of mud and sand. The tip of the long stalk reaches to the bottom of the burrow. When the animal is disturbed the stalk contracts, drawing it down into the safety of the burrow.

Simple life history

Lampshells are usually male or female, although there is no obvious difference between the sexes, but a few species are hermaphrodite. The eggs, heavily charged with yolk, and the sperm are passed out through the kidneys and shed into the sea where fertilisation takes place. The fertilised eggs develop into tiny larvae that swim around for a day before settling on the sea-bed and becoming fixed. In some species the larvae look like miniature lampshells with a pair of valves and a stalk, which is coiled in the back of the mantle cavity. The larval lophophore is simple; its cilia are used not for feeding but for driving the larva through the water. A few lampshells brood their eggs in the mantle cavity and some of these have a special pouch, or they may brood them actually in the kidneys.

Few enemies

The living lampshells number fewer than 300 species compared with 30 000 known species of lampshell fossils. In past ages they must have been as numerous as molluscs are today and in some parts of the world whole layers of rock are made up of little else than fossil lampshells. The earliest known animal fossil is a lampshell, and the group as a whole reached its peak during the Ordovician period, which lasted from 500 million to 440 million years ago. *Lingula* was one of the earliest and it has persisted virtually unchanged throughout this long period of time. Other groups of animals have come and gone, flourished and died out, but *Lingula* has gone steadily on. Apart from its simple way of life one reason for this is that it can live in foul water that few other animals can tolerate. So it has few competitors for the available food and very few enemies.

There has been more change in those lampshells that look more like cockles and

△ Opened lampshell shows feathery lophophore, which sorts sand from food particles.
▽ Lingula lampshells showing attachment stalks.

other clams. Their shells mainly have altered, some being ribbed or folded or ornamented with spines. Such changes are largely superficial but they have their uses. One of the main interests in lampshells is that they are especially useful in helping the geologist to identify and date the rocks in which he finds them.

phylum	**Brachiopoda**
class	**Articulata**
order	**Atremata**
genera	*Lingula, Crania*
class	**Inarticulata**
genera	*Terebratulina, Terebratella*

Abalone

A genus of single-shelled molluscs related to the limpets. Also known as ormer, sea ear, or earshell, the abalone (four syllables, the final e being sounded) somewhat resembles a snail, the body being little more than a muscular foot with a head at one end, bearing a pair of eyes and sensory tentacles. The body is also fringed with tentacles.

Over the top of the shell lies a line of holes, through which water is exhaled after it has been drawn in under the shell and over the gills to extract oxygen. New holes are formed as the shell grows forward, while the old holes become covered over, so that only a few younger holes are open at any one time, the rest appearing as a line of bumps.

Some abalones are among the largest shellfish: they range in size from the 1 in. long and very rare **Haliotis pourtalese** to the red abalone of California, which is a foot across.

Abalone showing edge of foot and its frill of tentacles which seek out its seaweed food.

Distribution, habitat and habits

Abalones are to be found in many parts of the world: along the coasts of the Mediterranean, Africa, Australia, New Zealand, the Pacific islands, and the western coast of North America. In the Atlantic they are found as far north as St. Malo and the Channel Islands. The rare species *Haliotis pourtalese* is found off Florida. It is known mainly from specimens washed up on the shore, as it lives at depths of 350–1 200 ft. It is thus the deepest-living of all abalones; the rest live between the extreme low-water mark and a depth of about 60 ft along rocky shores where there is no sand to clog the gills or in rocky pools large enough not to be heated too quickly by the sun. The only other exception is the black abalone, which lives in the splash zone where waves breaking against rocks alternately cover and expose it.

Unlike their limpet relatives, abalones have no 'home', no spot on a rock where they always return after feeding. They simply hide up in a crevice or under a rock, avoiding the light and coming out at night. When disturbed an abalone grips the rock face, using its foot as a suction pad: the two main muscles of the body exert a tremendous force—up to 400 lb in a 4 in. specimen. Unlike the limpet, the abalone cannot bring its shell down over the whole of its body: the edge of the foot, with its frill of tentacles, is left sticking out.

Abalones move in the same way as limpets and snails. Waves of muscular contraction pass along the foot, pushing it forward. As each part expands it is fixed to the ground by slimy mucus: the part in front, expanding in turn, is pressed forward and then itself stuck down. Abalones differ from limpets and snails in having a sort of bipedal movement. Alternate waves of movement pass down either side of the foot, so that as a part of one side is moving the corresponding part on the other side stays fixed.

△ *Left: Mother of pearl, used in making jewellery, lines the inside of the abalone shells. Right: A black abalone without encrusting seaweeds which grow on most other species.*

▽ *The starfish is one of the abalone's main enemies. It uses its hundreds of sucker feet to prize the abalone away from its rock. The starfish then turns its stomach inside out and pushes it beneath the abalone's shell to dissolve away its flesh.*

△ *The abalone breathes through the line of holes in the top of its shell. As it grows, new ones form and others are covered over.*

▽ *The remarkable teeth of a radula, the mollusc tongue, magnified 1,450 times by using a deep field scanning electron microscope.*

The rate of travel is very rapid for a shellfish: a speed of 5–6 yd/min has been recorded—although no abalone would cover this distance in one dash.

Many-toothed tongue for feeding

Abalones are vegetarians, crawling over rock faces and browsing on seaweeds that they seek out with their sensitive tentacles. Their favourite foods are the delicate red weeds and green sea lettuces, although they also scrape tissue off fragments of kelp that have been torn away by waves. Young abalones eat the forms of life that encrust rocks, such as the coral-like plant *Corallina*.

Food is scraped up and chewed into small pieces by the rasp-like action of the radula, a tongue made up of large numbers of small, chalky teeth.

100,000 eggs laid

Some molluscs are hermaphrodite but all individual abalones are of one sex or the other. They reach sexual maturity at six years. The germ cells, or gametes, are shed directly into the sea, causing great wastage. Thus a female will liberate 100,000 or more eggs, and the sea around a male turns milky over a radius of 3 ft when he sheds his spawn. To reduce wastage, however, the female does not shed eggs until induced by the presence of sperms around her.

The fertilised eggs are covered by a gelatinous coat and float freely in the sea until they hatch a few hours later as minute trochophore larvae. These trochophore larvae are top-shaped and swim around by means of a band of hair-like cilia around the thickest part. Within a day the trochophore develops into a veliger—a miniature version of the adult complete with shell but still with the band of cilia. Two days later it loses the cilia, sinks to the bottom and starts to develop into an adult, a process that takes several weeks.

The free-swimming larvae have advantages in that they are the means by which the otherwise rather sedentary abalones can spread, but they are very vulnerable and are eaten in their millions by plankton-eating fish like anchovies and herrings.

Enemies everywhere

Although mortality is heaviest during the free-swimming stage, adult abalones also have several enemies. Fish, sea birds, sea otters, crabs and starfish dislodge the abalones or chew bits off them. Their only protection lies in their tenacity in clinging to rocks and the protective camouflage of the shell and foot. This camouflage is improved by the seaweeds and sedentary animals that settle on the shell. Also, it has been found that when young abalones feed on red weeds their shells become red.

On the other hand abalones are more vulnerable due to the boring sponge *Cliona lobata*, which erodes holes in their shells and so opens them up to other predators. In the Channel Islands as many as 95% of a sample of abalones have been found to be infected with boring sponges.

Dark pearls, called blister pearls, are sometimes found in abalones. Like the real pearls of oysters, these are formed by the animal to cover up a source of irritation—in this case a minute parasitic clam, *Pholadidea parva*, that bores through the abalone's shell and into its tissues.

Prized for shell and meat

The shells of abalones are prized because, although they are superficially rough and dull, cleaning reveals the gleam of mother of pearl. This and the large size of the shell make abalones popular with shell collectors, and they are also used for making costume jewellery. The body itself is much esteemed as food. The large foot is cut into strips, beaten with a mallet to make it soft, and then fried. The edge of the foot is trimmed off to make chowder.

The popularity of abalones and the ease with which they can be collected from the shore has led to stocks being severely depleted. In California, which is the centre of the abalone industry, only strict laws have prevented its extinction. As abalones do not breed until they are six years old and perhaps 4 in. long, there is a minimum length at which they can be taken: for the common red abalone this is 7 in., corresponding to about 12 years of age. There is a close season—though it now seems that abalones breed all the year round—and catches are limited to five a day and can only be taken by a licence-holder.

Finally, abalone meat cannot be exported from the State of California. This does not mean, however, that it cannot be obtained outside California, as tinned abalone meat is exported from Mexico and Japan.

phylum	**Mollusca**
class	**Gastropoda**
order	**Prosobranchiata**
genera	*Haliotis rufescens* (red abalone) *H. fulgens* (green abalone) *H. cracherodii* (black abalone) others

Cone shell

There are 500 to 600 species of cone shells — sea snails named for the shape of their shells. As in an ordinary snail, the shell consists of a tube wrapped round a central column. In the cones the tube is flattened making a long, tapering shell. The cone is formed by the large outside whorl of the tube, with its narrow, slit-like opening extending to the tip of the cone. The base of this cone is formed by the short, and sometimes almost flat, spire formed by the exposed parts of the inner whorls. The surface of the shell is generally smooth with a dotted or lacy pattern of brown on white.

The cones range up to about 9 in. long, the majority being much smaller. Attached to the foot of the mollusc is an elongated operculum, the horny lid or door that seals the aperture of the shell when its owner retires inside. When the snail is active, a pair of sensory tentacles and a long siphon protrude from the front of the body. Water is drawn in through the siphon by the cilia and passed over the gills in the cavity within the shell.

Habits

The cones are found in tropical and sub-tropical waters, mainly in the western Atlantic and around the Philippines and the Malay Archipelago across the Indian Ocean to East Africa, up the Red Sea and in the Mediterranean. They live in shallow water to a depth of several hundred feet. Some live in coral reefs, others in coral sand or rubble. They are active mainly by night, coming out to feed after lying up in crevices or under stones during the day, or burying themselves in the sand with only the siphon showing.

Hunts with a poison harpoon

The cones are carnivorous, feeding on worms, other molluscs or even live fish such as blennies or gobies, each species having its own preferred prey, which it first paralyses and then swallows whole. Capture of the prey is accomplished by means of a snout-like proboscis armed with long poisonous teeth. The teeth are basically the same structures as those on the tongue or radula of other snails, like the abalone (see page 31) or banded snail. In most snails there are many small teeth forming a file for scraping off particles of food, but in the cones there are only a few teeth, each as much as $\frac{3}{8}$ in. long. Each tooth is a long, barbed, hollow

harpoon mounted on a mobile stalk. Associated with these teeth is a poison gland, connected by a long tube to the teeth. The viscous, milky white poison is squeezed out by the contraction of muscles around the poison gland.

Cone shells detect scent particles secreted by their prey with a sense organ called the osphradium, which 'tastes' the water as it is drawn through the siphon. A fish-eating cone shell will respond if water from a tank containing fish is put in its own tank.

The cone will either track down its prey, if it is another slow-moving animal such as a worm or mollusc, or lie in wait. The final stages of attack are controlled by touch. The proboscis is brought out of its sheath and held poised, then brought rapidly down onto the prey. At the same time a single tooth is everted and thrust into the victim's body. In seconds it is paralysed by the poison and the cone shell can eat it at leisure. The mouth at the end of the proboscis dilates and engulfs the victim's body, rapid muscular contractions forcing it down the gullet with the help of a lubricating secretion. Swallowing and digestion may take several hours, and during this time the snail cannot retreat into the shell.

The tooth usually breaks off when it has been used and another is brought forward

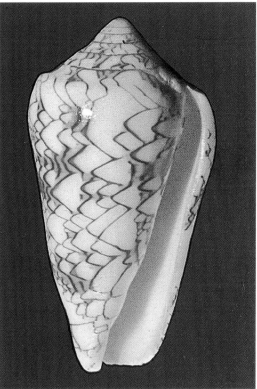

*The marble cone, **Conus marmoreus**, a common inhabitant of coral reefs of the Indo-Pacific, is up to 4 in. long. It feeds on other cones.*

*The poison teeth of the striated cone, **Conus striatus**, are used as miniature harpoons to kill small fishes, such as blennies and gobies.*

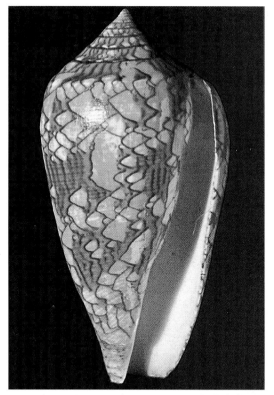

Conus textile, one of several sea snails of tropical seas, known as cone shells. These molluscs are carnivorous, and have poison glands associated with their radula teeth, for killing prey.

Another example of *Conus textile* which, when compared with the first, shows how patterns vary from one individual to another within the same species. *Textile* is Latin for a piece of cloth.

for the next victim. The poison is related to curare (the famous arrow poison of American Indians) and paralyses the victim's muscles. If the prey is another mollusc the paralysis makes it lose its grip on its shell so the cone can draw it out.

Breeding

The eggs are laid in vase-shaped capsules of a hard, parchment-like material. The capsules are attached by their bases in lines or groups to the coral or rock. They hatch in about 10 days.

The Glory of the Sea

Their beauty has resulted in cones being used for money, in the manner of cowries, and Rembrandt was sufficiently impressed by the marbled cone *Conus marmoreus* to depict it in his etching of 1650, 'The Little Horn'. Careful as ever to etch his signature in mirror image, he neglected to do the same for the shell which therefore twists the wrong way in the print.

The shells are also highly esteemed by collectors and of all shells the one that has been held most precious is the rare Glory of the Sea, *Conus gloriamaris*. Its shell has a fine network pattern of pink-brown on a light background. Although a most beautiful

shell, it was its rarity that once tempted an American collector to pay $2 000 for a specimen, and others regularly change hands for several hundred dollars. The earliest record of the Glory of the Sea is in a catalogue of 1757 when a specimen was sold at the Zoological Museum of Copenhagen. A few other specimens were found later, but towards the end of the 19th century the species was considered by some people to have become extinct as a result of the destruction of the reef which was its only known home. In fact, specimens had been found elsewhere before this, but many years passed before the next came to light in 1957, when one was found in the Philippines. Since then a number of others have been found off Indonesia, the Philippines and in the sea east of New Guinea, so that by 1966 over 50 had been found and the Glory of the Sea was no longer the most prized of shells.

The poisonous teeth with which the cones despatch their prey present a great danger to the collector who must pick up the living animals with extreme caution. Some, like the Mediterranean species *C. mediterraneus* are too puny to be troublesome and others may sting no more severely than a bee, but in other cases the pain may be excruciating and even fatal, death ensuing in 4 or 5

hours. One survey gives the death rate as 20% of all people stung, higher than that due to cobra or rattlesnake. When the cone stings it does so very rapidly and the victim may at first be unaware of the attack. Pain comes later, together with numbness, blurred vision and difficulty in breathing. A Japanese collector who was stung by the geographer cone *C. geographus* was able to walk just over a mile before collapsing, and dying of heart and breathing failure. The Glory of the Sea and many others are also very poisonous, and with the increase in the number of people collecting shells with aqua-lung apparatus, the number of deaths is sure to rise.

phylum	**Mollusca**
class	**Gastropoda**
sub-class	**Prosobranchia**
order	**Neogastropoda**
family	**Conidae**
genus	***Conus***

Giant snail

A pest in many parts of the world, **Achatina fulica** *is a large land-living snail, native to East Africa. With its pointed shell, 5 or even 8 in. long, it weighs about ½ lb. This species deserves the title of giant snail, although there are other large terrestrial snails in many of the warmer countries, because of its notoriety and economic importance. The fact that even larger snails live in the sea seems somehow less remarkable.*

In other respects, there is little of note in the appearance of the giant snail as compared with the snails of our gardens.

Dusk feeder

The giant snail feeds mainly by night or at dusk, usually returning after its forays to a regular 'home'. However, it will also come out by day if there is rain or if the sky is overcast. For continued activity, dampness and a temperature above about 24°C/75°F are needed. On the other hand, during dry or cold periods it remains inactive, often deep in some hollow log or under a rock and withdrawn into its shell, the aperture closed off with a thin membrane. This state of inactivity, or aestivation as it is called, has been known to last for as long as a year —a long enough time, but not to be compared with the 6 years recorded for an individual of another species of snail. When so much time can be spent in suspended animation, records of longevity have little meaning, but one specimen is recorded as having lived 9 years in captivity.

Voracious feeders

To a large extent the giant snail feeds on rotten plant matter and dead animals but it will also feed voraciously on the leaves, fruit, bark and flowers of a great variety of plants—including, unfortunately, crops like beans, breadfruit, cabbage, cacao, citrus trees, melons, yam plants and rubber. Needing calcium to form its shell, it may even climb walls of houses to ravage the whitewash on them for its lime content.

Pea-sized eggs

These giant snails begin breeding when about a year old and, like their smaller relatives, are hermaphrodite. They lay eggs the size of small peas, like miniature bird's eggs with lemon-yellow shells. These they deposit, 40—500 at a time, in or on the soil, doing so every 2 or 3 months. The young hatch in 1—10 days. A single snail can apparently lay eggs without mating after months of isolation, for evidently sperm can be stored for this time before being used. One result is that a single snail can suffice to found a new colony if it was fertilised before being transported.

Growth of a pest

In its East African home, the giant snail is hardly a pest, but it has spread from there to many of the warmer parts of the world, becoming in most of them a considerable pest. Like the rabbit in Australia, it is one of too many examples of animals or plants, originally fairly innocuous, that have become pests outside their native lands. Everything about this snail, such as its ability to eat almost any plant material and its high rate of reproduction, combined with its hardiness and a scarcity of natural enemies, favour its chances of colonising new areas, provided that the climate is suitable. Just a few individuals need be introduced—even one is enough.

The spread of the giant snail started in about 1800 when some were taken to Mauritius by the wife of the governor on doctor's orders (medicinal properties have been ascribed to these snails as to others). There they multiplied and became a pest. Some were taken to the island of Réunion and to the Seychelles and, in 1847, some were released in Calcutta. From then on the snail has appeared in more and more countries—particularly in the Indo-Pacific area, including Malaya, Indonesia, the Philippines, Thailand, Vietnam, and China.

Sometimes introductions have been accidental, the snails being transported while aestivating in bananas, in soil, or in motor vehicles. Sometimes they have been deliberately introduced. In 1928, for instance, they were introduced to Sarawak to be used as poultry feed and in 1936 to the Hawaiian islands by a lady wishing to keep two in her garden as pets. The Japanese forces took them as food for themselves into New Guinea and elsewhere and, before the Second World War, they were eaten by Malays and by Chinese in various places. Other related giant snails are important as food in parts of West Africa. In Ghana they are the greatest single source of animal protein. The value of snails as food, however, even to those willing to eat them, is more than offset by the damage they can inflict on crops and gardens, for they can occur in huge numbers, like apples under an apple tree.

The nuisance does not end there, for in places the ground may become slippery with slime, excreta and dead snails, and roads in Sri Lanka and Saipan have been turned into 'stinking nightmares' as more and more were attracted to their crushed fellows. Worse still, the slimy mess provides breeding grounds for disease-bearing flies. With others dying in drinking wells, devouring with impunity the warfarin bait and springing the traps put out for rats, it is hardly surprising that much effort is devoted to their control. Poisons have been used as well as various predators—including other carnivorous snails—but always there is the danger in these methods of upsetting the balance of nature in yet other ways, such as the controlling predators attacking innocuous species, and so becoming pests themselves. The best method of all, if it can be used in time, is a rigorous system of control to prevent the spread of the snail. It is encouraging that, in some areas, after an initial heavy infestation, the population diminishes to a steady level at which they are not such serious pests.

phylum	**Mollusca**	
class	**Gastropoda**	
order	**Stylommatophora**	
family	**Achatinidae**	
genus	***Achatina fulica***	*East Africa*
& species	***A. achatina***	*West Africa*

This West African giant snail has a pointed shell 5—8 in. long and weighs about ½ lb. Introduction into many parts of the world mainly for its food value has resulted in it becoming a pest.

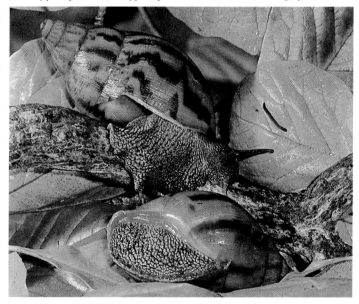

Limpet

'Limpet' is a term applied to various kinds of snails which, while not necessarily closely related, have two features in common. They cling tightly to rocks or other surfaces and they have a shell that is more or less tent-shaped. The best-known is the common limpet, flither or papshell, and related to it is the pretty little blue-rayed limpet or peacock's feathers, found on some of the large brown seaweeds at low tide, and the tortoiseshell limpet *Acmaea tessulata*. The keyhole limpet *Fissurella costaria* is named for the hole in the top of its conical shell and the slit limpet *Emarginula elongata* for the slit at the front. The Chinaman's hat *Calyptraea chinensis*, which retains a trace of its spire, is classified in the separate order Mesogastropoda. The limpet form has also been evolved independently in certain relatives of the pond snails. This repeated emergence of the limpet form in the evolution of snails is due to the advantage it gives in withstanding the action of fast-moving or turbulent water. It is particularly advantageous on rocky, wave-battered shores and it is on these that the common limpet, the main subject of this article, is so successful and abundant.

Under the protection of its ribbed, conical shell, which may reach nearly 3 in. in length, the common limpet has a grey-green oval foot with a large flat adhesive surface. At the front is the head with its big ear-like tentacles, each bearing an eye near its base. Lining the shell around its margin is the thin layer of tissue that secretes it and all around this skirt and lying in the space between it and the foot are many small ciliated gills and short tentacles.

Limpets are not suckers

The common limpet may occur in great numbers on rocky shores, from low water even to above the highest tide levels, provided the rocks are well splashed and shaded. As well as being resistant to wide temperature fluctuations limpets may flourish where the sea is greatly diluted with fresh water. Shells high up on the shore tend to be taller and thicker, especially near the apex, than those living lower down or in rock pools. Limpets are very difficult to dislodge, unless taken by surprise, and Reaumur found that a weight of 28 lb could be supported when attached to the shell.

Carving itself a niche

As well as giving resistance to wave action the ability to cling serves to protect limpets from predators. They are, however, a favourite food of oystercatchers and rats may take them in large numbers, dislodging them by a sudden movement of the jaws. It has been known for the tables to be

△ Chain of slipper limpets (with shore crabs). The slipper limpet forms chains of eight or nine, one on top of the other.
▽ Flattened delicate tortoiseshell limpet.
▷ ▽ The blue-rayed limpet with its rows of vivid blue spots.
▷ Village of common limpets.

turned and for a rat to become trapped with its lip under the shell, and birds have been caught by their toes. That man at one time ate them in large numbers is evident from the shells in his old kitchen middens.

A further advantage is that the limpet can seal a little water amongst its gills and so avoid drying up when the tide is out and in this, as well as in its clinging, it is helped by the close fit of shell to rock. This comes about in the first place from the choice of a suitable resting place, but it is improved both by the growth of the shell to fit the rock and by the abrasion of the rock to fit the shell. Each limpet has a definite 'home' to which it returns after each feeding excursion. Often the rock becomes so worn the limpet comes to lie in a shallow scar of just the right size and shape.

How limpets get home

Limpets leave their 'home' when the tide is in and the water not too rough, also when the tide is out at night or if they are sheltered by seaweeds. They feed by rasping at the small green algae on rocks, moving around with head and tentacles protruding and swinging from side to side. Large seaweeds are not often eaten but these may be prevented from colonising areas of rock through being devoured when small. On the return journey, the limpet tends to retrace its outward track at least in part. It seems to have some kind of directional

memory for feeling its way about like a blind man as it can still return even if its tentacles are removed and its outward track is obliterated by scrubbing with detergent or chipping away stone placed in its path. The journey may cover 2 or 3 ft and limpets moved farther away rarely return home.

Cold-weather larvae

The common limpet breeds during the colder months—September to April—shedding its eggs freely into the sea. The tiny trochophore larvae hatch out about 24 hours after fertilisation. Each is $\frac{1}{120}$ in. across, with a belt of long cilia around its middle, a tuft of them on top and short cilia covering the surface between the two. A day later, the larvae become veligers with little shells. These settle and grow to about an inch long in a year. Limpets may live as long as 15 years.

Changeable sexes

Most limpets start life as males and remain this way until they are 1 in. long. As they get older, however, the proportion of females increases as the limpets reverse their sex. This has gone much further in the slipper limpet *Crepidula fornicata*, a native of North American seas which was accidentally introduced into British waters in a cargo of oysters and has since made its way round the English coast. It is not related to the common limpet, and its shell resembles a rounded slipper when laid on its back. The slipper limpet forms chains of up to eight or nine, one on top of another. It is a serious pest of oyster beds and its arrival was first noted in Britain in the 1880's and since then it has become very well established on some parts of the coast and it has spread from there to other parts of Europe. In a chain of slipper limpets, the bottom ones are females and the upper, younger ones, males: those in between are of inter-mediate sex. It is believed that the females release a substance into the water that causes young limpets to stay in the vicinity and to develop male characters. Young males may later move off, however, and become fe-males, and immature individuals that settle on rock and not on females may themselves become females with only a short male phase, or none at all. Slipper limpets do not move about in search of food, but strain it from the water.

phylum	**Mollusca**
class	**Gastropoda**
subclass	**Prosobranchia**
order	**Archaeogastropoda**
family	**Patellidae**
genera & species	***Patella vulgata*** *common limpet* ***Patina pellucida*** *blue-rayed limpet, others*

Slug

Broadly speaking a slug is a snail without a shell. This is, however, not strictly correct because it may have a vestigial shell, usually hidden within the body. Slugs belong to the Pulmonata, a large group of land and freshwater molluscs that breathe by means of a lung. There are three types: keelback slugs, roundback slugs and shelled slugs, forming the families Limacidae, Arionidae and Testacellidae respectively. The first are named for the ridge or keel on the upper surface of the body towards the hind end. Behind the head with its four tentacles the back is covered by a roughly elliptical mantle-shield perforated by the respiratory pore on its right margin. In the keelback slugs this opening lies behind the middle of the mantle shield. In the roundback slugs the pore is farther forward. The tiny shell is a flattened oval, horny and with little lime in it, hidden under the mantle shield in the keelback slugs, but usually reduced to a number of separate chalky granules in the roundback slugs. An exception is seen in the North American roundback slug **Binneya** *in which there is an external spiral shell. The largest of these slugs may be 8 in. long, as in* **Agriolimax columbianus** *of North America.*

In the third group, the shelled slugs, there is a small shell visible on the surface towards the rear of the animal. A shelled slug may be anything up to 5 in. in length. Its mantle, heart and kidney lie under the shell towards the broad rear, instead of towards the front as in the other two families and a groove runs forward from the mantle on either side of the body, giving off branches to the back and flanks.

△ *Month-long incubation nearly over,* **Limax flavius** *eggs with embryos visible (approx* ×5*).*

▷ *A roundback,* **Arion ater**. *Although called the large black slug, its colour is very variable.*

Tree climbers

Through having such a useless, almost non-existent shell a slug is more vulnerable to predators and, more important, perhaps, to drying up. However, the animal's load is lightened, its need for calcium is much less and it can creep through much smaller holes than a snail. So slugs live in damp places and some species spend most of their lives underground. They are most active at night, or by day when it is wet, and some regularly return to the same 'home' after feeding. Though most feed near ground level, some are good climbers and regularly ascend trees to heights of 30 ft or more; the tree slug, *Lehmannia marginata*, formerly known as *Limax arboreum*, and field slug, *Agriolimax agrestis*, are two such climbers. The silver trails of slime running up and down some tree trunks attest to these activities, but the slug may take a more rapid route for the descent and lower itself many feet through the air on a string of slime. Such slugs spend the day in knotholes, coming down to the ground at dusk and climbing up again about dawn.

Other food than seedlings

Although hated by the gardener slugs may be vastly more numerous in his garden than even he is aware and, taking them as a group, very little of their food consists of the plants he has cultivated, except where there are few alternatives. Some slugs feed almost entirely on fungi, eating little or no green food and then only when it is dying or rotting. Many slugs are omnivorous and are attracted by fungi, greenstuff, tubers, carrion, dung, kitchen refuse or the metaldehyde-baited bran put out to kill them. They are drawn to such foods over distances of several feet by the odour, a slug's organs of smell being in its tentacles. In confinement, slugs may turn upon each other, but the shelled slugs are particularly notable for their predacious habits. They are most common in well-manured gardens and live underground most of the time. They feed by night on earthworms and to a lesser extent on centipedes and other slugs, seizing them with their needle-like teeth and swallowing them whole.

Aerial courtship

Slugs are hermaphrodite and although self-fertilisation can occur a two-way exchange of sperm between mating pairs is usual. In the first stages of mating, roundback and keelback slugs typically trail around each other in a circle, constantly licking each other and devouring each other's slime until they come to lie side by side. The great grey slug *Limax maximus*, up to 4 in. long, concludes this circling in a particularly spectacular manner. Climbing first up a tree or wall, the two slugs circle for a period of ½–2½ hours, flapping their mantles and eating each other's slime. Then suddenly they wind spirally around each other before launching themselves heads downward into the air on a thick cord of slime perhaps 18 in. long. Now the penis of each is unrolled to a length of 2 in. and entwined with the other into a whorled knot. Sperm masses are exchanged after which the slugs either fall to the ground or re-ascend their life-line, eating it as they go. The eggs are laid soon afterwards in some damp recess such as under a stone or among roots. The soft amber eggs hatch in about a month.

Many enemies

Despite their unpleasant slime, slugs are eaten by a variety of predators, including frogs, toads, hedgehogs, ducks, blackbirds, thrushes and other birds. Ducks are especially good for controlling the numbers of slugs. Slow-worms and various insects also take their toll. Though sheep are not deliberate predators of slugs, they do eat them accidentally and in doing so may become infected with lungworm, a parasitic nematode, whose larvae have formed cysts in the foot of the slug.

Universal panacea

For many centuries slugs have been regarded in folk lore as a sovereign remedy for a variety of ailments, eaten alive or boiled in milk for the cure of tuberculosis, for example, or in the form of ashes to relieve such diverse ills as ulcers, dysentery or hydrocephalus. The internal shell, or the little chalky grains representing it, were often regarded as particularly efficacious and, as Pliny recorded, quick relief could be obtained if the granules were placed in a hollow tooth. Warts even now are the target of various odd forms of treatment and one in recent use, at least until the turn of the century, if not later, involved the use of slugs. The method was to rub the wart with the slug and then to impale the mollusc on a thorn. As it died and withered away, so did the wart. One may doubt the value of these old remedies, but there are many people today who seek 'solace in a slug'.

phylum	**Mollusca**
class	**Gastropoda**
subclass	**Pulmonata**
order	**Stylommatophora**
family	**Limacidae**
genera	*Limax, Agriolimax, Lehmannia, Milax*
family	**Arionidae**
genera	*Geomalacus, Arion*
family	**Testacellidae**
genus	*Testacella*

Cockle

Of the various cockles the commonest by far is the edible cockle. Although its scientific name is now **Cerastoderma edule**, it is referred to in many books by the older name of **Cardium edule**, a name that reflects the heart-shaped appearance of the pair of shells viewed end-on, as well as the tastiness of their contents. The cockle is an unusually globular bivalve mollusc and the two 'valves', or shells, are similar in shape, unlike those of the scallop which, however, they resemble in being radially ribbed.

There are ten other British species of cockle in the superfamily Cardiacea. The largest, growing to a length of 4 in., is the spiny cockle, or red-nose, **Acanthocardia aculeata (Cardium aculeatum)** found mainly on the South Devon coast. It is named for the spines along the ribs on its shell and for its cardinal-red foot. Another spined species, smaller and more widely distributed, is the prickly cockle **A. echinata**. There are other bivalves that are known as cockles, but belong to other groups of molluscs, including the large heart cockle, **Glossus humanus**, **Cyprina islandica**, **Isocardia cor** and others.

The 200 or so species of cockles in the Cardiacea have a world-wide distribution and 11 occur around the coasts of Britain. The edible cockle is found from high-

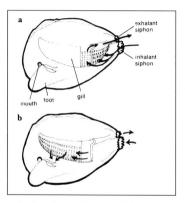

Above right: Cockle's siphon mechanism. **a:** Water is sucked in by one siphon and expelled by another, after passing through the gill. **b:** Trapped food drawn in with water is passed to the mouth by cilia. Below: Spiny cockle with siphon on right and pink foot showing between edges of mantle.

tide level down to 8 000 ft deep, lying
obliquely not more than 2 in. below the
surface of clean sand especially but
also in mud or muddy gravel. Generally
the average size increases from high to
low water. It is particularly common in the
sheltered waters of bays and the mouths of
estuaries, as many as 10 000 having been
recorded to a square metre. Although
cockles do live in estuaries, the largest,
about 2 in. long, are found far from fresh
water. Dilution of the salt water with
fresh has the curious effect of producing
a less regularly shaped shell which is
thinner and has fewer ribs than usual.

Digging with its foot

A cockle, in a most remarkable piece of
behaviour for a mollusc, may sometimes
skip upwards, bending in the middle, its
orange, tongue-like foot protruded between
the two valves and pressing the tip into the
sand before suddenly straightening it.
Usually, however, this merely rolls the
cockle over a few times. More often if the
cockle has been dislodged and has to move
it will creep along with its foot and re-bury
itself.

It has been suggested that the 20—24
ribs that radiate out from the hinge region
help to hold the cockle firmly in the mud or
sand in which it is usually just buried, and
that the globular shape helps to protect the
animal should it be dislodged and rolled
about by wave action.

At the back of the body is a pair of short
tubes, or siphons, joined at the base like the
legs of a pair of trousers. Water containing
oxygen and the plankton and organic matter which are the food of the cockle, is
drawn in through the lower one, that far-
thest from the hinge. Through the upper
sweeps an outgoing jet, carrying wastes. The
siphons are the only parts of the buried
animal to project above the sand, and so
they are an appropriate site for the eyes.
These are small but surprisingly complex,
with retinas and lenses, and are mounted on
sensory tentacles. They enable the tentacles
to be withdrawn if a shadow falls on them,
so protecting them from predators, but presumably eyes can have little other use in
such a sedentary, filter feeding animal.

To see what drives water through the
siphons, one must open the valves which
can be done when the cockle is clamped
shut, by cutting through the two muscles,
the adductors—one on each end and on
either side of the hinge—that pull the valves
together. If the cockle is dead, the valves
may have already been forced partly open
by the elastic ligament associated with the
hinge which opposes the action of the
muscles. The shell opened, the gills are revealed as a pair of flaps of tissue on each
side of the foot, covered with countless tiny
cilia whose beating sets up currents of water
and propels the particles of food towards
the mouth.

Usually a cockle stays in one place, and a
tuft of algae may grow on it as if it were a
stone. When the tide goes out the siphons
are withdrawn but the site where the cockle
is buried just below the sand may be revealed by the tuft of algae.

*Close-up of a cockle's siphons shows the eye-
bearing tentacles at their tips.*

Conveyor belt digestion

Cockles feed on the small plant particles
that abound in the water: single-celled
plants such as diatoms and the spores and
fragments of larger algae. There is little
selection of what is eaten, however, and the
stomach usually contains much sand and
mud as well. The water bearing these particles enters through the lower end of one
of the siphons and out by the other after
passing through the fine latticework of the
sieve-like gills. The cilia, as well as creating
this current, also act to propel the trapped
food towards the mouth, itself flanked by a
pair of cilia-covered lips. In the stomach is
a curious structure found in molluscs only,
a rotating coiled rod 20—26 mm long called
a 'crystalline style', turned by cilia lining the
pocket which secretes it. The crystalline
style, made up of digestive enzymes, gradually wears away and dissolves at the tip. Its
rotation serves to draw along the food particles trapped in strings of mucus, as on a
windlass, and at the same time its enzymes
help to digest the food.

Chancy breeding

Though some related species are hermaphrodite, the sexes are separate in the
edible cockle. Spawning begins at the end of
February or early in March and continues
till June or July, the eggs and milt being released freely into the water. Such eggs as
become fertilised by this uncertain means
develop into minute, free-swimming 'veliger' larvae, propelled by the beating of
cilia. Eventually each develops a shell and
foot, if it has not been eaten, and the resulting young cockles, still less than 1 mm long,
settle on the sea bottom, some falling on
stony ground and others on the sand or mud
in which they can grow to maturity. The success of spawning varies from year to year
and populations tend to be kept up by particularly good 'spat falls' perhaps once in
3 or 4 years.

As the shells grow, fine concentric grooves
appear, marking former positions of the
shell edge and providing a guide to age. The
groove reflects the slower growth of the
shell in winter when lack of sunshine means
there is less plankton food available. A full-
grown cockle has some 3—6 grooves and is
about that many years old.

*Cockle graveyard. Cockleshells are distinguished
by their 20—24 radiating ribs.*

Many enemies

For those cockles that escape man, life is still
precarious, for they may be attacked by
various parasites from within and by other
creatures from without: snails that bore
holes through their shells, starfish that pull
open the valves by sheer persistence and
push out their stomachs between them (see
abalone, page 31), gulls that attack when the
tide is out and flatfish, like plaice and dab,
when the tide is in. In addition, cockles can
be stranded above high tide level by storms
or carried away to other unsuitable areas.
They may be killed, like other shore creatures, by excessive heat or cold as in the
winter of 1904—5 when the Lancashire
coasts were covered with ice floes and hundreds of tons of dead cockles were washed
up the beach.

Athletic cockles

It has often been said that cockles can leap
across the sand. A naturalist in the early
years of this century used to entertain his
friends with a story about cockles hitting him
in the back. As he was walking up the beach
he felt something, perhaps a stone, hit him
in the small of the back. He turned about,
to find nobody in sight. Continuing up the
beach he was again hit in the back. Again he
turned and could see nobody. This time,
however, he saw one of the cockles leap, and
realized what was happening. He did not
say what kind of cockles they were, however.

Admittedly, this naturalist was not a tall
man, but his story may have made up for his
own lack of inches. From what we now
know, the spiny cockle does leap, but to
nothing like that extent. It has a very long
red foot, much longer than most other
cockles. When the tube-feet of a starfish, the
cockle's hereditary enemy, touch its shell
the spiny cockle leaps—for a distance of 8 in.

phylum	**Mollusca**
class	**Bivalvia**
subclass	**Lamellibranchia**
order	**Heterodonta**
family	**Cardiidae**
genus & species	***Cerastoderma edule** others*

Mussel

Various kinds of bivalve molluscs are known as mussels, including horse mussel **Modiolus modiolus***, fan mussel* **Pinna fragilis** *and the freshwater swan mussels* **Anodonta spp.** *The best known, however, is the common or edible mussel* **Mytilus edulis***, a species widely distributed over most of the temperate and subtropical coasts of the northern hemisphere, where it is found in very large numbers on the shores and down to about 30 ft. There are closely related species in other parts of the world. Both 'mussel' and 'muscle' derive from Latin* **musculus***, a small mouse.*

The adult edible mussel is 2 – 5 in. long but may be much smaller in some localities or, exceptionally, nearly 9 in. Typically blue or purple, or sometimes brown or with radial dark brown or purple markings, each of the two valves making up the shell is broad at the hind end and narrow at the front. Near the front end is the hinge and the elastic ligament that pushes the shell open when the muscles inside relax. There is one of these 'adductor' muscles at each end, running from one valve to the other, that at the hind end being largest and strongest. Their points of attachment can be seen as 'scars' inside empty shells, together with those of other muscles that withdraw the foot. When the mussel is submerged, this long brownish foot may be seen protruding from between the valves. Not only is it used for moving about, but also for making the tough protein threads, forming the byssus or beard, with which the mussel is normally anchored.

△ *A series of attachments. Mussels, themselves now covered by small organisms, coat the mooring chain of a ship in the Mediterranean.*

▽ *Permanent fixtures. Once anchored, adult mussels rarely move about although the young often do so for short periods.*

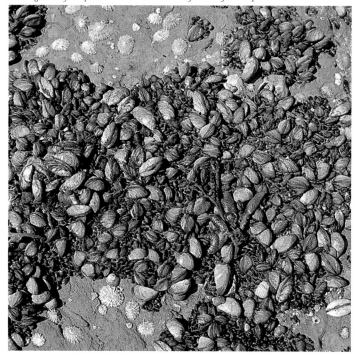

Millions of mussels

Secured by their byssus threads as by guy ropes, edible mussels are found from high on the shore to a depth of a few fathoms, principally near low tide mark, on rocks, pier piles or stones lying in mud or gravel. Few molluscs can rival them in abundance. Exceptionally, concentrations of 16 000 to a square foot have been seen and in some parts of the coast there may be 20 million in a mile stretch. In the northern hemisphere they range from the Kara Sea to the Mediterranean, on both coasts of North America and around Japan, as well as in a few other localities outside these areas, but not in the high arctic. The other species, such as the California mussel, *M. californianus* and the Australian mussel, *M. obscurus*, are so like the common mussel of the northern hemisphere that only an expert can tell them apart. Mussels can live in sea water considerably diluted with fresh water and can tolerate even further dilution for a while by clamping their shells. The adults rarely move about but the young do so fairly often, sometimes freely by means of their long extensible foot and sometimes by throwing out fresh byssus threads to pull themselves along with and then cutting loose the old byssus threads.

Water purifiers

Mussels feed by straining fine particles from the water together with small floating organisms like diatoms. On each side of the foot is a large gill, each double so there are actually four similar 'gill plates'. Each bears countless cilia beating in such a way as to draw water in at the hind end of the body, through the gill plates and out through a special opening at the rear. The inhalant and exhalant currents do not pass through siphons as well-developed as those of the cockle (page 40). As the food particles hit the gills they are caught up in mucus given out by the gills and are driven with it by cilia to the edges. Here the mucus enters special ciliated channels and moves forwards towards the mouth. On either side of the mouth are two much smaller gill-like flaps that sort the particles, directing the indigestible matter out along special rejection paths and the digestible into the mouth. All this requires the coordinated action of several different kinds of cilia with different functions. Some indication of what happens may be obtained by opening a mussel (cutting the adductor muscles), scattering powder on the gills and watching how it is carried along by the cilia.

Mussels and other animals feeding on microscopic particles are ultimate scavengers in the sea. Some idea of the effect they have can be gauged from an incident that took place at the Millport Marine Biological Station, in Scotland. There was a tank containing a number of common mussels and although there were other animals in it the mussels kept the water so clean that anyone looking down on it from above was unaware that there was any water in the tank. One day a visitor to the Station leaned over this tank and to get a closer look at the animals on the bottom of it, he lowered his face — right into the water!

Only one month's freedom

The breeding season varies with the locality, and also with the temperature of the water. Each egg is only about $\frac{1}{500}$ in. across but a single female may release 5 – 12 or even 25 million of them. The eggs are grouped together in short pink rods when they are shed, but these break up on sinking to the bottom. They are fertilised by sperm also released into the water and give rise to free-swimming ciliated embryos after about 5 hours. Towards the end of the second day, the shell appears, at first horn yellow and without a hinge. At this stage, the larvae feed and propel themselves by means of ciliated lobes projecting from their shells. Later the young mussels lose these lobes and improve their buoyancy by giving out a bubble of gas between their valves. Later, this is released, the larvae sink to the bottom, settle and give up their floating life. The free larval stage lasts about a month and by the time of settling, the larvae measure about $\frac{1}{50} - \frac{1}{25}$ in. Having settled, the young mussels may glide about rapidly on their ciliated feet or they may simply anchor themselves with the byssus threads. Until they are about $\frac{1}{8}$ in. long, they have the choice to do either of these, and they sometimes do them even at the surface of the sea, presumably held there by surface tension.

Mussels **Mytilus edulis**, barnacles and a colony of tunicates grow side by side but independently.

The world is against them

Mussels have many enemies, including dog whelks, herring gulls, oystercatchers, ducks and walruses as well as fish such as flounders and plaice. Starfish are often their chief predator, however, apart from man. Mussels are considered large enough to eat when just over 2 in. long and two or more years old. They are generally collected by dredging or raking, but in France they are farmed by a method said to have been invented in 1235 by a shipwrecked Irishman whose original intention was to construct a trap for sea birds. In this, tall hurdles are planted in the mud on the foreshore and on these the mussels are hung in bags of netting which eventually rot away after the molluscs have fastened themselves to the hurdles. For commercial purposes mussels are carefully washed and care must be taken by anyone collecting mussels for themselves, since their method of feeding is ideal for concentrating the bacteria in sewage, including those of typhoid. Sometimes, too, mussels produce an alkaloid that can cause death by stopping the breathing. As well as being sold as food, mussels are useful as bait in long-line fishing, as fertilisers, as chicken feed and sometimes for stabilizing the foreshore. At St Anne's-on-Sea, in Lancashire, mussels settle every 2 years on a gravel bed. During the next 2 years they form a mass of mussels and mud 2 ft deep. Then heavy seas roll the whole mass up like a carpet and smash it to pieces, after which the gravel is repopulated with mussels and the process starts all over again. Even so, the mussel carpet protects the foreshore from violent erosion.

Cloth of gold

The byssus threads are so strong that they can be woven into cloth. There are in various museums objects made from the beards of common fan mussels, for example gloves. The cloth woven from the larger bivalves was extensively used centuries ago to make some garments that had a golden sheen, and were used by the aristocracy especially those of southern Europe. The Field of the Cloth of Gold was an historic meeting between Henry VIII and the King of France. It was so called because so many of the nobles assembled there wore tunics made from the beards of bivalves. It had nothing to do with gold thread. Some other bivalves themselves make unusual use of their own beards. One *Modiolaria* lives embedded in a nest of its own byssus threads. The file shell *Lima* a relative of the scallop, builds a similar nest up to 10 in. across by darning bits of sea-bed debris together.

phylum	Mollusca
class	Bivalvia
sub-class	Lamellibranchia
order	Anisomyaria
family	Mytilidae
genus & species	*Mytilus edulis*

Oyster

△ *Gourmet's delight, an oyster lies in its larger left valve, pinky white and glistening.*

▽ *The highly convoluted shell with a fan-shaped base is the home of* **Ostrea gigas.**

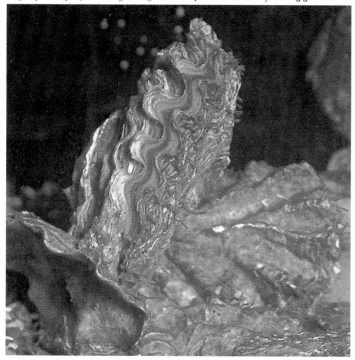

The true oyster of the family Ostreidae is the European flat oyster, **Ostrea edulis.** Its well-known shells are untidy and irregular in outline (often made more so by a variety of encrusting animals and plants growing on them) and there are such big local differences in appearance that with experience one can sometimes tell in which bed a particular oyster lived. The two valves are unlike, the right one being flat and the left convex. They are hinged in the pointed region of the 'beaks', held together by the triangular elastic ligament. There are no hinge teeth such as are found in many bivalves. On each valve a series of wavy ridges centres around the beak, marking former positions of the margin. Ill-defined ridges radiate from the beak of the left valve, while the other valve bears horny scales, which are less rigid than the rest of the shell, allowing the valves to make good contact around the edges when pulled together. Oysters are unusual for the soft porous chalky masses laid down within the substance of the shell. Often, also, in the convex valves of older oysters, there are chambers filled with sea water smelling of hydrogen sulphide. These chambers are the result of the mantle surface shrinking during life, and they get their smell from the putrefaction of organic matter.

Looking between the valves when they are agape, one sees just the edges of the mantle—the tissue that lines, and secretes, the inside of the shell. This thickened mantle edge has short sensory tentacles and a muscular fold that controls the flow of water. Opening the shell farther with a knife, one sees the large central adductor muscle that closes the valves against the pull of the hinge ligament. Arranged more than half way around this and the general body mass are two double crescentic gills.

The oyster family includes two other genera, **Pycnodonte** and **Crassostrea** (formerly **Gryphaea**). Amongst the latter are the American, Portuguese and Japanese oysters more of which are eaten than of the sweeter European flat oyster. The Portuguese oyster, **C. angulata,** introduced into France in 1868, has been relayed, during the last few years, to beds on the east coast of Britain, but it seldom breeds there. **Crassostrea** is easily distinguished from **Ostrea** since its shell is elongated rather than round, its left valve is more deeply convex and the muscle scars inside are deep purple. Apart from these true oysters, there are other bivalves bearing the name of 'oyster'. These include the tropical pearl oysters **Pinctada** which are closer to the mussels and are, like them, attached by byssus threads, the thorny oysters **Spondylus,** and the saddle oysters **Anomia** which live attached to rocks by thick calcified byssuses which pass straight through a notch in the lower valve.

Several ways of feeding

The European flat oyster occurs down the Atlantic coast of Europe from Norway (latitude 65°) to Morocco and also in the Mediterranean and Black Sea. When it first settles as spat, it becomes attached by its convex left valve, but later it may become detached and turned over. The adult oyster then stays in one place, feeding by filtering small particles from the water. By beating the cilia on its complex, lattice-like gills, it draws a current of water in at a rate of perhaps 2 or 3 gallons an hour. The food particles, caught in mucous strings on these ciliated sieves, are wafted either to the bases or to the free edges of the gills and thence forwards to the mouth via the palps which sit either side of it and have a sorting function. Once in the digestive tract, the particles continue to be propelled by cilia to the elaborate ciliated stomach. It is in the stomachs of bivalves and of a few snails that there occurs perhaps the only truly rotating structure in the whole animal kingdom. This is the crystalline style, a rod of solid digestive enzymes, rotated by cilia in the sac that secretes it, dissolving at the tip where it rubs against a piece of cuticle, the gastric shield, and helping to wind in the strings of mucus in the manner of a windlass.

Not only does digestion take place in the cavity of the gut, but cells lining it also take in particles and digest them in their cytoplasm. Furthermore, some of the particles are engulfed by amoeba-like blood cells that come out into the gut cavity through the stomach walls and then migrate back with the food particles trapped in them.

At times the oyster is in danger of becoming clogged with sediment in its mantle cavity and at such times the valves are clapped shut which suddenly expels the water and sediment. This sudden 'cough' contrasts with the sustained closure of the shell in response to dangers from outside. The adductor muscle is in two parts, different to the naked eye as well as in microscopic structure. One part can contract rapidly; the other is able to remain contracted for long periods without tiring.

Male or female

An oyster may change sex many times during its lifetime. This is not unusual amongst bivalves and the reproductive systems are so simple that the change involves little reorganisation. Maturing first as a male, the oyster takes some weeks to become a functional female but recovers his virility within a few days of discharging her eggs. In the cold waters off Norway, an oyster may change sex once a year, but in warmer waters, many times. Spawning occurs in summer when the temperature of the water exceeds about 15°C/60°F. The eggs pass through the gills against the water current and are fertilised in the mantle cavity by sperms carried in by the feeding current. They are not freed for about another 8 days. Then the shell is opened wide and closed violently and each time expelling clouds of larvae. Up to a million larvae may be incubated at a time, a large enough number, but small compared with the American oyster, *Crassostrea virginica*, which does not incubate its eggs but can release over a 100 million eggs at a time.

△ *All valves shut tight, a bed of European flat oysters lies exposed on rocks at low tide.*

The eggs of the European flat oyster are about $\frac{1}{200}$ in. across and as they develop within the shell of the parent they change from white to black. At one time, 'whitesick' and 'blacksick' oysters were thought to be males and females respectively.

Explosive spawning

When released, the young, then known as a veliger larva, has a tiny shell with two adductor muscles, a ciliated tuft, or velum, for swimming and feeding, and a foot. For between 1 and 2½ weeks the larva swims in the plankton, but when ready to settle, it protrudes its foot and grips any solid object it should touch. It then starts to crawl, but if the area is unsuitable, it can swim off again. Eventually, however, if it survives, the larva sticks itself down by its left valve using a drop of cement from the glands that in other bivalves secrete the byssus threads. At this stage, the oysters, about $\frac{1}{25}$ in. across, are known as spat. Now the shell grows rapidly and the body changes dramatically; foot, velum and eyes are lost, together with the anterior adductor muscles, the gill is increased and the mouth moves around through a right angle to the adult position.

It is important that males and females should spawn at the same time and to some extent this is aided by the dependence of spawning on temperature. In *Crassostrea* at least, however, chemical stimulation is also important. The sperms carry a hormone-like substance that stimulates spawning in both sexes and the males are also stimulated to spawn by the presence of eggs and by various organic compounds, including one present in seaweed. Thus one spawning individual can cause the whole population to release their eggs and spawn.

Downfall of the oyster

Great mounds of shells in coastal regions all over the world testify to the importance of oysters in the diets of many prehistoric communities. In Brittany there are banks 15 yds high, 700 yds long and 300 yds wide, containing shells of oysters, scallops and mussels. The Romans delighted in oyster orgies and were sufficiently impressed by English oysters to export them to Rome. Pliny records that the first person to establish artificial beds was Sergius Orata. During much of the 18th and 19th centuries, British beds were the most productive in Europe and vast quantities of this poor man's food were eaten. Today that huge harvest has dwindled so much that few can afford the price of a dozen oysters.

phylum	Mollusca
class	Bivalvia
subclass	Lamellibranchia
order	Eulamellibranchia
family	Ostreidae
genus & species	*Ostrea edulis* *European flat oyster, others*

Octopus

The name 'octopus' means literally 'eight feet' and the animal, indeed, has eight arms, joined at their bases by a web, and surrounding a beaked mouth. Octopuses differ most obviously from squids and cuttlefishes, the other well known members of the Cephalopoda, in lacking the extra pair of long tentacles. Moreover, their suckers, which run right along the arms, are not strengthened by the horny rings seen in the suckers of squids. Other differences are that octopuses have no trace of an internal shell and their body is short and rounded instead of being streamlined.

*The 150 species of octopuses are distributed throughout the seas of the world, but are especially numerous in warm seas. The smallest is **Octopus arborescens**, less than 2 in. across. The largest is the Pacific octopus, **O. hongkongensis** which reaches 32 ft across the arms although its thimble-shaped body is only 18 in. long. Another giant is **O. apollyon**, of the North Pacific, 28 ft across. The Octopoda also include species that are very different in form. One is the argonaut. Another is the blind deep-sea **Cirrothauma** of the North Atlantic, which has two large fins on its body. The web between its arms reaches almost to their tips and it swims by opening and closing this umbrella. Besides the suckers on the undersides of its arms, it has rows of filaments which are believed to be used for catching food particles. Its body has the texture of a jellyfish and it is said to be so transparent one can read newsprint through it. The common octopus, the species mainly dealt with here, lives off the coasts of tropical and subtropical Africa and Atlantic America, is especially numerous in the Mediterranean, and reaches the southern coasts of the British Isles. It may, exceptionally, reach a span of 10 ft but is usually much smaller. The lesser octopus, ranges from Norway to the Mediterranean. It is rarely more than 2½ ft across the widest span of its arms and can be readily recognized by the single row of suckers on its arms, instead of the double row in the common octopus.*

Master of disguise

The common octopus lives among rocks in shallow water, spending much of the time in a hole in the rocks or in a 'villa' built of stones. When outside, it creeps about on its arms most of the time, using its suckers to grip, though it can also swim. It usually swims backwards with its arms trailing, by blowing water out through its siphon. As in cuttlefish and squid, this water is blown out from the mantle cavity which houses the gills and the openings of the kidneys, rectum, reproductive organs and ink sac. Like cuttlefish and squid it can send out a cloud of ink to baffle pursuers.

There is no evidence that octopuses react to sound. However, the arms are very sensitive to touch and taste, and the eyes are well developed. The importance of vision is reflected in their outstanding ability to change colour. This is done with two kinds of chromatophores, or pigment cells, in the skin that vary in colour according to how much they are expanded or contracted. One kind varies from black to red-brown and the other from red to pale orange-yellow. Beneath these chromatophores is a layer of small bodies known as iridocytes that reflect white light or give a blue or green by refraction. The variation in appearance is not, however, just a matter of colour patterns but also of posture and of general texture. The arms may be extended, tucked underneath or curled stiffly back over the body as armour and the suckers may be out of sight or protruded to give the arms a wavy outline. By suitable adjustments in colour, posture and texture an octopus can merge completely with its background so it is extremely difficult to see. Octopuses also have a conspicuous display that often gives them away to fishermen searching for them. This is the so-called dymantic display, given when octopuses are frightened by large objects. The animal flattens out, coiling its arms in beside the body and extending the web between them. The body grows pale but dark rings develop around the eyes and the edge of the web also becomes dark. Presumably the purpose of this display is to deter predators, at least long enough for the octopus to change colour, blow ink and shoot away. With their large brains and adaptable behaviour, octopuses have been the object of a number of revealing studies on learning and brain function in lower animals. In captivity they rapidly settle down and become used to their captors.

Octopus attack

An octopus usually attacks only moving objects. It glides smoothly to within a few inches of its prey, collects itself together and then jumps forwards at it with a sudden backwards spurt from the jet. Small prey, mainly fish and crustaceans, is trapped beneath the expanded web between the arms, and then seized with the parrot-like horny beak around its mouth. At the same time a poison is given out that paralyses the prey. An average-sized octopus eats perhaps two dozen small crabs in a day. There are many reports of people being seized and held by octopuses and there is little doubt this does happen, perhaps rarely, and especially in warm seas. It seems, however, that these are not deliberate attacks but more a matter of investigating a moving object, and people have found that if they keep still, the octopuses will 'feel' them for a short while, then let go.

Coldblooded courtship

In mating, which may take several hours, male and female sit apart. There is almost no courtship display, although the male may expose certain particularly large suckers near the base of the second pair of arms, as if 'making a pass' at the female. The only contact he has with her is through a single arm which he extends to caress her. This arm is always the third arm on the right side which is specially modified for the purpose and has a spoon-shaped tip. It is called the hectocotylus arm. The tip of this arm is placed in the female's gill cavity

▽ *Smoke screen: an octopus ejects a cloud of ink to deter a predator and to escape behind.*

▷▽ *Tiny suction pads to grip the rock cover the tentacles which surround a central mouth.*

▷ *A cruel but beautiful animal, an octopus glides effortlessly through the deeps.*

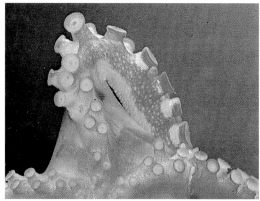

△ *Blue-ringed octopus* **Hapalochlaena maculosa** *swimming backwards, its arms trailing.*

◁▽ *An all-seeing eye of an octopus. The siphon blows out water from the mantle.*

△ *Sea-spider: blue-ringed octopus. It usually attacks only moving objects.*

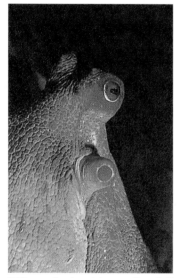

and the sperms are deposited near the opening of her oviduct in elaborate packages called spermatophores.

A female lays about 150 000 eggs in about a week, each in an oval capsule slightly smaller than a grain of rice. They are attached by short stalks to long strands that festoon the mother's lair. The mother broods over the eggs for several weeks, often cleaning them with her arms or blowing water over them with her funnel. During this time, she eats little. Indeed, she may fast completely for weeks, or for as much as 4 months in one species, and a brooding female in an aquarium has been seen to remove food placed near her and drop it well away from her. The short-armed young hatch at about ⅛ in. long and drift around for a while before they start their own life on the bottom, by which time they may be ½ in. long and several weeks old. The common octopus rarely, if ever, breeds on the coasts of the British Isles although, year after year, larvae migrate across the Channel from Brittany. Sometimes after a mild winter, the numbers of octopus may reach plague proportions, to the detriment of the crabs and lobsters.

True or false?
It is sometimes said that octopuses can feed on bivalve shellfish by jamming stones between the valves to stop them closing. Pliny, the Roman naturalist, recorded this

and in 1857 Jeannette Power, the French naturalist, wrote of an octopus, failing to force open a large mussel, picking up a stone and inserting it when the shell next opened.

This is a very pretty tale and not to be discounted out of hand, but several zoologists have watched in vain for this behaviour, and some have experimented with octopuses in aquaria but without result. Moreover, it is unlikely that the octopus, for all its relatively capable brain and sensitive arms, can ever perform such skilled manipulations. The trouble is that the shape of the body is just too variable, so the nervous system would need to be very complex to take into account all the bends and twists in the arms, and at the same time monitor and control such an intelligent action.

phylum	**Mollusca**
class	**Cephalopoda**
order	**Dibranchiata**
suborder	**Octopoda**
family	**Octopodidae**
genera & species	***Eledone cirrosa*** *lesser octopus* ***Octopus vulgaris*** *common octopus, others*

▽ *The ever-changing octopus camouflages itself as coral, altering both its shape and colour.*
▷▽ *The focal point. The well-developed eyes of the octopus have a large cornea which gives them a range of vision of 180 degrees.*

Earthworm

The earthworm, so familiar to gardeners, has many varieties, and the two dozen British earthworms are not all easily recognised at a glance. The brandling **Eisenia foetida** has alternating bands of red-brown and yellow and a strong smell, and has always been sought by anglers as a potent worm bait. It lives in dung and compost heaps, as does the gilt-tail **Dendrobaena rubida**. Another distinguished by its colour is the green worm **Allolobophora chlorotica**. The species usually referred to as the earthworm is, however, the large **Lumbricus terrestris**, up to 10 in. long (rather short by comparison with the 11ft earthworms of Australia). The reddish tinge of this and other earthworms is due to the oxygen-carrying pigment haemoglobin in the blood. The long body is divided into ring-like segments (150 of them in **L. terrestris**) and some of the internal organs, those for excretion for example, are duplicated in most of these segments. At the tapering front end is the mouth with its overhanging prehensile lip, but with no teeth or jaws. Around the body, like a cigar band (segments 32-37 in **L. terrestris**) is what is sometimes taken for a scar, where the worm has been cut in two and healed again. It is in fact a special gland, the saddle or clitellum, which secretes the cocoon.

How the earthworm burrows

An earthworm moves along by waves of muscular contraction travelling back along the body. Each body segment acts as a unit lengthening as it becomes narrower under the action of circular muscles, becoming broader as it shortens, pulled in by longitudinal muscles. When a group of the segments are pushing out sideways into the wall of a burrow, holding the worm firm at that point, elongation of the foremost segment of the group pushes forwards the segments in front. At the same time another segment, in the group at the rear, becomes shorter and fatter. This continues until the whole worm has moved forwards.

Extra grip is given during crawling, especially on the surface of the ground, by short, backwardly-directed bristles, which can be pushed out as required. There are four pairs on each segment except the first and last. These can be felt on the underside, more easily than seen, by drawing a worm backwards through the fingers.

Tree-climbing earthworms

Although a worm burrows partly by pushing soil aside, it also eats much of it. In some species, swallowed soil is voided at the surface in the familiar worm casts, though this is not true of L. terrestris which seldom makes casts. Some earthworms, like the gilt-tail, climb trees and may sometimes be found under the bark. The brandling, too, often scales trees and fences. After heavy rain in India, earthworms have been seen

△ *Worm casts – soil drained of humus and nourishment by the earthworm's gut – on a lawn.*

▽ **Lumbricus terrestris** *is the familiar garden 'lobworm', the angler's heavyweight worm bait.*

migrating uphill and even up trees, presumably to avoid immersion. They were, however, probably in no danger of drowning, since earthworms can be kept under water for months and still survive. Those found dead in puddles have probably died from other causes. Getting too dry is more dangerous for a worm than getting too wet. In dry weather and in winter, worms may burrow as much as 8 ft below the surface. At such times, they may pass into a state of inactivity in mucus-lined chambers in the ground.

Fleeing from moles

Earthworms have no ears or eyes but their surfaces – especially the upper – are sensitive, even to light. A worm can detect the vibrations from a mole digging, and large numbers of earthworms will come to the surface, as if in panic, when a mole is working nearby. Pushing a stick into the ground and wriggling it about also brings worms to the surface. Should an earthworm fall foul of a predator, it may lose only part of itself, torn or cast off by reflex action (autotomy). The remaining portion of worm can often regrow the lost part. The amount of this regrowth varies from one species to another, but it is usually limited to a few segments at the front end and slightly more at the hind end.

Rudimentary intelligence?

The chief food of earthworms is decaying plant matter although they sometimes eat small dead animals, such as other worms, and droppings. Some food is taken in with soil swallowed in burrowing, but vegetation lying on the ground near the mouth of the burrow is also important. This is pulled into the burrow and to some extent pre-digested by digestive juices from the mouth before being eaten. Charles Darwin in *The formation of vegetable mould through the action of worms*, a book published in 1881 just before his death, showed that leaves, pine needles and even paper would be drawn in and used to line the upper parts of the burrows. In spite of the fact that worms are blind, the leaves and paper triangles with which he experimented were usually drawn in by their pointed ends. Clearly it is easier to

draw in a leaf by the tip than by the edge, and Darwin reasoned that this behaviour showed rudimentary intelligence. Several biologists have since looked into this and it seems clear now that leaves are pulled down in the way which is mechanically most efficient, that is, by the tips. The worms reach from their burrows, grasp leaves at random, and pull. If the leaves meet with resistance they let go and try again. Success comes when they happen to grasp the tip of the leaf, and so they do this largely by simple trial-and-error and not by intelligent action. There is, however, more to it than this, for worms respond to some of the chemicals in the vegetable matter, showing a preference for the chemicals of the leaf tips rather than those of the bases and stalks.

A worm's castle

It is not unusual to find heaps of pebbles on gravel paths, as if torrential rains had washed the gravel uneven. This is probably the normal interpretation. But if one takes a closer look it is possible to see that around each hillock there is bare earth, and in this are impressions of the outlines of pebbles on the heap nearby, showing that something has lifted the pebbles up carefully and placed them on the heap. If one of these heaps is carefully taken apart we find a worm-cast at the centre and beneath it a small mound of earth forming the core of the heap. The heap will consist of up to 200 pebbles of a total weight of about 22 oz, the pebbles ranging from pea-sized to 1½ in. across and weighing 1½ oz.

The best way to see what is making these heaps is to go out after dark after a light shower of rain with a red lamp, walking carefully so as not to cause vibrations in the ground. From each heap a worm will be seen stretching out, anchored by its tail in the centre of the heap, and with luck one may see a worm pressing its mouth against the surface of a pebble to form a sucker. It is not easy to catch the worm actually in the act of moving the pebble but one can hear, as one stands silent, the occasional chink of a pebble being moved, and there is the impression in the surface of the soil, already mentioned, showing the outline of a pebble now lying on top of the

heap, to give evidence that it has been moved gently.

We know that worms will pull leaves into the burrow, and they will also drag in small sticks, feathers, even pieces of wool lying on the ground. We can only surmise that it is necessary for the worm to clear part of the earth's surface to feed. On a piece of ground without pebbles it is possible with care to watch earthworms feeding by stretching out from the entrance to the burrow and running the mouth over the surface of the earth rather like the nozzle of a vacuum cleaner while swallowing movements can be seen, as if the worm were sucking in minute particles of soil or food material as part of a meal.

Economical breeding

A visit to a lawn on a warm, still night that is not too dry will show worms joined in pairs, each with its hind end in its burrow. Some species pair below ground. Each worm is hermaphrodite and sperms are exchanged during the three or four hours in which the pairs are united, held together by slime from the clitellum and by certain of the bristles.

Egg-laying begins about a day after mating, and this may continue for several months without further pairing (belying the view of Gilbert White, the 18th-century English clergyman and naturalist, that the earthworms are 'much addicted to venery'). As they are laid, the eggs become enclosed in a cocoon secreted by the clitellum and are fertilised by sperm stored in it – not, as one might expect, from inside the body. The cocoon of *Lumbricus terrestris* is pea-sized and dark brown. Although several eggs are laid in each cocoon, together with a thickish albumen, only one embryo usually survives. The young worm emerges after 1 – 5 months and is ready to reproduce after another 6 – 18 months. How long worms usually survive is uncertain but *L. terrestris* has been kept 6 years in captivity and *Allolobophora longa* 10¼ years.

Churning up the soil

Estimates of earthworms to the acre have been as high as 3 million, or 15 cwt. Without their continual action in aerating and drain-

An earthworm's main nerve (centre) branches off into each segment of its body. Septal branches run next to each dividing wall; interseptal branches run into the middle of each segment. The 'brain' (not shown here) consists of 2 knots of nerve cells above the gullet.

Two blood vessels run the length of a worm, one above, one below. Connecting these like the hoops of a barrel are circular vessels; 5 pairs of these (in segments 7 – 11) are dilated and pulse rhythmically forming the 'pseudo hearts' (ringed in the horizontal section below).

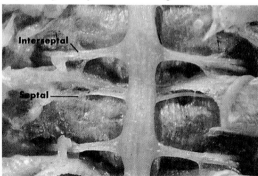

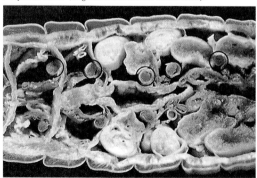

50

△ *Earthworms mating; the process takes 3–4 hours, during which the couple both keep their hind ends in their respective burrows.*

▽ *Sweating it out; to conserve moisture in a dry spell, an earthworm coils itself in a small chamber which it lines with its own mucus.*

ing, pulling down leaves and throwing up worm casts, the earth, or at least uncultivated land 'would soon become cold, hardbound, and void of fermentation; and consequently sterile', as Gilbert White wrote in 1777, a time when 'gardeners and farmers express(ed) their detestation of worms'.

Darwin pointed out, however, that the action of earthworms may be harmful on sloping ground and assist in denudation, the soil brought up from below the surface being washed or blown downhill.

Worms occur in the highest numbers in grassland, where there is plenty of food and no disturbance, and the population declines drastically if the ground is dug or ploughed. There is a limit to the earthworm's toleration of soil acidity and, if this is exceeded, vegetation accumulates on the surface as a mat which eventually becomes peat.

From the weights of daily collections of worm casts, Darwin estimated that $7\frac{1}{2}$ to 18 tons of soil can be thrown up per acre each year, equivalent to $1-1\frac{1}{2}$ in. over 10 years. One result is a very fine surface layer of soil and, at the same time, large stones tend not only to be buried under the collection of casts but also to be undermined. This is why some of the outer stones of Stonehenge have started to disappear – the present rate of covering there is estimated at about 7 in. per century, a rate considerably exceeded in some of Darwin's experiments. This also explains why so many Roman remains are now buried. In a ditch at Verulamium (St Alban's) which had been sealed over by the floors of successive buildings during the first 4 centuries AD – with no apparent way in or out – have been found certain 'mud worms' *Eophila oculata*. These require very little oxygen and had plenty of food.

phylum	**Annelida**
class	**Oligochaeta**
order	**Prospora**
family	**Lumbricidae**
genus & species	*Lumbricus terrestris others*

To add to the worm's grip while tunnelling and crawling, pairs of bristles (setae) grow through the skin (top left). The central gut is buckled, increasing the surface area.

An earthworm strains liquid waste through tubes (nephridia) inside the body wall, one pair per segment. Also shown below is the ventral nerve cord below the central gut.

In the worm's 13th segment the ovaries flank the ventral nerve cord (centre, with one of the two main blood vessels above it). Eggs are laid in a cocoon already containing sperm.

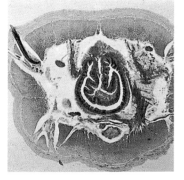

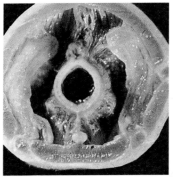

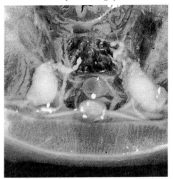

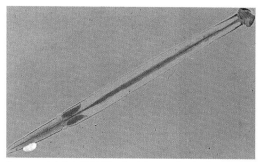

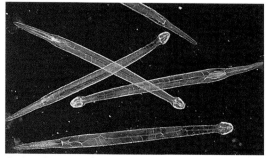

Arrow worm's body is divided into head, long trunk and tail. A jaw-hook and spines can be seen on the head; and two ovaries, full of eggs.

Sagitta elegans × 3½. *The silvery network in the trunk is the nervous system. Millions drift passively with the currents in the sea's plankton.*

Arrow worm

Among the myriads of tiny animals that float in the sea and are known as plankton, there are some with narrow, transparent bodies ¾ in. – 4 in. long. These are the arrow worms.

At certain times of the year a tow net will catch vast quantities of them, but, when one looks down into the water, they will be very difficult to see. Their bodies are transparent, save for a pair of minute black eyes on the head, and can be seen readily only with food inside them.

When taken into the laboratory and coloured with special dyes, an arrow worm's body can be seen to have three sections: a short head, a long trunk comprising most of the body and a short tail. Arrow worms swim by up-and-down movements of the trunk and tail, aided by fins on the side of the body. **Sagitta**, *the common arrow worm around the British Isles, has two pairs of fins on the trunk and a single, paddle-like fin on the tail.*

The mouth is surrounded by a thin hood covering two sickle-shaped hooks that serve as jaws. On the hooks and around the mouth there are sharp spines which are used for capturing food when the hood is drawn back to expose them.

Throughout the oceans

Almost any bucketful of sea water will contain arrow worms. Most species live near the surface of the open seas but others live around the shores or at great depths, where they may be a beautiful golden-orange. They can swim by flexing their bodies but they cannot travel far on their own accord. Usually they swim passively in the water drifting with the currents.

Although the ocean appears to be the same in any part of the world, parts of it are as different as jungles and deserts on land. Throughout the ocean, the temperature and salt concentrations vary, and the distribution of the different animals varies with them, each animal being restricted to areas where conditions suit it. This is not strictly true for all marine animals, as the common mauve jellyfish *Aurelia* is world-wide, but it is true for arrow worms.

Arrow worms often migrate vertically, from the surface layers to deeper water and back. This is a habit of many planktonic animals and it is thought that many of them swim down to get away from too bright a light during the day. Arrow worms sink during the day and night, coming to the surface at dawn and dusk so that they are always in the most suitable dim light intensity.

Voracious feeders

Arrow worms are voracious creatures. They hang motionless in the water and dart at their prey, propelled by rapid flicks of the body. In a flash, they cover distances several times their own length, an unusual turn of speed for a planktonic animal, many of whom can barely swim at all but merely drift about. The prey is grappled by the bristle-covered jaws and hauled into the mouth where a sticky secretion, from special cells in the lining of the mouth, at once immobilizes it by gumming up its legs. It also acts as a lubricant to ease the passage down the gut.

Any small animal is taken, including other arrow worms, while herring larvae larger than the arrow worm itself are eaten in large numbers, especially in January and February when just hatched.

Not all arrow worms chase their prey. *Spadella* from the shores of south-west England lives in pools, attached to rocks or seaweed by special suckers on its tail. As a small crustacean swims past its head the arrow worm strikes at it with its jaw, without releasing its hold on the rock. The prey is worked round by the spines until head or tail can be dragged into the mouth.

Breeding

Like many invertebrate animals, arrow worms are hermaphrodite, that is, each individual has both male and female reproductive organs. In arrow worms the ovaries lie in the trunk and the testes in the tail. Eggs of one individual are usually fertilised by sperms from another, but self-fertilisation occurs in some species. The eggs are released into the sea where they develop into larvae, that later change into adults. Correct water temperature during the breeding season appears to be important to many arrow worms. If the sea currents carry them too far north, into colder waters, they fail to breed and, instead, grow to twice their normal size.

Guide to ocean currents

If a plankton net is towed up the English Channel from the open Atlantic Ocean the arrow worm *Sagitta elegans* will be caught in large numbers, but, just as the ship nears Plymouth, it disappears, to be replaced by another species *Sagitta setosa*. The change is so abrupt that on one occasion a marine biologist was able to catch *elegans* from the bows of his ship and *setosa* from the stern. The two look very much alike but can easily be told apart because if dropped into weak formalin preservative *setosa* remains transparent while *elegans* becomes opaque. This is a great convenience to the biologists of the Marine Laboratories at Plymouth because they can instantly distinguish between water from the channel, called *setosa* water for convenience, and water upwelling from the Atlantic, *elegans* water.

To the man in the street it may appear a matter of little importance whether one kind of arrow worm is found in one part of the Channel and not another, but in fact this knowledge helped to account for an otherwise baffling problem. During the first part of this century, fishermen used to put out from Plymouth to catch herring that appeared in the Channel off Cornwall every winter. During the 1920's the herring gradually ceased coming up the Channel and in a short while no more herring boats were to be seen. The fishermen, deprived of a means of livelihood, were unable to say where the herring had gone. For some years at the Plymouth Marine Laboratory routine tow-nettings were made and samples of plankton were brought back to the laboratory and analysed. These showed that *Sagitta elegans* was gradually moving further up the Channel. This could mean only one thing: that oceanic water was coming in from the Atlantic across the fishing grounds. Herring are very sensitive to changes of temperature. It became clear that the loss of the herring fishery off the south coast of England was due to the herring being driven away by the shift in the water currents.

phylum	**Chaetognatha**
genus & species	**Sagitta setosa** **S. elegans**

Pogonophore

The name of these marine animals means literally 'beard-bearers', and if the name sounds mildly ridiculous, this is in keeping with the whole history of the group. The pogonophores represent a branch of the animal kingdom that was completely unknown until 1914, and which attracted little attention even among marine zoologists until about 25 years ago. Yet they seem now to be the most widespread and abundant sea animals.

The 100 or more known species of pogonophores are worm-like and extremely slender; a 5in. individual being ⅟₅₀ in. thick. Most are a few inches long; the largest is just over a foot. Each lives in a transparent horny tube little wider than itself, but five times as long, which has ring-like markings at intervals along its length. The animal itself is made of different sections, each having a slightly different shape. In front is a long tentacle or tentacles—there may be as many as 200 or more in some species—fringed with pinnules. At the rear end are spines, or short bristles, like those on the bodies of

earthworms and marine bristleworms. They probably help the animal to move up and down inside its tube. No mouth or other special organs have yet been identified.

These animals have now been found in all oceans, mainly at great depths, down to 25 000 ft, but in recent years some have been discovered in shallower water.

Mystery tube-dwellers

Dredged up and kept alive for only a few hours, living pogonophores are difficult to observe. Their way of life has to be deduced from what can be seen in the dead animal. They live only where the seabed is fine mud, and seem to spend most of their time inside semi-permeable tubes, through which water can pass. This may be important to the animal inside the tube because incoming water would bring oxygen for breathing. Studies at very high magnification with electron microscopes have shown a complicated body structure, including a nerve network and blood vessels containing red blood with haemoglobin. No digestive organs have been seen. The nearest thing they have to a brain is a group of nerve cells, the ganglionic mass. Tests made with living pogonophores showed that they reacted only slightly to being touched.

A question of feeding

There has been much speculation about the way pogonophores feed, as to whether they take particles of food from the water by gripping them with the pinnules on the tentacles or whether the pinnules give out a sticky secretion to which the particles adhere. Another suggestion has been that the tentacles may sweep the surface of the mud for particles. Where there are many tentacles they form tubes or complicated spirals, and it is believed food may be caught and digested in these, as in a sort of external stomach. These tentacles may also secrete fluids which digest the food externally, the nutrients being absorbed through the skin. The most favoured view is that these animals absorb nutrients dissolved in the seawater through their skin, but all these suggestions are no more than inspired guesses.

*Overleaf: The single tentacle of **Siboglinum** often coils up into this shape. Along its length is a double row of fine unicellular pinnules.*

*▽ A rare photograph of the pogonophore **Oligobrachia ivanovi** from the north east Atlantic. This large pogonophore is seen partly removed from its tube, its seven tentacles coiled up into an orange mass (× 10).*

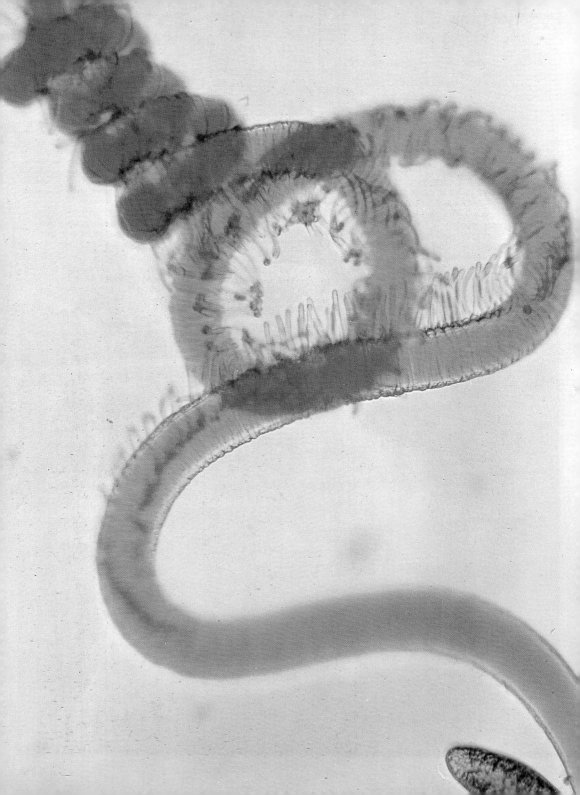

Unknown breeding habits

Some pogonophores that have been examined have contained large yolky eggs, others have had sperms enclosed in capsules, or spermatophores. There is nothing to show whether the sperms are merely liberated into the sea to find their way to ova in other individuals, or whether pogonophores join together in some simple form of mating. Estimates have been made of how densely they live. These vary from 50 to 500 per sq yd, but even the more densely crowded would have difficulty in contacting each other. The most reasonable assumption seems to be that the sperms are liberated into the sea, yet the fact that they are in a capsule, would suggest that the male places them on the female, or in her tube. Embryos and larvae have been found in some of the tubes. The embryos are rounded, with two girdles of cilia around the front and the rear ends. As the cilia beat in a wave-like action the embryo slowly revolves on its axis. Later, the embryo grows longer, into what may be called a larva, in which the future hair-like adult pogonophore is foreshadowed.

Ancestral pogonophore – the tapering tube of the fossil **Hyolithellus**, *buried over 500 million years ago in Cambrian rocks in Greenland. The indentation above the tube probably marks the position of the animal when feeding (× 8).*

The youngest phylum

The very existence of the phylum Pogonophore was entirely unknown and wholly unsuspected until 1914, when specimens were examined by the French zoologist Professor M Caullery. These were collected by the Dutch research ship *Siboga* dredging in the seas of the Malay Archipelago. He worked on them from 1914 to 1944 but was unable to find any relationship between them and other animals. He named them *Siboglinum* after the Dutch ship, *linum* being Latin for flax or linen thread. Then, in 1933, more were dredged up in the Pacific, and the view began to be taken that they were degenerate bristleworms. Soviet research ships began to find large numbers of pogonophores in the Sea of Okhotsk and later in the Indian Ocean, Antarctic and Atlantic Oceans. The Russian zoologist AV Ivanov decided, in 1955, that they represented a new phylum, which he named the Pogonophora. In plain terms an entirely new section of the animal world had been discovered.

The pogonophores have been described as looking like threads, like bits of string, or like trawl twine – or even contemptuously as

A developing ciliated embryo of **Siboglinum** *removed from its mother's tube. There is a broad ciliated band on the protosoma below the apical cone, and another smaller band at the end of the body on the metasoma (arrowed) (× 160).*

looking like chewed string! We know now that research ships at sea had been finding masses of these tangled threads in their dredges. They cluttered the decks when the dredges were emptied onto them and on a British research ship they were given the name of the Gubbinidae – and shovelled back into the sea ('gubbins' is a slang name, often used by scientists, for unidentifiable 'insignificant' rubbish!). This alone shows how abundant they are on the ocean bed. It also shows why nobody took any notice of them; they looked like fibrous rubbish.

There is a great deal yet to be learned about the pogonophores. Some of it may shed light on the evolutionary history of the vertebrates. The current opinion is that they are most closely related to the supposed forerunners of the vertebrates, such as the acorn worm.

phylum	**Pogonophora**
order	**Athecanephria**
order	**Thecanephria**

Tree-like tube of **Polybrachia**, *this middle section has membranous frills. Like many small pogonophores it has ring markings and is divided into segments. The rigid tube is composed of chitin and proteins (× 5).*

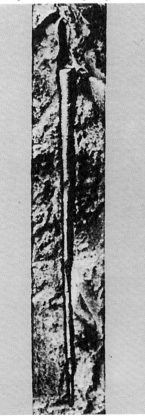

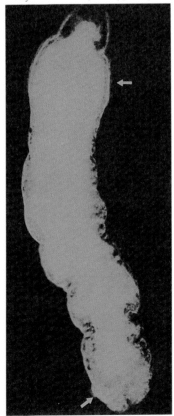

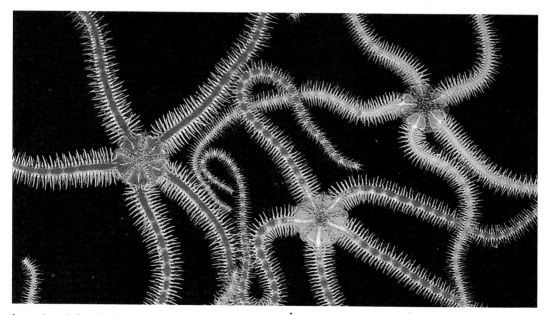

*In some places, the floor of the English Channel is carpeted with masses of common brittlestars, **Ophiothrix fragilis**. These are shown here at about the size of the largest specimens, but they are usually half this size. The name refers to the ease with which the arms fall off when handled.*

Brittlestar

*These are echinoderms closely related to the basket stars and somewhat more distantly related to the starfish. Like the latter, they have five arms joined to a central body, although some species may have more arms. The body, or disc as it is known, is button-shaped, and the arms are snake-like, hence the scientific name of its class, Ophiuroidea, from the Greek **ophis**, serpent. The English name alludes to the ease with which the arms fall off. Any that do come off are regrown.*

Some brittlestars are a light grey in colour but many are delicately coloured. The largest brittlestars have discs of 4 in. diameter with a spread of 2 ft across the arms. Another has a disc only ½ mm across.

The arms are covered with rows of hard plates and spines, while running down their centres are 'vertebrae' forming a flexible structure very much like our backbone. Muscles controlling movement are attached to these vertebrae. Along the underside of the arms are rows of tube-feet, or podia. These are badly named as they are used for feeding. Similar structures in starfish are used for walking.

Widely distributed

Brittlestars are found in seas all over the world from the tideline to deep water. One species is almost cosmopolitan, being found off the shores of Europe and New Zealand and on both east and west coasts of America.

Many species of brittlestar live on the seabed, burrowing into it if it is muddy.

Others live amongst seaweeds and corals, climbing around the fronds by grasping them with their flexible arms rather like a monkey swings through the trees. On the seabed they move by waving the arms in a rowing action. Either two or four arms work together in pairs. The fifth is held out in front or trails behind, sometimes assisting in the motion by a beating action. By this means brittlestars can travel at speeds of as much as 2 yd/min, which is quite fast compared with the slow crawls of other echinoderms such as starfish or urchins which drift along on their tube-feet.

Two ways of feeding

Brittlestars have two basic feeding methods. They capture small particles on the arms, which are then passed to the mouth that lies on the underside of the disc, or they tear off lumps of dead flesh or seaweed with the tube-feet and teeth around the mouth.

Collecting small particles is a passive method of feeding. The brittlestar rests on the seabed or burrows down into the mud, leaving only the arms from which long sticky mucous threads wave about in the water. Organic debris in the mud or floating in suspension, as well as minute planktonic animals and plants, are trapped in the mucus.

The skin around the arms is covered with cilia (protoplasmic hairs) which sweep the mucus and the entrapped particles in towards the tube-feet on the underside of the arms. The tube-feet also help in this movement by 'licking' around the parts of the arm within reach. In this way they become covered in a mixture of mucus and particles. This is then wiped off against a spine near each one and the resulting mass transferred on the tip of the tube-foot to another nearer

the mouth. As the mass is moved inwards more is added and it is patted by the tube-feet to form a compact ball. Eventually it is brought to the root of the arm, where it is transferred to tube-feet around the mouth. These taste the ball and, if it is acceptable, they force it into the mouth. If unpalatable, they reject it, pushing it back onto the arm. It is then passed back down the arm and released to drift away.

Brittlestars also feed on larger animals or carrion. Large lumps of food, up to 1 in. across are caught, wrapped in an arm and held by the tube-feet. The arm then curves over to carry the food to the mouth. Smaller lumps are grasped by the arm then transferred along it by the tube-feet in the same way as the mucous ball. Lumps of food still smaller are merely grasped by the tube-feet without the arms flexing over to hold them.

Brittlestars can detect the presence of food, provided it is upstream of them, presumably by 'tasting' chemicals liberated from the food. The arms wave about. Then having found out in which direction the food lies, the brittlestar moves towards it.

Simple sexual organs

In most species, eggs and sperms are merely shed into the sea, where fertilisation takes place. The sexual organs are, therefore, very simple. There are genital openings at the base of each arm through which the sex cells are discharged. There may, however, be a bag, or bursa, just inside the slit, into which the cells are discharged from the gonads.

The fertilised eggs develop into delicate larvae with long arms, stiffened with fine rods, and covered with cilia whose beating keeps the larva from sinking. The larva is called an *ophiopluteus, pluteus* meaning easel-like, an apt description. After floating about for some time, the larva develops into the adult form and settles on the seabed.

A few brittlestars do not have free-swimming larvae but retain their eggs in the bursae or in the ovaries, where they develop into small adults before crawling out through the genital slits. These species are often hermaphrodite, having both male and female sex organs, but they avoid self fertilisation by the cells of one sex ripening before the other.

Lost arms replaced

Brittlestars fall a prey to fish such as plaice and dab, that feed on the sea bottom. The species that burrow into the mud avoid predation to some extent, apart from having their arms bitten off which is of no great importance as the arms are readily regrown.

Some brittlestars have light-producing cells on the spines of the arms and when one arm is bitten off, the others produce a flash of light as the brittlestar withdraws. This, presumably, deters the predator from following up the attack (and may even put it off attacking any more brittlestars).

Brittlestars cling together

Around the shores of the eastern coast of the United States there is a brittlestar that normally lives amongst the stems of eelgrass, hanging onto them by its arms. In winter the eelgrass dies back and the brittlestars twine their arms around each other to form a tight bunch. This habit has been examined in the laboratory. Whenever they are deprived of eelgrass the brittlestars bunch together, but it has been found that if vertical glass rods are placed in the aquarium, the brittlestars treat them as substitute eelgrass and twine their arms around them.

It seems, then, that the brittlestars have some need to twine around something and when there is no eelgrass or artificial substitute they will cling to each other. This contrasts with the usual gatherings of animals which are normally only for breeding or feeding.

The bunches form by random movements of the individuals, the more active ones clinging to the inactive ones, reacting to them as if they were a piece of glass or eelgrass. When gathered together, the bunch is drawn tighter and tighter. Brittlestars in bunches live longer than isolated ones and they are less likely to shed their arms. When curled around an object a brittlestar is exerting tension and the rate at which its body functions work goes up. For some reason that is not properly understood, this enables them to live longer. Therefore it is an advantage to cling to any object, so, without the normal solid supports, they cling to each other.

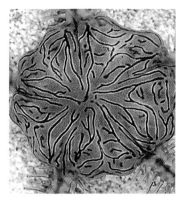

△ *Central disc of brittlestar magnified 12 times.*
▽ *The star-shaped mouth is on the underside.*

△ *Closeup of mouth, armed with spines serving as teeth, which leads directly into the stomach.*

phylum	**Echinodermata**
class	**Ophiuroidea**
order	**Ophiurae**
genera	***Ophiura, Ophiothrix, Amphiura,*** *others*

Sea urchin

Sea urchins — or sea hedgehogs — are the spiniest of the Echinodermata or 'spiny-skins', the group that includes starfishes, brittlestars, sea lilies and sea cucumbers. Their internal organs are enclosed in a test which typically takes the form of a more or less rounded and rigid box made up of chalky plates fitting neatly together. There are, however, sea urchins with leathery, flexible tests. In sea urchins with the rigid box the shape may be nearly spherical, rounded and somewhat flattened, heartshaped, or like a flattened disc, as in the sand dollar. In most sea urchins the test is covered with spines, which may be short and sharp, long and slender or thick and few in number. When the spines are removed knobs can be seen on some of the plates. These form part of the ball-and-socket joints on which the spines move. Also seen when the spines are removed are the double rows of pinholes arranged in a series of five, forming a star in the heart urchin or running from the bottom to the top of the test when this is spherical. In the living sea urchin the tubefeet project through these pinholes. Among the spines are small jointed rods with two or three jaws at the top, which act like tiny pincers. These are known as pedicellariae, and each moves like the spines on a ball-and-socket joint. Sea urchins are not only attractive in appearance when living, but their tests, cleaned of their spines, are collected because of the beauty of their design. In life they are attractively coloured from greens to yellow, red, orange and purple. The smallest sea urchins are barely ½ in. across, while the largest are up to 1½ ft across, including the spines.

The 800 species have a worldwide distribution, mainly in shallow waters, usually at less than 600 ft although some live down to 1 500 ft.

Burrowing through steel

In addition to the spines and the pedicellariae, the teeth of a sea urchin play an important part in its life. These too are objects of beauty. Over 2 000 years ago Aristotle wrote of the teeth as resembling a horn lantern with the panes of horn left out. There are five vertical teeth supported on a framework of rods and bars, and the whole structure, teeth and supporting skeleton, is now called Aristotle's lantern. Some sea urchins move freely over the seabed using their tubefeet to pull themselves along. When walking the tubefeet are pushed out, their suckers take hold and then the tubefeet shorten, pulling the body along. Its course is usually an erratic one, as first the

△▷ Pink pin cushion: an edible sea urchin **Echinus esculentus** *on* **Laminaria**. *Only the ripe ovaries are eaten, raw like caviare, or cooked.*
▷ Sea mine: small spines surround the bases of the larger primary spines of a **Cidaris cidaris**.

tubefeet on one side are pushed out, then the neighbouring tubefeet, each side pulling the sea urchin in a slightly different direction. Other sea urchins use their tubefeet, assisted by the spines, while yet others walk on the spines in a deliberate way, pursuing a steady course, and when viewed from the side the animal appears to be walking on many stilts. There are also sea urchins, including the heart urchins, so named from their shape, that plough through sand and burrow into it, using their spines. *Echinocardium* sinks vertically into the sand, to a depth of 8 in. — twice its own length or more. It lines its vertical shaft with mucus and pushes several very extensible tubefeet up the shaft to the surface of the sand to breathe. It also keeps a horizontal shaft open behind it with other tubefeet, to receive its excrement, while tubefeet in front are picking up particles of food and passing them to the mouth. As the *Echinocardium* moves forward it abandons the vertical shaft by withdrawing its tubefeet, then pushes them up through the sand, making a new vertical shaft to the surface.

There are sea urchins that burrow into soft rock, using their spines to scrape away the surface, some using their teeth as well. *Echinostrephus molaris* of the Indo-Pacific makes cylindrical burrows several inches deep. When feeding it comes up to the mouth of the burrow. Should anything disturb it, it merely drops into the burrow and wedges itself in with its spines. On the Californian coast steel pier piles put in position in the late 1920s were completely perforated by the sea urchin *Strongylocentrotus* in 20 years, the steel being ⅜ in. thick. In other places the anti-corrosive surface layer of the steel piles was abraded and polished by the sea urchins' spines.

Surface cleaning pincers

Sea urchins are mainly vegetarian, chewing seaweeds with the teeth of their Aristotle's lantern. Burrowing forms eat fragments of dead plants in the sand, but probably also take animal food. All get some food as a result of cleaning their tests. The pincers of the pedicellariae are constantly moving about picking up grains of sand that fall on the skin covering the test and also any tiny animals that settle, such as barnacle larvae. These are passed from one pedicellaria to another to the mouth.

Free-swimming larvae

Male and female sea urchins shed their sperms and eggs respectively into the sea where fertilisation takes place. The larva, known as an echinopluteus, is like that of other members of the Echinodermata, with slender arms covered with bands of cilia. Before it settles on the seabed it already has a mouth surrounded by a few tubefeet and spines and the arms are shorter. It is when the arms are too short for swimming that the tiny sea urchin, barely half-formed, settles on the bottom.

Protected from predators

Sea urchins are eaten, especially when small, by bottom feeding fishes but have relatively few other enemies when fully grown. The roes of *Echinus esculentus* have long been eaten in Mediterranean countries and other species have been fished in the Caribbean, South America, Malaya and Japan. Off Barbados they are fished by naked divers with handnets. Most echinoderms have unusual powers of regeneration which sea urchins lack. They can re-grow tubefeet and pedicellariae and if one of the plates in the test is cracked it will be cemented and healed. If a part of the test becomes pushed in, however, the damaged plates will be merely cemented together but will not be pushed out into their normal position. Nevertheless, what sea urchins lack in healing powers they make up for in armaments. In many species the spines are sharp, hollow and brittle, and readily break off. Bathers getting such spines into their feet can sustain painful wounds, and in some places sea urchins are so numerous on the seabed it is practically impossible to put a foot between them. We can be fairly sure that most animal predators treat them with as much respect as the human bather or diver. Many, as we have seen, burrow in sand or rock. Others hide by day under rocks coming out at night to feed. This is purely a reaction away from the light but the practical effect is to keep the animals hidden. Those that do not hide from the light, including the European *Psammechinus miliaris*, hide by holding pieces of seaweed over themselves with their tubefeet. *Diadema* of the Caribbean has light-sensitive cells scattered all over its test. It also has long needlelike spines. Any shadow falling on its body makes the spines in the shaded area point towards the object causing the shadow, thus presenting a formidable array of weapons to a potential attacker.

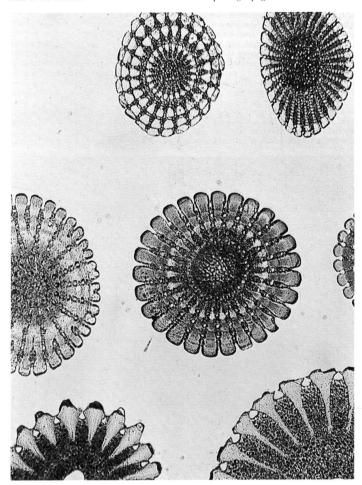

phylum	**Echinodermata**
class	**Echinoidea**

◁ *Natural radial symmetry — a section through the spines of various sea urchins (approx × 20).*

The Higher Invertebrates

The single phylum containing all the higher invertebrates is known as the Arthropoda or 'jointed-legged' animals. Since we normally expect a leg to be jointed it should be explained that in these animals, which include insects, crustaceans, millipedes, centipedes, spiders and a few others, the legs are typically many jointed. The phylum is enormous, both as to species and populations, comprising nearly a million known species.

The progression towards bilateral symmetry, a segmented body and a well-defined nervous system with special sense-organs, noted in the introduction to the previous section, takes an important stride forward in the Arthropoda. The members of this phylum also have in common a chitinous exoskeleton. That is, instead of an internal skeleton of hard material, such as bone, the body is encased in an outer covering of chitin, a nitrogenous carbohydrate similar in consistency to horn. This not only supports and contains the body as a whole, but affords attachment on its inner surface for the muscles.

It is very clear from the structure, particularly of some of its members, that the arthropods must be evolved from worm-like ancestors. Millipedes and centipedes, for example, are elongated with obviously segmented bodies that recall the form of an earthworm. This is reinforced by the shape of peripatus, the unusual and primitive arthropod, as well as by some of the more primitive insects. In most arthropods, however, the segments tend to be reduced in number, as in familiar insets, such as beetles and bees, and even more so in spiders, ticks and mites.

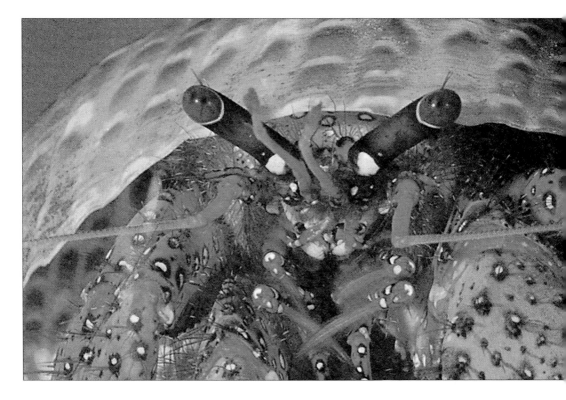

Fossils of the earliest arthropods are found in the rocks of the Cambrian period laid down over 500 million years ago. They included mainly small crustaceans and the trilobites. These were all aquatic. Some 150 million years later, in the Devonian period, there were land-living arthropods, including millipedes, mites, spiders, and wingless insects. Winged insects, in the form of dragon flies, have been found in deposits of the Carboniferous period, 50 million years later.

The lower invertebrates are all aquatic, living in the sea or in freshwater, or in damp situations on land. Among the arthropods, crustaceans are also typically aquatic, most numerous in the sea, and generally require a damp environment in those instances in which they have become land-living. Insects and spiders, by contrast, can tolerate a dry environment and, having thrown off the shackles of a life spent totally in a fluid medium, have been a able to extend the range of their activities. The whirligig beetle, for example, can survive in air, can fly or live on the surface of water or even dive and remain submerged, taking its air supply down with it, like a scuba-diver.

The arthropods are a good example of proliferation of animal forms. They have produced species numerically almost without an end, for almost every kind of habitat and diet, to almost every kind of parasitism and symbiosis. More than that, they give us examples of how a small increase in the proportion of nervous tissue in the body can lead to an integrated structure, as in termites, bees, ants and wasps, and to an appearance of intelligence which, although illusory, is none the less remarkable. Perhaps the most

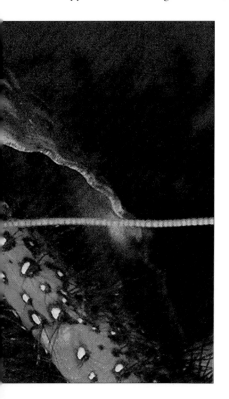

remarkable discovery in biology of this century is that concerning the methods of communication used by honeybees and their almost incredible ability to navigate by the sun.

The classification of the Arthropoda, showing the classes, is as follows:

THE CLASSIFICATION OF THE ARTHROPODA	
Phylum Onychophora (peripatus)	100 species
Phylum Merostoma (horseshoe crabs)	4 species
Phylum Pycnogonida (sea spiders)	600 species
Phylum Symphyla	120 species
Phylum Pauropoda	400 species
Phylum Diplopoda (millipedes)	8,000 species
Phylum Chilopoda (centipedes)	2,750 species
Phylum Crustacea (crabs, lobsters)	30,500 species
Phylum Insecta (insects)	750,000 species
Phylum Arachnida (spiders, ticks, mites)	66,000 species

Bird-eating spider

Among the largest of living spiders are the so-called bird-eating spiders of the family Theraphosidae. The largest, from the Amazon basin, can attain a length of 3½ in. with a leg span of 10 in. The body and legs are hairy and the hairs have an irritant effect on the human skin. The theraphosids, which belong to the order **Orthognatha**, differ from the more numerous and generally smaller **Labidognatha** in having four lungs instead of two, four spinnerets instead of six, and jaws that work vertically instead of sideways.

There are over 600 species, all living in the tropics. A number of other spiders, in related families, have also been called bird-eaters, and there are others, only distantly related, that are referred to by this name.

The bird-eating spiders are sometimes referred to as tarantulas, especially by American writers. The true tarantula, however, is a wolf spider, **Lycosa tarentula**, found in Southern Europe. Some trapdoor spiders, for example, will kill small birds and there are a number of spiders of the genus **Nephila** that spin such a stout web that small birds are trapped and accidentally eaten.

Hairy night-hunter
During the day the bird-eating spider hides in a rock crevice or a hole in a tree and comes out into the Amazon jungle at night to hunt. With its legs spreading 7½ in. or more (as wide as the span of a man's hand) it does not spin a web but runs down its prey or seizes it by a sudden silent dash, to catch small mammals or drag hummingbirds from their nests. In spite of its size and

the revulsion most people feel on seeing this spider, it is not especially dangerous to humans. It is not easily provoked into attack and its venom is usually no more troublesome than a bee sting. On the other hand the whole body and legs are covered with fine hairs which can be very irritant. A curator of the insect house at London Zoo was once injured so badly by handling one of these spiders that his hand was red, swollen and painful for several days and one of his fingers remained permanently crooked.

Fangs for stabbing prey
Once the prey is captured it is instantly stabbed by the sharply-pointed hollow fangs and a fluid injected. It is not clear whether this fluid is a venom or merely the first of a series of injections of digestive juices. It is said to be very mild as a poison, neither killing nor paralysing the prey and yet it can cause a painful local reaction in man, which suggests that it could be a protein-splitting digestive enzyme. Most spiders digest their prey by injecting powerful digestive juices which liquefy the victim's body and then they suck out the contents. Early stories of bird-eating spiders tell of them chewing their food as well as liquefying it, but it is now known that movements once mistaken for insertions of the fangs are really repeated insertions of the fangs to liquefy more of the victim's body during the lengthened feeding process.

Female spider guards her babies
The bird-eating spider's instinct to attack and eat any moving thing it can manage is so strong that the male has to approach the female very cautiously during the brief courtship. To avoid being eaten he grasps her fangs with his front legs and after mating he eases himself away from her, then hastily retreats. It is not known whether he finds his mate by smell or touch but his sight is poor.

Each female lays 500–1 000 eggs in sum-

△ The fangs of the bird-eating spider are sharply pointed and hollow. As soon as the prey has been caught and quickly stabbed, a fluid is passed down the hollow fang. It is not clear whether this fluid is a venom or merely the first of a series of injections of digestive juices.

mer, in a loose cocoon, which she guards by resting with her front feet on it or sitting on it as a hen broods her eggs. If disturbed, she spreads her fangs in a threatening posture. After three weeks white baby spiders hatch from the eggs but stay in the cocoon for up to five weeks. When they leave the cocoon, they are brown with a black spot on the abdomen. They stay near the cocoon for a further 3–12 days, then they scatter.

Baby bird-eating spiders feed at first on very small, slow-moving insects, and grow from 4 mm to 16 mm in the first three years, and increase in weight from 0·0052 gm at birth to 0·8 gm. When adult these large spiders have been known to fast for nearly two years; and they can live for 30 years. They moult about 4 times in each of the first

Bird-eating spider
(family Theraphosidae)

three years, twice in each of the fourth and fifth years, and after that once a year. During the moult the senses of sight, hearing and touch are suspended, and the spider remains motionless for several hours.

Enemies

The bird-eating spider has few enemies, largely, it is claimed, because of the irritant nature of its hairs, which it is said to scrape from its abdomen with its hind legs so releasing a cloud of fine hairs which blind and stifle its pursuer. Its main, and probably the only effective, enemies are the hunting wasps, against the paralysing sting of which it is defenceless. The most the spider can do is to rise high on its legs and spread its fangs, in a threat display, which the wasp ignores.

In spite of the parental care enjoyed during the first weeks of life, it has been estimated that not more than 0·2% of bird-eating spiders reach adulthood.

An artist vindicated

The first person to record the carnivorous habits of the bird-eating spiders was Maria Sibilla Merian who, in 1705, published in Amsterdam, a large book called *Metamorphosis Insectorum Surinamensium.* She was an artist and worked in what was then Dutch Guiana. In her book, which was mainly devoted to insects, was a picture showing a large spider dragging a hummingbird from its nest. Beside it was an account of how these spiders take small birds from their nests and suck their blood. No one believed her and in 1834 WS Macleay, an Australian zoologist, made a vitriolic attack on Madame Merian's book, and it was not until 1863, when HW Bates watched spiders killing finches in the Amazon Valley, that Merian's account was fully accepted.

phylum	**Arthropoda**
class	**Arachnida**
subclass	**Araneae**
order	**Orthognatha**
family	**Theraphosidae**
genus	***Theraphosa,*** *others*

△ ▷ The bird-eating spider has few enemies, largely it is assumed, because of the irritant nature of its hairs. The main and probably only effective enemy of this spider is the hunting wasp whose sting paralyses it.
▷ Mother with baby bird-eating spider hatched at the London Zoo in October, 1966. The parents were brought back from Guyana earlier in the year. The female laid over 50 eggs in cocoons she had woven and hidden amongst the vegetation in her cage. On hatching, because of the danger of cannibalism between the young, they were each put in a separate glass tube where they were fed on fruit flies (life size).

△ *Black widow, sitting on its web with the feet touching the silken strands, waits for a victim (× 6).*

▽ *The spider begins to wrap and secure its victim by using quantities of silk from spinnerets (× 18).*

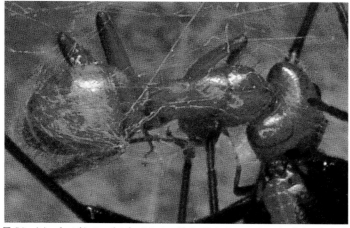

▽ *Often it is only at this stage that the victim is stabbed with the fangs and paralysed, then the back legs are skilfully used to enshroud almost completely the ant victim in the viscid silk (× 6).*

Black widow

*This name is given to a number of species of spiders widely distributed over the warmer parts of the world. The North American species **Latrodectus mactans** is especially noted for its powerful venom, a reputation which is not fully justified. The female is about ½ in. long, a shiny velvety black with a red hour-glass mark on the underside of her almost spherical abdomen. The male is much smaller. The size and colour of the female has led to the alternative names which include shoe button spider, red mark, red back, jockey and also hour-glass spider. The more familiar name of black widow is based on her colour and on the reputation she has for eating her mate as soon as he has fertilised her. It seems possible that the strength of the venom varies with the species and the one inhabiting the southern United States seems to be the worst.*

Painful but not fatal

The black widow spins a coarse irregularly designed web which often has a short funnel of silk, usually in the more elevated area. The male spins a similarly textured web but much smaller. Cool dark places are chosen, in cellars, outbuildings, ruined or abandoned houses, under doorsteps and porches, beneath floorboards or in piles of rubbish. Among the outbuildings must be included the primitive latrine where, it seems, most human victims have been attacked. Proportionately with the large numbers in which it exists the number of people who fall victim is surprisingly small. The known cases of injury or death in the United States for the 217 years between 1726 and 1943 are 1 291, only 55 of which are known to have been fatal. That is, one death in every 4 years and half a dozen injuries per year. Moreover, the evidence suggests that a high percentage of injuries have been sustained in rural areas where the plumbing is primitive, and even there the victims are mainly children or elderly or unwell people. Above all there seems a strong suggestion that when death does occur shock is a contributory factor if not the sole cause. Nevertheless, the non-fatal consequences are unpleasant enough. The poison is a neurotoxin which attacks the nerves to cause severe pain, muscular cramp, paralysis and hypertension. Fortunately the spider itself is retiring and more concerned with avoiding people than with attacking them. And only the females are troublesome as the male is too small to have enough venom to have any significant effect on humans.

With the exception of one family all spiders have poison glands. These lie in the cephalothorax, the smaller and front portion of the two parts that make up a spider's body, and the poison passes through slender ducts to the fangs. In all but a few spiders, the black widow being one, the venom is effective only against small animals such as insects. It is introduced into their bodies by a stabbing action rather than a bite since no jaw mechanism is involved, the mouthparts of a spider being capable only of sucking.

Paralysed victim enshrouded in silk

As with other web-weaving spiders the black widow sits on the web with her feet touching the silken strands. When an insect flies into the web and starts to struggle the vibrations are detected through the feet of the spider who immediately runs out, and by skilfully using her rear legs and quantities of the viscid silk from the spinnerets, quickly binds and secures it. Often it is only at this stage that the victim is stabbed with the fangs and paralysed, subsequently to be almost completely enshrouded in silk. Meanwhile a drop or two of saliva containing a protein-splitting ferment is exuded from the spider's mouthparts into the insect's body, the contents of which are therefore digested externally. This takes an hour or two, at the end of which the spider, by using its muscular stomach as a pump, sucks out the 'soup', leaving behind only the husk of its prey. This the spider finally cuts away and lets fall to the ground.

Pedipalp sperm reservoir

When adult, the male seeks a mate but before doing so he spins a very tiny web, rubs his abdomen against this and ejects on to it a drop of seminal fluid. This he then takes up in his pedipalps, a pair of specially adapted appendages situated near the mouth and resembling short legs. In mating the male merely transfers the sperm from the reservoir in the pedipalp to the female's body, only one mating being necessary for several bouts of egg-laying, since the female stores the sperm and uses it over a period, often of months. The eggs are laid in silken cocoons and the spiderlings hatching from them are, apart from colour, more or less replicas of the parents and independent from the start.

Self imposed widowhood

Almost everyone believes that the female spider invariably eats her spouse after mating. Even some of those who study spiders join in the chorus possibly after having occasionally seen this happen. This, it is said, is the reason for naming this most venomous spider the black widow. Certainly few people have ever sat down and watched hundreds of spiders mating to see whether the male is invariably eaten. Therefore this idea that the female always eats her spouse is based on this act of cannibalism being occasionally seen. There is, however, a more reasonable explanation. For example, we are told by one expert after another that when the male spider has transferred his sperm to a female he replenishes the reservoir in his pedipalps and will do so several times. This is consistent with the accepted and oft-repeated statement, that male spiders are polygamous—a polygamous male obviously cannot meet his death at each mating. The more likely explanation, and one consistent with the facts, is that after several matings the male becomes enfeebled, is indeed moribund, and then it is that the female devours him, as she would any similar small animal that came her way.

It is a fact that in the insect house at the London Zoo where black widows have been bred in large numbers for many years, individual male spiders have often been mated many times.

phylum	**Arthropoda**
class	**Arachnida**
subclass	**Araneae**
order	**Labidognatha**
family	**Theridiidae**
genus & species	***Latrodectus mactans***

Black widow with her completed cocoon. On hatching the spiderlings, apart from colours, are more or less replicas of the parents and independent from the start. The name widow comes from the belief that the female eats the male after mating. This does happen, but only occasionally.

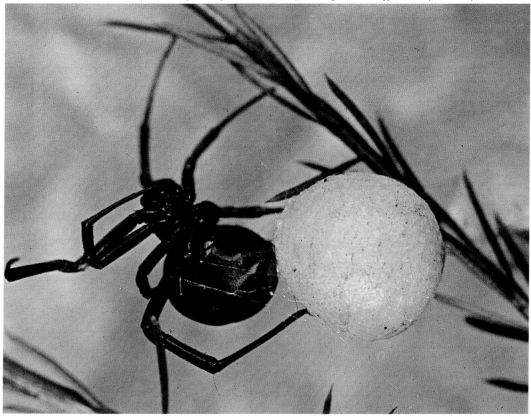

Crab spider

*Crab spiders are so called because of the length and curvature of their legs and the way they scuttle rapidly sideways, like the true crabs of the sea shore. Crab spiders are all much alike wherever they are found. Many are found in flowers, the colours of which they often match to perfection. They make no web but lie in wait for their prey. They are represented in Britain by 41 species, many rare or of local distribution, and they range from very tiny to not much more than $\frac{1}{4}$ in. All but one of these belong to the family Thomisidae, there being a single representative of the family Sparassidae, the beautiful, green **Micrommata virescens** which is comparatively large, the female being $\frac{1}{2}$ in. long, the male $\frac{1}{3}$ in.*

Beauty lies hidden

Crab spiders' colours or marks blend with their surroundings and this helps in capturing prey. Some spend most of their time in flowers, others lurk among leaf litter or low vegetation, and some lie along the stems or leaves of plants, head-downwards with the legs on each side held together in the same plane as the piece of foliage. Many combine effective camouflage with considerable beauty. *Thomisus onustus*, for example, is often a bright pink, blending perfectly with the flowers of the bell heath or certain orchids. Another, *Misumena vatia*, sometimes called the 'white death', occurs only in white or yellow plants, the white forms being found in flowers like the butterfly orchis, yellow varieties in mullein and gorse. If one of these spiders is transferred to a flower of a different colour, it quickly leaves it and seeks out another flower to match its own hue.

Danger in a flower

As the crab spider seizes its prey it pumps a poison into the victim's body along ducts in its sharp-pointed jaws. This quickly affects the insect's nervous system or its blood, or both at once. The paralysed prey is then drained of its body fluids through the cuts made by the jaws. The husk is discarded. A wide variety of small insects and other invertebrates is taken.

Those crab spiders which lurk in flower heads often take insects like hover-flies, bees and butterflies which visit the flowers for nectar. Sometimes the prey is bitten in a non-fatal part, such as the abdomen, in which case the spider manipulates it until it is able to administer the *coup de grâce* in the head or thorax where the central nervous system can be more directly reached.

Captive courtship

A few days before the male undergoes his final moult he builds a small band of web on which to discharge a drop of seminal fluid. This he takes up into each of his two palps and then goes in search of a mate. There is little preliminary courtship, only tentative caressings with the legs which enable the two partners to recognise each other and which stimulate the female to

An example of crab spider technique on a flower in the Transvaal veld: sudden death for a honey bee. In this case the spider has selected a flower in which its own colour will not be noticed by the victim until too late. Crab spiders kill by striking at the victim's head and thorax.

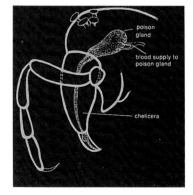

▷ The crab spider's hypodermic. The venom is held in the sac-like gland, which is covered with secretory cells. Muscle fibres encircle the gland; when they are contracted, venom is forced down the long duct running through the chelicera (fang).

poison gland

blood supply to poison gland

chelicera

△ The face of an assassin: head-on view of a crab spider showing groups of eyes and pedipalps hiding the chelicerae or poison fangs.
▽ Female crab spider, with male. Like other spiders, mating is fraught with peril for the male crab spider, for the female will often seize and kill the male. In one species the male ties down the female until mating is completed and he can make good his escape.

accept the male. Grasping the female by a leg the male inserts the sperm into her genital aperture. If she has already mated she will not allow the male to approach but menaces him by raising her front legs and jerking her body. If he persists she may well seize and kill him. Mating may last for less than a minute or go on for several hours.

In one species *Xysticus cristatus* the male employs a device to prevent the female from seizing him. He binds her legs to the ground with threads of silk, after caressing her into accepting his initial advances. When mating is over the female is delayed just long enough in freeing herself from her bonds to allow the male to make good his escape.

Most crab spiders lay their eggs in early summer. The female makes a silken saucer into which to lay her eggs. This she then covers with another silken layer, forming a cocoon. It may be built between leaves lying on the ground or among foliage. Sometimes the female makes a silken tent within which she sits guarding the eggs. Many females eat nothing during the period of incubation, becoming extremely emaciated. Others capture prey as usual, though never straying far from their eggs. Young crab spiders are hatched as miniatures of their parents, though often differing considerably in colour. As in other spiders they grow by shedding their skins at regular intervals.

Many enemies

Spiders have many enemies. Small mammals, birds, reptiles and amphibians eat them, as do beetles, ants, and centipedes. Certain species of wasps and ichneumon flies lay their eggs in living crab spiders. Not least, considerable spider mortality is caused by different species of spider killing and eating one another. Indeed, it is likely that spiders indirectly play a major part in controlling their own numbers.

WS Bristowe, distinguished student of spiders, once estimated that the spider population of England and Wales alone was probably of the order of 2⅕ billions (2 200 000 000 000) at any one moment — or some 40–50 thousand times the human population of Britain! If each spider eats only 100 insects a year, a conservative estimate, then the value of the service spiders render us in keeping insects down to a reasonable level is obvious. On a world scale it is incalculable.

△ The crab spider's sharp-pointed jaws inject paralysing venom. It then drains the helpless victim of its body fluids.

▽ Crab spiders specialise in camouflage; this species is a perfectionist, even matching the flower's yellow-pointed stamens.

phylum	**Arthropoda**
class	**Arachnida**
subclass	**Araneae**
order	**Labidognatha**
family	**Sparassidae**
genus & species	*Micrommata virescens*
family	**Thomisidae**
genera & species	*Thomisus onustus* *Misumena vatia* others

Scorpion

Scorpions are notorious for their stings, the venom of which, in some species, is fatal to man. They range in length from ¼ in. to as much as 8 in. in **Scorpio viatoris** of Africa. The body is segmented and bears a pair of powerful chelicerae or pincerlike claws similar to those of a lobster. The thorax has four segments each with a pair of walking legs on the undersurface and the abdomen has six segments tapering to a single sharp sting at the end with a small opening supplied by two relatively large venom glands. Such animals as the 8in. African scorpions have a very large sting and venom dangerous to humans.

The lobster-scorpion of Sumatra is even larger but as it lives in dense forest it is not often encountered by man. Although the United States has about 40 species, only two, the 2–3in. **Centruroides sculpturatus** and **C. gertschi**, have venom which can be fatal.

The 650 species are found in all the warm regions of the world. They are particularly abundant in deserts but are found only sparsely in the temperate zones. In America they are found as far north as British Columbia, and they also live in southern Europe. They are extremely adaptable and can stand fierce heat.

Dangerous in the house

One of the main dangers from a scorpion is its habit of living in human dwellings, crawling into beds, furniture, under carpets and into shoes. Away from houses they hide by day under logs or rocks, or in holes in the sand which they dig with their middle legs. Scorpions lead solitary lives, being very hostile to other scorpions, the females may even devour the males after mating.

Tearing their victims to pieces

Scorpions hunt by night. Their prey consists almost entirely of insects and spiders. They seize a victim with their large claws and tear it to pieces or crush it, extracting its body juices. If it offers any resistance the scorpion may then, and only then, use its sting by bringing its abdomen forward over the body and thrusting the poison-bearing tip into its prey. The prey is then slowly eaten, an hour or more sometimes being spent in consuming a single beetle. Scorpions can survive long periods without eating and it is said that they never drink, getting all the moisture they need from their food or from dew. This is not true. In captivity they will readily take water. The usual method of supplying a scorpion with water is to put a wad of wet cotton-wool in its cage, which it will visit regularly to drink.

▷△ *The sting, with its poison-bearing tip, is stabbed into any victim which puts up a fight.*
▷ *Young scorpions ride on their mother's back for nearly a week. These miniature adults are born alive over a period of several weeks.*

Some species of scorpions stridulate, or 'sing', by rubbing the bases of their clawed limbs against the bases of the first pair of walking legs. In some there is what is known as a rasp at the base of each claw with a 'keyboard' on the walking legs. In others the 'keyboard' is on the claw. Scorpions do not stridulate for the same reason as grasshoppers do. Their 'song' is used as a preliminary to attack or as a defensive warning. It is interesting that the positions of the claws differ: in the attack posture they are held wide apart with the claws open and pointing upwards, while in the defensive position the claws are held low and in front of the head. Only the pseudoscorpions have similarly enlarged pedipalps or claws.

Courtship 'dance'

Like spiders, scorpions indulge in a form of courtship before mating. Normally when the female is responsive the male first grasps her with his claws and then manoeuvres to face her, gripping her claws with his own. Sometimes when the female is not submissive and tries to pull away, the male raises his sting almost straight above his claws and the female does the same. It happens very rarely and then only for a few seconds. Having grasped the female the male drags or pushes her to a suitable place where he scrapes away the soil with his feet and deposits his spermatophore. Then, still holding her by her claws, he manoeuvres her over it so she can take up the sperma-

tophore with her cloaca. The two animals remain together for about 5 or 6 minutes before breaking away.

Development in scorpions is especially interesting because the entire order is either ovoviviparous or truly viviparous. The young scorpions are born alive, one or two at a time, over a period of some weeks. In some species a placenta-like tissue is formed in the mother's body through which food is passed to the growing embryo and waste products removed. After birth the baby scorpions ride around on their mother's back. Only after their first moult do they leave the mother and become independent. Some scorpions are known to live for as long as 5 years.

Danger when provoked

The ferocity of scorpions has probably been much exaggerated although there is no doubt that some species are very dangerous. They will not, however, use their sting against humans unless considerably provoked. The danger lies in their coming into houses and, where they are common, this can make living hazardous unless special precautions are taken. In the United States and Mexico it is estimated that more people are killed by scorpions than by snakes. In a town in Brazil, with a population of only 200 000, in 1954 alone nearly 200 people needed emergency hospital treatment for scorpion stings. It is much the same story in other tropical parts of the world and in some places the number of scorpions is amazingly high as shown by a report from Bombay in India. There, what was described as a casual hunt revealed nearly 15 000 scorpions in an area inhabited by only 13 000 people, and the writer of the report suggested that a closer search might have revealed even more.

A sting from one of the more dangerous species is often followed by collapse, profuse perspiring and vomiting, and the skin becoming cold and clammy. Even when drugs and oxygen are administered the patient has difficulty in breathing, with a profuse frothy fluid coming out of the mouth and nostrils. Even with modern medicines this usually ends in death.

phylum	**Arthropoda**
class	**Arachnida**
order	**Scorpiones**
genera	*Ospistobuthus* *Buthus* *Scorpio* *Tityus*

▽ *Battle in the sand. The triumphant victor of these two* **Centrurus** *grasps its overturned opponent's claw. The last two sections of the large pedipalps are modified and enlarged to form claw-like pincers. The overturned scorpion displays its segmented abdomen and the arrangement of legs on the thorax.*

Tarantula

Although everyone knows that the tarantula is a spider, few people are sure of its exact type; great confusion exists over the name. Originally, it referred to a small spider, belonging to the family of wolf spiders living in southern Italy. Its name was derived from the town of Taranto where legend stated that its bite was fatal unless the patient danced until exhausted, and the poison had been sweated from the system. The dance became known as the tarantella. All this happened in the Dark Ages, possibly earlier, and long before Columbus discovered America. Soon after that discovery the large bird-eating spiders of South America were called tarantulas. Their large size and, to most people, repulsive hairiness epitomized the popular horror of spiders and the image in many people's minds of the dreaded spider of southern Italy. Setting the seal on the confusion, certain harmless whip-scorpions that are not even spiders have been placed in a family named the Tarantulidae.

There are nearly a dozen species of the genus Tarentula, including the one that started all the fuss. This used to be known as Tarantula inquilina, then Lycosa narbonensis and now it is named Tarentula narbonensis. Its long, somewhat narrow, grey body is just over 1 in. in length, with dark spots, and its legs are hairy and about the same length as the body. Other European species are similar but only just over ½ in. long, or less, and one, T. fabrilis, has a dark, dagger-shaped mark on its abdomen. The tarantula of southern Europe is Lycosa tarentula.

A tarantula attacking a grasshopper. Tarantulas kill insects by injecting them with a poison.

Poison investigated

Tarantulas are found in different habitats according to the species, from lowlands to mountains up to and above 2 000 ft, on open country such as moors, heaths and grassland, and also in woodlands. They live in short burrows in the ground and spin no web but, like wolves, run down their prey which is mainly small insects. They kill them by injecting a poison. Henri Fabre, the famous French entomologist, found this was instantly fatal to insects, but he went further to investigate the potency of the poison in relation to the legend. He found the tarantula would bite a sparrow but that a young sparrow took 3 days to die, and a mole died in 36 hours. From this he concluded that the bite could be troublesome to people and that measures to counteract the poison should be taken.

Male tarantula dances

As in all spiders the courtship is elaborate, and, fittingly, in these species the male does a dance. WS Bristowe, in his *Comity of*

Spiders, has given a detailed description of what happens in some of them. In two species the male moves his palps up and down, slowly at first, then more quickly, and he begins to pulsate his abdomen. Then he walks around the female with jerky steps, with his front legs bunched up and pulsating both his palps and his abdomen, the latter making a tapping sound on the ground. In a third species the male paws the ground in front of him with his front legs, in the manner of a horse, and then starts to circle the female, getting slowly closer and closer to her. He rears up with his palps pointed upwards and his first pair of legs raised in a curve. He then jerks them upwards before lowering them, trembling, to the ground. The female eventually becomes receptive and the male transfers the packets of semen first from one palp, then from the other, to the female.

So far as we can see, these strange convolutions eventually bring the female into a mood to mate, and it is not without profit to recall that the human victim of the tarantula's bite, dancing to cure himself, infected those who watched. In his case, however, he produced a kind of mass hysteria, which has been called tarantism.

The female, like other wolf spiders, carries her eggs in a silken cocoon attached to the tip of her abdomen. When the 40 or so spiderlings hatch they ride in a crowd on the back of the mother's abdomen.

Disease and remedy

The bite of the tarantula was supposed to bring on a general melancholy which in the end proved fatal. The only thing for the victim to do was to call for one or more musicians who, with their pipes and fiddles, would play a succession of tunes until they hit upon one that set the patient dancing,

slowly at first but with more and more speed and vigour – rather like the male tarantula's wooing – until the patient finally fell sweating profusely, exhausted but cured. By that time all of his neighbours might be affected and they would take up the dance, and this might spread to other communities.

It sometimes happened that mass hysteria would break out and spread across Europe. The tarantula was blamed for this. By contrast we find Robert Burton, in his *Anatomy of Melancholy* (1621), recommending hanging the spider in a nutshell around the neck as a cure for the ague (malaria). He says he got this cure from his mother but seems to have been doubtful of its value until he found it had been recommended by Dioscorides, Matthiolus, Aldrovandus and other authors of high standing from the days of the Ancient Greeks onwards.

▷ *Tarantula: the spider that started all the fuss. T. narbonensis, poised menacingly above its burrow. Its long, hairy legs and body and beady stare make it easy to see why many people find it so repulsive.*

phylum	**Arthropoda**
class	**Arachnida**
subclass	**Araneae**
order	**Labidognatha**
family	Lycosidae
genus & species	*Tarentula barbipes* *T. cuneata* *T. pulverulenta* others

△ *Cracking the eggs. Millipedes hatching.*
▷ *Changing outline. A millipede of the order* **Spirobolida** *nibbles at an orange leaf.*
▽ *A pill millipede,* **Sphaerotherium.**

Millipede

Millipedes range from being soft-bodied and less than $\frac{1}{10}$ in. long, to heavily armoured forms exceeding 8 in. Many are poisonous. One of the most obvious ways in which they differ from centipedes, with which they used to be classified under the name 'Myriapoda', is in having two pairs of legs on most of their body segments—the first 4 segments have only single pairs—and in the variable number of segments. The head has short antennae, and some species have no eyes. The general body surface may, however, be sensitive to light.

Millipedes are typically light-shy, nocturnal animals living in moist soil, leaf mould and crevices. They feed on vegetable matter and though valuable in breaking this down, some cause much damage by attacking crops especially in wet weather. The $\frac{1}{2}$in. spotted snake millipede **Baniulus guttulatus,** *for instance, eats potatoes. The potatoes are probably attacked only when the tough skin has already been broken, for the jaws of these and other millipedes are not powerful. They then burrow inside, making them unfit for human consumption.*

Chemical warfare

In contrast with the fast-running centipedes, millipedes are built not for speed but for pushing their way powerfully through soil or vegetation. When walking, each leg is a little out of step with the one in front, so waves appear to sweep back along each side of the body. When attacked, some make a rapid escape without using their legs, writhing and wriggling their bodies through the vegetation, while others have a protective reflex of coiling up like a watch spring as soon as they are disturbed. The pill-millipedes curl into small balls, and in warmer parts of the world there are millipedes that roll into golf ball size. The usual defence of millipedes is, however, a row of poison glands down each side of the body. The secretion may be red, yellow, white or clear, but typically it is brown or yellow-brown and smelling of excrement, chlorine or prussic acid. The latter two are probably present, as well as iodine or quinine, so it is not surprising that some species are unpleasant to handle. Indeed, in central Mexico one species is ground up with various plants as an arrow poison. Usually the venom simply oozes from the glands, but some larger tropical millipedes discharge it as a fine spray, even to distances of up to a yard. Such millipedes may blind the incautious chicken molesting it, or it may discharge onto human skin, making it blacken and peel. Some of the large tropical

millipedes sport contrasting, bright warning colours. There are even a few luminous species. One, sometimes conspicuous at night in the Sequoia forests of California and aptly named *Luminodesmus sequoiae*, is blind and its light shines continuously from the time of hatching. The light is probably a warning signal to potential predators rather than a recognition sign for its fellow millipedes. That the warning is no mere bluff was shown by the death, from cyanide poisoning, of a bee accidentally imprisoned with one of these millipedes in a test tube.

Tents and mud huts

In mating, which may last for several hours, the male embraces the female, lower surface to lower surface. The genital openings are in pairs on the third body segment and fertilisation takes place inside the female. According to species, 10–300 eggs may be laid. Some millipedes simply coat each egg with soil and excrement, so disguising it, and leave it in a crevice in the earth, while the females of other species make elaborate nests and may remain coiled tightly around them for a few days. The nest can take various forms: a hollow sphere of soil and saliva, lined with excrement or a thin-walled dome of excrement, anchored to the substratum with a narrow tubular chimney, and covered with bits of leaf. The mother will replace these if they are removed. Some-

times the nest is a tent spun from silk. Some millipedes conceal themselves in such silken chambers or tents when they moult, for having cast their skins, they are temporarily very vulnerable to attack. Usually a millipede eats its cast skin, and also the silk tent. The young millipede starts life without the full number of legs, perhaps only three pairs, and acquires more at successive moults.

Millipedes by the million
In 1878, a train was brought to a halt in Hungary by a black mass of millipedes that carpeted the ground and made the wheels slip on the rails. Trains were again stopped in this way in northern France in 1900 and mass migrations of millipedes of various species have been recorded periodically in various countries, including once in Britain, in 1885, when a large number were seen crossing a road. More than a score of such phenomena have been recorded in the United States as, for instance, when 75 acres of West Virginia farmland were covered by these animals in 1918. Cattle would not graze and men hoeing in the fields became nauseated and dizzy from the smell. In the end, most of the millipedes, about 65 million, were killed when they were halted at a cliff bottom and were parched by the sun.

Such plagues are rare, but sudden attacks on crops in lesser numbers are familiar, and tend to occur in times of drought following damp weather. The size of millipede populations does not seem to be governed by predators and parasites, though there are plenty of these, including spiders, toads and birds, particularly starlings. The main controlling factors seem to be physical conditions. The best conditions for the buildup of a population occur when there is plenty of moisture and organic matter in the soil, as for example when farmyard manure has been spread. If the soil then becomes dry, the millipedes move to a more congenial environment. What then could be better than a damp cavity in a sugar beet? Sometimes the migrating masses of millipedes have been accompanied by centipedes and woodlice, for reasons far from clear. Conversely, it is not unknown for millipedes to accompany the marching columns of army ants. Again it is not known why, but millipedes are among the 'guests' to be found in the nests of ants and termites.

phylum	**Arthropoda**
class	**Diplopoda**

▽ *A long embrace. Millipedes, entwined around each other head to head and lower surface to lower surface, may take several hours over mating. These millipedes belong to the order Iuliformia.*

△ **Cylindroiulus.** *Walking is a serious business with so many legs — two pairs to a segment.*

Centipede

*There are many different kinds of centi-
pedes but as they are little noticed and
even less liked they do not have common
names individually — to most people one
centipede is much the same as any other.
Scientists, however, have divided them
into four orders, the Scolopendromorpha
(millipede-like forms), Lithobiomorpha
(living-under-stone forms), Geophilo-
morpha (earth-liking forms), and
Scutigeromorpha (shield-covered forms).
The first two include the active, elongate
but not very slender animals having
respectively 21 pairs and 15 pairs of legs.
The Geophilomorphs are slender, worm-
like centipedes with the pairs of legs
varying in number from 31 — 177, so that
some of them more than justify the name
'centipede' or 'hundred-legs'.*

*The Scutigeromorphs are very distinct
and curious. The body is cigar-shaped,
not sinuous, and the 15 pairs of legs are
very long and slender, enabling the
animals to run with remarkable speed and
agility. Their respiratory system and the
oxygen-carrying capacity of their blood is
more efficient than in other centipedes, a
feature related to their high rate of
activity. Although their appearance is so
distinctive, the Scutigeromorphs are allied
to the Lithobiomorphs, both orders having
15 pairs of legs.*

*As there are no common names the
scientific (Latin) names must be used.
The most familiar British species is*
Lithobius forficatus, *the dark-brown
centipede that scuttles away when a log or
a rock is lifted. Another common species,*
Lithobius variegatus, *with speckled
legs, is unusual in being apparently
confined to the British Isles. The long,
slender Geophilomorph centipedes are also
common in Britain and are most often
found when digging the garden. Most of
them are only 1 or 2 in. long, but the North
African species* **Oryza barbarica** *may
measure up to 7 in. Many of the
Geophilomorph centipedes exude a strongly
luminous fluid when molested or injured.*

*There are only three small Scolopen-
dromorph centipedes in Britain but in the
tropics they are very numerous and varied
and include giant forms. The tropical
American* **Scolopendra gigantea** *may
be 1 ft long and the common Asian species*
Scolopendra morsitans *reaches 8 in.*

*The long-legged Scutigeromorphs occur
in southern Europe, the United States
and throughout the tropics.*

Unwelcome visitors

The body covering of centipedes is not
waterproof and they easily die of desiccation. They are confined, therefore, to
humid surroundings and are commonly
found in leaf mould, compost heaps, under
logs and stones, beneath the bark of trees

and in the soil; they come into the open
only at night when the air is moist and cool.
One British Geophilomorph *Scoliophanes
maritimus* lives on the seashore under stones
that are covered at high tide. Centipedes
often enter houses and a long-legged centipede *Scutigera forceps* found in dwellings
in the warm parts of the world, is regarded
as beneficial as it preys on insects. In tropical
Asia the large and venomous *Scolopendra
morsitans* is often found in houses, but is by
no means a welcome visitor. Many caves in
hot countries harbour centipedes, especially
the long-legged Scutigeromorphs, which
look quite remarkable in the light of lamps
or torches, racing about on the floor and
up the walls.

Active hunters

Centipedes are active predators, hunting
insects, spiders, worms and other small
prey. The common *Lithobius forficatus* readily
accepts flies in captivity and a large tropical
Scolopendra kept for over a year in the
London Zoo fed mainly on small mice. In
the wild state these large centipedes prey
on big insects such as locusts and cockroaches and also on geckos and other
nocturnal lizards. The marine centipede
Scoliophanes maritimus has been seen eating
barnacles. Some of the worm-like Geophilo-
morpha feed partly on plant tissues.

Poisonous legs

The poison bite of centipedes is used to
paralyse and kill prey. All centipedes have
a venomous bite that is inflicted not by the
jaws but by the front pair of legs, which
are specially modified as 'poison claws',
being hollow and connected to poison
glands. The bite of the large tropical Scolo-
pendras is excessively painful and occasionally dangerous, though very few fatalities
have been recorded.

Breeding

The sexes are very similar and can usually
be distinguished only by microscopic exami-
nation. All centipedes lay eggs and in the
Lithobiomorpha and Scutigeromorpha when
the young hatch they have fewer legs than
the adult (7 pairs in *Lithobius*) and they
reach the full number in the course of
development.

Most centipedes merely lay their eggs in
the soil and leave them, but the big Scolo-
pendras brood and guard their eggs and
young, fiercely fighting any enemy which
attacks, and also protecting them from
fungal infection by mouthing and licking
them. If seriously disturbed they will often
eat the eggs or young, or may desert them,
and, unattended, the eggs always go mouldy
and die.

Centipedes are long-lived creatures and
even the little *Lithobius forficatus* may live
for 5 or 6 years. The big tropical species
probably take at least 4 years to reach full
size and may live for considerably longer.

Well protected from enemies

Small centipedes are readily eaten by birds
when exposed by spade or plough but they
are well protected from enemies of their
own size by their poisonous bite. One
Malayan monitor lizard, after dissection,
was found to have a stomach almost full of

large *Scolopendra* centipedes. Very few animals, however, have an appetite as robust as this, and these big centipedes must have few enemies. In staged combats they are almost always more than a match for spiders or scorpions of their own size.

Rapid movers

In the earlier days of zoology, the rapid movements of centipedes made the details of their locomotion something of a puzzle and the only conclusion reached was that if the animal stopped to think about how it should move its legs it would make poor progress. This situation has been celebrated in rhyme:

A centipede was happy, quite
Until a toad in fun
Said, 'Pray which leg goes after which?'
This raised her doubts to such a pitch,
She fell exhausted in the ditch,
Not knowing how to run.

The problem has been resolved by high-speed photography. In most centipedes the legs move rhythmically in waves which alternate on either side of the body, so that in any part, at a given moment, the feet will be bunched on one side and spread on the opposite side. When the legs bunch the tips often cross, but the centipede seems to be immune to the hazard of falling over its own feet. In the long worm-like Geophilomorph centipedes this pattern of movement is not seen; each leg seems to move on its own, picking its way independently of the others. Much of the movement of these centipedes consists of burrowing rather than running, and this sort of leg action is more suitable for such deliberate pushing along of the body.

phylum	**Arthropoda**
class	**Chilopoda**
orders	**Geophilomorpha**
	Lithobiomorpha
	Scolopendromorpha
	Scutigeromorpha

Centipedes paralyse and kill their prey with a venom from poison claws which are developed from the first pair of legs. The giant Malayan centipede (bottom right) may grow to 8 in. long and can inflict a very painful bite which has occasionally killed a human. The tropical American species of **Scolopendra**, *bottom left, may grow to 1 ft long. The young* **Lithobius** *centipede (top left) hatched from its egg with only seven pairs of legs. When fully grown it will have 15 pairs. This type is common in Britain and grows to only 1 or 2 in. long but it may live for 5 or 6 years. Centipedes are often confused with millipedes but they may easily be told apart as these pictures show: each segment of a millipede* **Polydesmus** *(top right) has two pairs of legs; centipedes have only one pair to each segment.*

These pictures of different centipedes show how they walk with rhythmic waves of leg movements alternating on either side of the body. At any one part of the body the feet are bunched on one side and spread on the other.

Kitchen nightmare: a common cockroach has a wash and brush-up after a meal of bread. These household pests have the depressing habit of fouling far more than they actually eat.

Newly-moulted cockroach larvae. They may moult 6 – 12 times before they are fully grown.

Cockroach

Cockroaches used to be classified together with the grasshoppers, crickets, stick-insects and others in one large order, the Orthoptera. This has now been split up into several separate orders of which one, the Dictyoptera, comprises the praying mantises and the cockroaches.

These are fairly large insects, flattened in shape, with two pairs of wings, the fore-wings being more or less thickened and leathery, serving as a protective cover for the delicate hindwings, just as the hard-ened forewings or elytra of beetles do. The hindwings of cockroaches are pleated like a fan when not in use; when expanded for flight they have a very large surface area. In the commonest European species, the black beetle as it is called, the male has very small wings, the female has

mere vestiges, and neither can fly. The female has reduced wings and is flightless in some of the other species also.

*The most familiar of the 3 500 species of cockroaches are those tropical and sub-tropical forms which have taken advantage of the warmth and the opportunities for scavenging afforded by homes and premises in which food is made or stored. By this means they have ex-tended their range into temperate and cold regions, and some of them have been artificially distributed all over the world. In the wild state, the great majority of species are tropical. In the outdoor fauna of Britain they are represented by 3 small species only, belonging to one genus, **Ectobius**.*

Three of the most common cockroaches are: Common cockroach, or black beetle **Blatta orientalis** length variable, averaging about 1 in., dark brown

(females almost black) wings not reaching the tip of the body in the male, vestigial in the female; both sexes flightless. A common pest in house. Now cosmopolitan in distribution, the region of its origin is unknown.

German cockroach, steamfly or shiner **Blatella germanica** about ½ in. long, yellowish-brown with two dark brown stripes on the prothorax, or fore-part, of the body. Wings fully developed. Almost as abundant as the common cockroach and certainly not of German origin; probably a native of North Africa.

American cockroach **Periplaneta americana** males nearly 1½ in. long, reddish-brown, with fully developed wings. Found mostly in sea port towns and on ships. In tropical countries it is the chief house-living cockroach. It is not an American insect and probably also originated in North Africa.

The young of the common cockroach are white on hatching, gradually becoming brown.

A brace of American cockroaches. Unlike the common cockroach, the American version has fully-developed wings. Despite its name it is not an American insect: it probably originated in North Africa.

They come out at night

In the wild, most cockroaches live on the ground among decaying vegetation or behind dead bark, and are coloured brown to match their surroundings. The 'domestic' species probably all lived in this way once. Some cockroaches are found among growing plants and are patterned in brown, yellow or green. The ground-living cockroaches are nocturnal, hiding away by day and coming out at night, just as the house-living ones do. Some of the large tropical species fly freely at night and are attracted to artificial light.

Their flattened bodies allow them to creep into cracks and crevices; in houses, cockroaches hide in inaccessible places and are not easy to get rid of.

Poisoned baits may be effective if used persistently, and insecticidal powders and sprays kill them if introduced well into their hiding places. Bad infestations, however, are best dealt with by professional pest controllers.

Unwelcome scavengers

In the wild, most cockroaches are scavengers on dead insect and other animal remains, fallen fruit and fungi; the transition to scavenging in human habitations is easy and obvious. Some of the wild species feed on wood, which they are able to digest with the help of protozoans, microscopical one-celled animals, in their intestine. Termites, which are closely allied to cockroaches, eat and digest wood by the same means.

In houses, cockroaches will eat any kind of human food that they can get at. They will also eat a variety of substances not generally regarded as edible, such as book-bindings, boot-blacking, ink and whitewash. Frank Buckland, in his *Curiosities of Natural History*, tells of a gentleman on his way home from India by ship who was much annoyed by cockroaches. At night, when he was asleep they 'came and devoured the little rims of white skin at the roots of the finger nails'. The harm they do is greatly increased by their habit of fouling, with their droppings, far more than they actually eat. The only good that can be said of them is that so far as is known they do not convey any disease.

Breeding

The eggs are enclosed in a purse-like capsule called the ootheca. In the common cockroach this is carried for a day or two, protruding from the body of the female, and then dropped, or sometimes stuck in a crevice, after which the insect takes no further notice of it. It is white when it first appears at the tip of her abdomen, but darkens later and, when deposited, is almost black and rather less than $\frac{1}{2}$ in. long. Normally an ootheca contains 16 eggs in 2 neat rows of 8, but there may be more or less than this. The eggs hatch 2–3 months after the formation of the ootheca, which splits to allow the young to emerge. The young of the common cockroach are about $\frac{1}{8}$ in. long on hatching, and white, gradually becoming brown as they grow. They resemble their parents in form, except that

79

the wings are lacking, and take 10 months
–1 year to reach maturity. Moulting of the
skin, or ecdysis, takes place anything from
6–12 times in the course of growth. The
breeding habits of the American cockroach
are similar.

In the German cockroach the ootheca is
carried by the female until a day or less before hatching, and the eggs may even hatch
while it is still attached to her. It is chestnut
brown and, a few days before hatching, a
green band appears along each side of it.
Hatching usually takes place 4–6 weeks
after the ootheca is formed and it normally
contains 35–45 eggs.

*Hated and loathed as a household pest because
of its habit of defiling food, the cockroach is
nevertheless one of the best examples of success
in surviving; and it has an important role in
the teaching of entomology.*
*This close-up shows the organs of special
sense: the eyes, which are compound, consisting
of many small elements; the palps and antennae,
which are organs of touch. On the highly
mobile antennae are structures which are used
for smelling. Above the front of the 'shell' are
the semi-transparent elytra, or wing cases.*

Living fossils

In a manner of speaking the world went
wild with delight when the coelacanth, a
living fossil, first came to light. The same
intense interest would be shown if another
living fossil were to be discovered. There is
something in the psychology of these events
which recalls the parable of the pieces of
silver that were thought lost and were
found again. Nobody but the most devoted
scientist, however, would think of rolling
out the red carpet for the roaches. Yet they
are extremely interesting and primitive
insects.

Many fossils have been found, showing
that there were already many species and
abundant populations of roaches at the
time when coal measures were being deposited, 300 million years ago. These cockroaches of the Carboniferous period look
similar to many of the present day ones and
the family as a whole must be regarded as
insects which, by adopting a simple and
secure way of life at an early period of the
earth's history, and never departing from
it, have inherited the earth by their very
meekness. As an example of success in survival they have few equals, but because they

intrude themselves on our notice in such an
unpleasant manner, few people find themselves able to regard them highly. Nevertheless, there are a few people whose sole purpose in life is to rear cockroaches.

Partly because they are so easy to obtain
and partly because their structure and
anatomy is so simple and generalised, cockroaches are widely used to introduce stu-
dents to the science of entomology, and
breeding them for this purpose is one of the
less well-known human occupations.

phylum	**Arthropoda**
class	**Insecta**
order	**Dictyoptera**
family	**Blattidae**

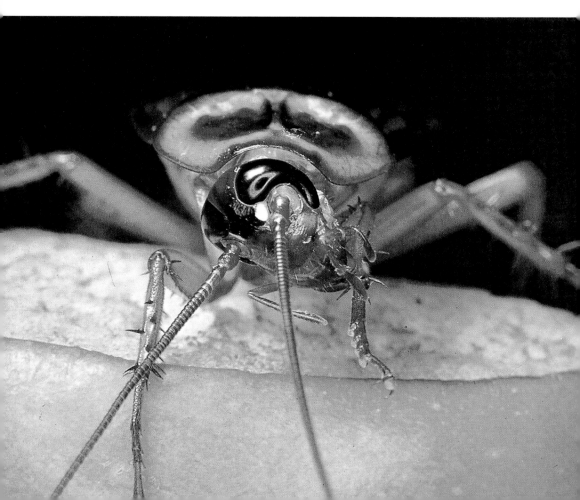

Grasshopper

As their name suggests, most grasshoppers
live among grass and herbage on the
ground. They are variously coloured —
mostly green and brown — and are protected
as long as they keep still by blending with
their surroundings. Grasshoppers are
active by day and if disturbed jump
suddenly and powerfully, using their
greatly-enlarged hindlegs. They can also
crawl slowly by means of the other two
pairs of legs.

Nowadays the term 'grasshopper' is
applied to the short-horned Acrididae,
while the long-horned Tettigoniidae are
called 'bush-crickets' because they are more
closely allied to the other main family of
the order Orthoptera (the Gryllidae or
true crickets) than to the Acrididae. In
all Orthoptera the forewings are leathery
and serve as coverings for the folded,
membranous hindwings which, in the
flying species, are the sole organs of flight.

Grasshoppers are mainly ground-living
insects, while most bush-crickets live in
the foliage of trees and bushes. Locusts,
which are in fact swarming grasshoppers,
will be dealt with under a separate
heading (page 84).

Fiddlers in the grass

The familiar chirping chorus in the fields
and hedgerows of the countryside is the
result of grasshoppers' stridulation. A row
of evenly spaced, minute pegs on the largest
joint of the hindlegs is rubbed over the more
prominent veins or ribs of the forewings.
Usually, but not always, only males can sing.
Each species has its own song, and these may
be learned, like the songs of birds, and used
in identifying the species. The colours of
species of grasshoppers vary so much that
their song is a better means of recognizing
them than their appearance.

Apart from stridulation, both pairs of
wings serve their usual function. In most of
the common species the hindwings are
fully developed in both sexes and the
insects can fly. One exception is the meadow
grasshopper Chorthippus parallelus in which
the hindwings are vestigial; even in this
species there are occasional individuals
in which the wings are fully developed and
functional. Among Orthoptera it is not
uncommon for species to occur in two forms,
winged (macropterous) or wings much reduced (brachypterous). The most usual
cases are like the one described, in which
occasional winged individuals occur in a
normally brachypterous population.

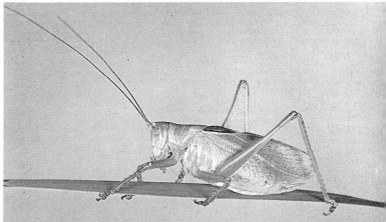

*Top right: Bush-crickets mating. Male (right)
is placing the spermatophore — package of
sperm — at the base of the female's ovipositor.
The blade-like structure of this organ is
typical of bush-crickets. Centre: Bush-cricket
Tettigonia cantans. Bottom right:
Short-horned grasshopper **Chorthippus
parallelus**.*

Openings to the hearing organs on the foreleg of a bush-cricket – sensitive enough to pick out the calls of different species.

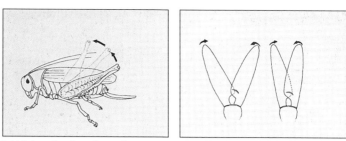

Stridulation – the voice of the grasshoppers. Left: Long-horned grasshopper rubs a hindleg over the ribs of the forewing. Right: Bush-crickets have one of the left wing ribs adapted to form a row of teeth, which is rubbed against the trailing edge of the right forewing to produce the sound.

Bush-cricket crawlers

Although some species live on the ground, most bush-crickets are at home in the foliage of trees and bushes. These tend to be mainly green while the ground-dwelling ones are brown or blackish. Unlike grasshoppers bush-crickets are not lovers of the sun, but become active in the late afternoon, or may be wholly nocturnal. Their hindlegs are adapted for jumping, but they have not the prodigious leaping powers of grasshoppers, moving mainly by climbing and crawling.

Singing a different song

They are also noisy and call by stridulating, but the mechanism is very different from that of grasshoppers. In the left forewing a rib, formed by one of the veins, has a row of minute teeth and this is rubbed against the hind edge of the right forewing. The arrangement is the same as in crickets except that the roles of the left and right forewings are reversed. Here again the species all have distinct songs, and there is good reason for this. In both bush-crickets and grasshoppers the song is mainly a courtship invitation addressed to the female, and it is important that the females should be able to recognise the call of males of their own species.

The great green bush-cricket *Tettigonia viridissima* ranges across Europe, Asia and North Africa. The female is 2 in. long, including the straight, blade-like ovipositor, and is bright green in colour. The male is a little smaller and his song is very loud and sustained, and uttered at night. In the late summer and autumn the speckled bush-cricket *Leptophyes punctatissima* is common in gardens and hedges. It is a plump, soft-looking insect, green with the wings reduced to small vestiges; the female ovipositor is broad and curved.

Two ways of laying eggs

Both grasshoppers and bush-crickets lay eggs. In the former they are enclosed in a tough case called the egg-pod, which the female buries in the ground. Each pod has from 5 to 6 or up to 14 eggs, more or less according to the species. Bush-crickets lay their eggs without any covering and usually singly, some putting them in the ground or crevices of bark, others inserting them in stems or leaves by cutting slits with the ovi-

Standing room only: a crowd of **Phymateus** *grasshopper nymphs. Wings show after moulting.*

positor. In both, the young hatch in the form of tiny worm-like larvae which moult immediately after hatching. They then resemble their parents except that they have no wings. With each moult (ecdysis) their size increases. The wings also appear and grow larger at each moult, becoming fully formed and functional, in the species that fly, at the last moult. Most of the common species have one generation a year.

Mainly vegetarian

Grasshoppers are entirely herbivorous and can be fed in captivity on bunches of grass tied with string and lowered into their home. The floor of the receptacle should be covered with 1½ in. of slightly damp sand, and in these conditions they will breed readily.

Bush-crickets are at least partly predatory and one species, the oak bush-cricket *Meconema thalassinum*, is entirely carnivorous and hunts caterpillars and other insects in oak trees. The others feed partly on grass and leaves and partly on insects. In captivity they must be given plenty of room; if they are crowded cannibalism will occur. Lettuce leaves seem to suit most of them, but they should have some animal food as well. Small looper caterpillars can usually be found by shaking bushes and branches into an open umbrella held underneath them.

Colour means nothing

Some grasshoppers show an extraordinary range of variation in the colour and markings on both legs and body. In the stripe-winged *Stenobothrus lineatus* and *Omocestus viridulus* there is a small number of well defined colour varieties, but in the common field and mottled grasshoppers *Chorthippus brunneus* and *Myrmeleotettix maculatus* there is almost every shade of colour: green, brown, yellow and red are the main colours and to these must be added extremely varied patterns of stripes, spots and mottling. As a result it is hopeless to try to tell a grasshopper by its colour.

class	Insecta
order	Orthoptera
family	Acrididae
genera	*Chorthippus, Omocestus, Stenobothrus, Myrmelotettix, Tetrix*
family	Tettigoniidae
genera	*Tettigonia, Leptophyes, Meconema*

Rhapsody in purple: an inch-long South African grasshopper of the family Eumastacidae.

Locust

Although the term 'locust' is loosely applied to any large tropical or subtropical grasshopper, it is better restricted to those whose numbers occasionally build up to form enormous migrating swarms which may do catastrophic damage to vegetation, notably cultivated crops and plantations.

Africa suffers most seriously from locust swarms and three species are of special importance. These are the desert locust, the red locust and the African subspecies of the migratory locust.

Both the red locust and the African migratory locust have their own regional control organisations which effectively prevent plague outbreaks. The desert locust, however, presents a real international problem which has yet to be solved and is the main subject of study of the Anti-Locust Research Centre in London. It will therefore be the main subject of this entry.

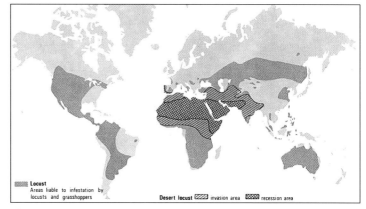

Locust Areas liable to infestation by locusts and grasshoppers

Desert locust invasion area recession area

The map above shows the wide distribution of locusts. In some places, like North America, cultivation of their breeding grounds has reduced their numbers. In Africa, however, the desert locust is public enemy number one. Other locusts are easier to control, because after their migrations they recede to small areas; the desert locusts' outbreak area is very wide, as indicated.

Locust or gregarious grasshopper

The vast plagues of locusts which periodically create such havoc in many regions of the underdeveloped world are really nothing more nor less than hordes of gregarious grasshoppers. For locusts can exist in two phases: a solitary, grasshopper phase, or a swarming locust phase. When the grasshoppers are crowded together they change their behaviour, and, if kept like this for a generation or more, also change their shape and colour to that of the swarming form.

Solitary locusts come together only for mating and then behave very much as other grasshoppers do. The eggs, the size of rice grains, are laid down to 4 in. below the surface of the ground. They are held together by a frothy secretion which hardens to form an egg-pod $1\frac{1}{2}$–2 in. long, which usually contains 80–100 eggs. Above the pod the

froth forms a plug which helps prevent the eggs from drying out and stops sand falling into the hole, so the hatchlings can escape. The egg stage lasts about 10–14 days in the main summer breeding areas but may be up to 70 days in the colder North African spring. The insects that hatch grow through a series of moults or skin-changes in the course of which they become gradually more like adult locusts and in the final 2 moults the wings form, becoming functional after the last moult, when the insect is adult. This takes 30–50 days, mainly depending on temperature. In a swarm the adults are pink at first, but after a few weeks or months, usually coinciding with the rainy seasons, they mature sexually and become yellow. The flightless immature locusts are traditionally known as 'hoppers'.

When they first hatch young solitary locusts disperse and unless some environ-

mental factor forces them together they never do begin to associate in bands but settle down to the solitary life of grasshoppers. These are usually green or brown, blending well with their surroundings.

Jekyll and Hyde phase-change

Under certain conditions, depending on many variable factors, often associated with the weather, scattered solitary locusts may become concentrated into favourable laying sites. With every female locust laying two or three batches of 70–80 eggs each the numbers after hatching will have multiplied at least 100 times. With many more hoppers crowded into the same area, groups coalesce and they are then well on the way to the all important phase change from solitary to gregarious type which leads eventually to hopper bands and locust swarms.

When crowded together their colour

Left: Immature pink adult female. Millions of these exist in vast swarms, which follow the wind to arrive in new breeding grounds soon after rain. Right: Hopper bands on the march, eating all the way. At first they move only a few yards a day, but in the later stages they hop for up to a mile.

changes to a bold pattern of black and orange or yellow stripes which probably helps them see one another and so keep together. The brightly patterned, crowded hoppers grow into pink adults which turn yellow at sexual maturity, solitary adults being sandy-coloured. Moreover, in the adults there are structural differences between the solitary and gregarious phases, notably in the wing, which is relatively longer in the gregarious phase. It is known that structural changes between one phase and another are associated with relative differences in the insects' hormonal balance.

Mutual stimulation leads to greater activity and they start to 'march'. Because an urge to keep close together is induced by development in the gregarious phase they march together in bands.

As adults they continue to migrate, and the urge to crowd together is maintained, but they are now airborne and move much faster. Weather conditions too can lead to the development of gregarious locusts and swarm formations. Scattered flying locusts fly downwind towards frontal systems of converging airflow and thus tend to accumulate in rainy areas. As the region inhabited by the desert locust is mainly arid, the result of persistently flying with the wind is to concentrate large numbers of locusts in areas when rain is likely to fall and provide them with food in the form of a flush of desert plants springing up after the rain. The gregarious phase develops in the offspring and migration then takes place in the usual way, following the prevailing wind and the favourable weather.

Locust plagues

When the swarm descends the locusts devour everything green. After mating takes place each female lays several hundred eggs. The young that hatch are still crowded and behave in just the same way, but the swarm that results can be many times larger. This swarm continues to migrate and again descends and multiplies its numbers. In this way a swarm may cover vast areas and build itself up into an aggregate of thousands of tons of locusts resulting in plague conditions. Plagues eventually come to an end due to adverse weather. The few survivors revert to the solitary phase, in which they are relatively harmless.

Perhaps the most important discovery made by the Anti-Locust Research Organisation has been that the African migratory locust and the red locust change from the solitary to the gregarious phase only in certain limited outbreak areas. These areas are effectively policed by regional locust control organisations and plague outbreaks have been prevented since 1944.

The desert locust is the locust of the Bible, and now by far the most damaging of all. It is hard to control because it has no geographically determined outbreak areas. It ranges over a vast area, from southern Spain and Asia Minor, the whole of northern Africa, through Iran to Bangla Desh and India, an area comprising about 60 countries. Between plagues lasting 6 or more years there are equally long recessions when only solitary locusts are to be found. The last plague ran from 1950 to 1962 and another showed all the signs of building up rapidly after the spring rains of 1967. In 1968 the situation looked very serious but by mid-1969 it was much quieter than expected 6 months previously. The last outbreak was in 1973–4 in New South Wales, Queensland and Victoria.

Natural enemies

If all the locusts in a swarm only 2 miles square were to breed successfully, in only four generations there would be a severe infestation of the whole 196 million square miles of the earth's surface. Fortunately there is enormous mortality from natural causes. Winds may fail to carry the locusts to a suitable breeding area. The soil may not be moist enough for the eggs to hatch. Or they hatch to find insufficient plant growth for their food or to protect them from the heat of the midday sun. There are also many predators, parasites and diseases of locusts. A little fly *Stomorhina* lays its eggs on top of the locust egg pods as soon as they are laid and the fly's grubs eat up the eggs. Larvae of the beetle *Trox* can destroy an egg field completely and ants have been seen waiting at the top of an egg froth plug and carrying away all the hatchlings. Flocks of birds often accompany both hopper bands and adult swarms and they can account for enormous numbers of hoppers. At this stage hoppers are particularly vulnerable and their predators take advantage of the feast.

Control by man

Concentrated insecticides and highly efficient spray gear using both aircraft and ground vehicles are used in enormous campaigns against desert locusts. One of the most effective, because it is simple and cheap, uses the exhaust gases from a Land Rover to produce a fine spray of poison. This will drift over the vegetation in the path of hoppers and is a very quick and economical way of killing hopper bands. Aircraft can match the mobility of a migrating swarm; searching greater areas, finding and following swarms and spraying them in the morning and evening when they fly low and are most vulnerable to spraying. A single light aircraft carrying 60 gallons of insecticide can destroy 180 million locusts.

Migrating swarms of locusts commonly travel between 1 000 and 3 000 miles between successive breeding areas and naturally cross many international frontiers. Regional locust control organisations within the desert locust invasion areas pool resources and facilitate the movement of supplies across frontiers. These organisations in turn are coordinated by the Food and Agriculture Organisation (FAO) of the United Nations with its headquarters in Rome. FAO cooperates with the Desert Locust Information Service run by the Anti-Locust Research Centre in London.

phylum	**Arthropoda**
class	**Insecta**
order	**Orthoptera**
family	**Acrididae**
genera & species	**Austroicestes cruciata**
	Australian plague grasshopper
	Chortoicetes terminifera
	Australian plague locust
	Locusta migratoria manilensis
	Oriental migratory locust
	Locusta migratoria migratoria
	Asiatic migratory locust
	Locusta migratoria migratorioides
	African migratory locust
	Melanoplus spretus
	Rocky Mountain locust
	Nomadacris septemfasciata
	red locust
	Schistocerca gregaria
	desert locust

Left: Close-up of a yellow and black hopper. Right: Trio of swarming hoppers. These come together to form dense groups, which join others to become a massive band.

Like an unknown monster from outer space the mantis cradles a day-flying moth in its spined forelegs and delicately and neatly eats its live victim.

Mantis

The name Mantis is derived from a Greek word meaning 'prophet' or 'soothsayer' and refers (as also does the epithet 'praying') to the habitual attitude of the insect – standing motionless on its four hindlegs with the forelegs raised as if in prayer – it is waiting for unwary insects to stray within reach. The forelegs are spined and the joint called the tibia can be snapped back against the femur, rather as the blade of a penknife snaps into its handle, to form a pair of grasping organs which seize and then keep a hold on any unfortunate victims.

Mantises, or praying mantises as they are often called, feed mainly on other insects, and are found mostly in tropical or subtropical countries. Most of the smallest are about an inch long. They have narrow, leathery forewings and large fan-shaped hindwings, which are folded beneath the forewings when not in use. Most mantises can fly, but they do not readily take to flight and seldom go far.

About 1 800 species are known, the most familiar species being the European mantis **Mantis religiosa**, which lives in the Mediterranean region and has been introduced into eastern North America.

Hidden terror

Most mantises spend their time sitting still among foliage, or on the bark of trees, waiting for insects to stray within reach of a lightning-quick snatch of their spined forelegs. Nearly all are shaped and coloured to blend with their surroundings. Many are green or brown, matching the living or dead leaves among which they sit, but some have more elaborate camouflage which serves two purposes. First, because they do not pursue their prey but wait for it to stray within reach, they need to stay hidden. Secondly, their grasping forelegs, although formidable to other insects, are usually useless against birds and lizards, and since mantises are slow-moving, they must be concealed to avoid being caught and eaten.

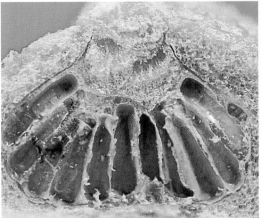

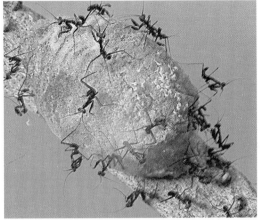

Mantises never take plant food. They seize their insect victims in their spined forelegs and eat them alive, neatly and delicately. Some of the largest species occasionally catch and eat small birds and lizards in the same way.

Unusual mating habits
To a female mantis a male is no more than just another piece of food. He must, therefore, be careful in his approach if he wishes to mate, rather than be the next meal. On seeing a ripe female, the male, justifiably enough, freezes, then starts to creep up on her with movements almost too slow for the eye to follow – sometimes taking an hour or more to move 1 ft. Once within range, he makes a short hop and clasps the female, to mate. If the pair is disturbed or the female sees her suitor, she will eat him, starting by biting off his head. As he loses his head, so he loses his inhibitions, because mantis copulation is controlled by a nerve centre in the head which inhibits mating until a female is clasped. If this nerve is removed (by an experimenter, or by a female mantis) all control is lost, and the body continues to copulate. The female, therefore, has much to gain from attacking and eating males; she ensures both fertilisation of her eggs and nourishment for her developing ovaries.

Eggs in a bag
The female lays 80 – 100 eggs at a time in tough, spongy capsules which she attaches to twigs, and she may produce 20 capsules in her lifetime. While laying her eggs she gives out a liquid which she stirs into a froth by movements of her body. The eggs become enclosed in this while it is still plastic, then it quickly hardens and dries.

The young mantises hatch together and at first hang from the egg capsule by silken threads which they give out from the hind end of the abdomen. After their first moult they can no longer make silk. They grow by gradual stages, moulting up to 12 times before becoming adult. The wings, tiny at first, grow with each succeeding moult.

The egg capsules are a protection against insectivorous animals and birds, but they are no protection against parasitic wasps of the ichneumon type, which are probably the most serious enemies of mantises.

Fatal flowers
Some mantises are even more deceptive, taking on the appearance of flowers and so luring insects such as bees and butterflies within reach. The orchid mantis of Malaysia and Indonesia, in its young or subadult stage, is coloured pink and the thigh joints of the four hindlegs are widely expanded so they look like petals, while the pink body

resembles the centre of the flower. When the mantis reaches the adult stage, however, its body becomes white and elongated as in a normal mantis. It still has the expanded, petal-like legs but its resemblance to a flower is largely lost. The African 'devil's flower' has expansions on the thorax and the forelegs which are white and red. It hangs down from a leaf or twig, and catches any flies or butterflies attracted to it.

When they are frightened, many mantises will suddenly adopt a menacing posture, rearing up and throwing their forelegs wide apart. One African species *Pseudocreobotra wahlbergi* improves on this display by spreading its wings, on which there are a pair of eye-like markings, so the enemy is suddenly confronted with a menacing 'face'.

class	**Insecta**
order	**Dictyoptera**
suborder	**Mantodea**
family	**Mantidae**
genera & species	***Hymenopus coronatus*** orchid mantis
	Mantis religiosa European mantis ***Idolum diabolicum*** African devil's flower, others

*Incredible birth: this **Bactrododema aculiferum** has just hatched from its tiny egg shell, having first pushed off the top of the egg, the operculum.*

Stick-insect

*Stick-insects are today more commonly kept as pets than probably any other insect. They are sluggish and live among the foliage of trees and bushes or in low-growing herbage, relying for protection on their resemblance to their surroundings. They are always long and very slender, usually with smooth bodies, although some species are spiny. The larger kinds look like twigs and may be green or brown; the small species and the young of the larger ones are usually green and resemble the midribs of leaves or the stems and blades of grass. Some are very large and the Asian species **Palophus titan** is the longest living insect, sometimes exceeding a foot in length.*

Some stick-insects have wings but many are wingless, a condition that enhances their resemblance to twigs.

*Stick-insects, with the leaf-insects, comprise an order, the Phasmida, once included in the Orthoptera together with the grass-hoppers, mantids, cockroaches and others, but this group has now been divided into several separate orders. About 2 000 species of phasmids are known, the majority being found in the Oriental tropics. One species, **Bacillus rossii**, is native to Europe, ranging as far north as central France. Two kinds of stick-insects from New Zealand have become established in the extreme southwest of the British Isles: the prickly stick-insect **Acanthoxyla prasina** in Devonshire and on Tresco in the Scilly Isles, and the smooth stick-insect **Clitarchus***

*hookeri also on Tresco and on an island off County Kerry, Eire. The so-called laboratory stick-insect **Carausius morosus** is an Oriental species often kept in schools and laboratories and more generally as a pet. It is a very easy insect to keep and breed and can be fed on leaves of privet, ivy or lilac. It cannot, however, survive out of doors through the cold winter in northern Europe and it is important that it is kept inside during this period.*

Dazzle and hide

Most stick-insects feed and move about only at night. By day they remain motionless and often appear to be 'feigning death'. In fact they pass into a hypnotic or cataleptic state during the day. When they are in this condition the limbs can be moved into any position and will stay there, rather as if the joints were made of wax. Some of the winged species are active by day. In many of these the hindwings—which are the only ones developed for flying—are brightly coloured but are entirely concealed when the insect is at rest. If it is disturbed the wings are suddenly unfolded and the resultant flash of bright colour is confusing to a searching predator. Then, when the wings are closed again, the bright colour suddenly disappears, so the exact position at which the insect has alighted is effectively concealed. This is a well-known protective device and is called 'flash coloration'.

All stick-insects are plant eaters and occasionally they become numerous enough to defoliate areas of woodland. In Australia there are two species which occur in swampy areas but also feed on agricultural crops where they sometimes cause serious damage.

Eggs like raindrops

All the phasmids lay rather large, hard-shelled eggs which look very like seeds. In some cases they closely resemble the actual seeds of the plant on which the insect feeds. The eggs are dropped by the females at random. The tap of falling eggs is often heard from the cages of captive stick-insects and a North American species *Diapheromera femorata* is sometimes so numerous that the sound of thousands of its eggs falling on the forest floor is as loud as that of rain.

Several hundred eggs are usually laid, a few each day, and they take a long time to hatch. Those of the laboratory stick-insect hatch in 4–6 months at ordinary room temperatures, but this can be speeded up to 2 months by extra warmth or retarded to 8 months by cold conditions such as an unheated room in winter. The eggs of the Madagascar stick-insect *Sipyloidea sipylus* will hatch in as little as one month if kept at $24°C/75°F - 27°C/80°F$, but at lower temperatures may lie dormant for up to a year. The young look very like the adults in all except size and, in the case of the winged species, in lacking wings, which develop gradually during growth.

Many stick-insects reproduce by parthenogenesis, that is the females lay fertile eggs without mating. In these species the males are usually rare; in cultures of the laboratory stick-insect, for example, they number about one in every 4 000 females. Of the two New Zealand species already mentioned, the male of the prickly stick-insect is unknown and possibly does not exist. In New Zealand, males of the smooth stick-insect are almost as common as females, but no males have been found in the small British colonies of the same species and the eggs develop without fertilisation.

Odd colours

The laboratory stick-insect occurs in various colour forms ranging from green to shades of brown. The colour is determined by green, brown, orange-red and yellow granules in the cells of the surface layer of the skin. Pure green individuals cannot change colour, but the others regularly change, becoming darker at night and paler by day. The change is brought about by movement of the pigment granules within the cells. Brown pigments may move to the surface and spread out, making the insect dark in tone, or they may contract into lumps and move to the inner part of the cell so the insect becomes pale. The orange-red granules can also move about in this way, but the green and yellow ones are unable to move about at all.

The alternation of colours becomes established by exposure to normal day and night, but once established it continues as a rhythm governed by the time cycle of 24 hours. A stick-insect conditioned to normal light change and then kept in permanent darkness will continue for several weeks to change colour every 24 hours, just as it did before. If it is kept in the dark by day and exposed to artificial light at night a reversed rhythm will develop in response to these conditions. This also persists for some time when the insect is kept continually in darkness with no light at all.

phylum	**Arthropoda**
class	**Insecta**
order	**Phasmida**
families	**Bacteriidae**
	Phasmidae

△ *Remarkable camouflage: head of* **Bactrododema aculiferum** *with its ear-like projections looking very like broken-off twigs.*
▷ *Rare shot: 7-inch* **Clemancatha regale**.
▽ *Precarious upside-down mating of* Gratidia *spp. The female holds onto the stem as the male clasps her — both beautifully camouflaged.*

Termite

Termites, often incorrectly called white ants, resemble true ants in their way of life, although less so in appearance, and the two are very distantly related. Ants are related to bees and wasps and termites are near relatives of cockroaches. Most of the 1 700 species live in the tropics, but a few are found in southern Europe and 55 in the United States. They are absent from northern Europe and are the only important order of insects not represented in northern Europe.

Fossil termites date back at least 250 million years. One very primitive genus **Mastotermes**, surviving in Australia, is very similar to a cockroach in the form of its hindwings and also in the way the female lays her eggs, these being arranged in groups of 16 and 24 in two rows.

Termites and ants often resemble each other in being social insects living in colonies numbering hundreds or thousands of individuals. In both, the colonies consist of large numbers of 'workers' and 'soldiers' which are non-reproductive, and a few, or even just one, reproductives, the 'kings' and 'queens', which are the parents of all the others and may be very long-lived. In both, the non-reproductives are wingless, but the functional males and females have wings and fly in swarms from the nest. Before founding new colonies, or re-entering existing ones, they break off their wings. Both ants and termites have the habit of trophallaxis or mouth-to-

*Harmonious community (above). A winged reproductive termite, two soldiers and two white workers: **Calotermes flavicollis** (×15).*
*Nest of activity (right), harvester termites **Trinervitermes trinervoides**. Note the long snout on the head of each soldier which can secrete a toxic liquid to repel enemies (×6).*

mouth feeding. The 'royal' individuals are fed entirely in this way. Termites and ants are also alike in having some species that cultivate fungi underground for food.

The life histories of the two insects are, however, very different. In ants there are distinct larva and pupa stages and the larvae are helpless and have to be fed by the workers. In termites the young hatch as minute replicas of the adults and do not change their form as they grow. They

are first fed by trophallaxis, but soon learn to feed themselves and can take an active part in the work of the nest long before they are fully grown. Ant workers and soldiers are all non-reproductive females; in a termite nest all the castes are composed of both sexes. The queen ant mates only on her nuptial flight and is not joined by the male when she founds a colony. The king and queen termite, on the other hand, cooperate in founding the colony and live together in the nest, mating at intervals and being fed by the workers.

A termites' nest

One of the most intensively studied of all termites is the black-mound termite *Amitermes atlanticus*, investigated by Dr SH Skaife in the Cape Province of South Africa.

The nests consist of black, rounded mounds, 2 ft or less in diameter. The nest is made of a cement of the termites' faeces. It is watertight and very strong; a pickaxe or hammer is needed to break it. When broken open it has a sponge-like appearance, consisting of innumerable cells an inch or less in size connected by openings just big enough for the termites to creep through. The inhabitants of the mound live in a perpetual warm, moist fug, with 5–15% of carbon dioxide always present in the air. A man confined in such an atmosphere would soon lose consciousness. The temperature varies far less than that of the outside air. In extremes of heat and cold the termites huddle to the centre; when the sun re-warms a chilled nest or the summer dusk cools an overheated one, they crowd to the periphery. The king and queen black-mound termites are not confined to a 'royal

chamber' as in some termites, but move about from cell to cell through temporary enlarged openings made by the workers.

The outside crust of the nest consists of sand grains stuck together with faecal cement, and any break in it is quickly repaired with this same material. During the spring months of August and September the nest is enlarged about an inch all round.

Division of labour

The queen is $\frac{1}{2}$–$\frac{3}{4}$ in. long, depending on her age, which may reach 15 years. The king measures only $\frac{1}{4}$ in. Both had wings and flew at one time, but they broke their wings off when founding the colony. In addition to these 'primary reproductives' there are 'secondary reproductives', individuals of both sexes with rudimentary wings, which can produce fertile eggs if the primary pair meet with an accident or become infertile with age. They are stimulated to do so by special feeding, but are never as prolific as a primary queen, and her place is taken not by one but by a number of female secondaries. In some nests a third, wholly wingless type of reproductive is found, but these are rare. The non-reproductives are either workers or soldiers. These go out at night for food, which in this species consists of decaying vegetation. The soldiers are simply a bodyguard against attack by ants, the arch-enemies of termites. They cannot even eat the natural food themselves but are fed, as the reproductives are, by the workers. A black-mound termite nest may last 40–50 years.

A two million termite tower

The more primitive kinds of termites, including *Mastotermes* and the family Kalotermitidae, live in wood, excavating galleries and chambers in it and feeding on it. Their natural role is to break up fallen timber and return it to the soil, but when they turn their attention to the timbers of buildings or to stored wooden crates and boxes they work havoc and are a serious problem in all tropical regions. Some of the more advanced types of termites make immense nests, towering as much as 20 ft above the ground and containing perhaps a couple of million inhabitants. When ground is being levelled in tropical Africa for cultivation or building, the large termite nests sometimes defy even bulldozers and have to be destroyed with explosives. In northern Australia the remarkable compass termite *Amitermes meridionalis* makes termitaria 10–12 ft high. They are shaped like a flat wedge with its edge uppermost and stand in an exact north and south position, with the flat sides facing east and west. It is not certain how this arrangement benefits the termites, or how they manage to build with such exact orientation, although it has been suggested that the termites build to make full use of the sun's warmth.

Some termites make underground nests with little or no visible superstructure, others build carton nests of chewed wood pulp in trees, very like wasps' nests.

Need help to digest

Termites are primarily vegetarians. Those that live in wood and feed on it have microscopic protistans in their intestines which break down the cellulose of the wood, enabling the termites to digest it. The subterranean and mound-building termites subsist on various kinds of vegetable matter,

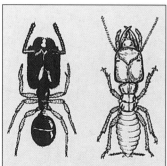

◁ *Comparison between a soldier ant* **Pheidole instabilis** *(left) and a soldier termite* **Archotermopsis**. *Both social insects, ants and termites live in colonies, each member or caste of the colony with a specific job. The soldiers, as their name implies, defend the colony. The most notable difference between these two soldiers is that the abdomen of the ant is waisted.*

▽ *Rulers of the colony, king and queen termites,* **Macrotermes natalensis,** *the longest lived members of the society. The king looks a mere weakling beside the queen who has her abdomen swollen disproportionately with eggs. Once fertilised she does nothing but lay eggs, the king staying with her, which is unusual among social insects, to help expand the new colony (approx × 2).*

living, dead and decaying. The fungi which are invariably present in decaying wood or leaves are probably important to many if not most termites, and some cultivate fungi in large chambers underground, just as the leafcutter ants do.

In a termites' nest of the black-mound type nothing is wasted. The bodies of the dead are devoured and excrement is eaten over and over again until every particle of nourishment is extracted from it. The paste that remains is used for building.

Free-for-all feast

When the winged males and females swarm out of the nests every termite's enemy. Birds, small mammals, lizards, toads and even some sensible opportunists among humans have a feast. Only a tiny fraction of the fragile fluttering princes and princesses live to become kings and queens. A few highly specialised mammals, such as anteaters, pangolins, the aardvark, and aardwolf, can break into the termitaria using strong claws and sweep up the termites with long sticky tongues. The termites' arch-enemies are, however, ants; a permanent state of war exists between the two insects. Termite soldiers are really specialised ant fighters. Some have powerful jaws which can snap an ant in two. Others have no jaws but instead the head is drawn into a spout-like snout from which an intensely sticky liquid can be squirted that effectively gums up any ant it touches. In spite of their seemingly effective armament, however, no termites are a match for ants in open battle, and they rely on the massive defences of their nests for their continued existence.

The long-lived queen

Most people know what a queen termite looks like—a great sausage-shaped egg-factory. Queen termites are unique among insects in growing after their last moult. The skin between the abdominal segments stretches, leaving the original segmental coverings as brown islands on the pale, bloated back. The queen black-mound termite can live 15 years; others, of larger and more highly developed species, may live longer. In Australia, in 1872, the top of a large termite nest had to be broken off to allow telegraph wires to pass over. In 1913 and again in 1935 the nest was examined and was found to have a flourishing population, although the broken top had not been renewed. No secondary reproductives have ever been found in nests of this species (*Eutermes triodiae*), so the original king and queen, founders of a nest already 14 ft high in 1872, were probably still alive in 1935. It is possible the original population had died and the nest had been recolonised, but it was more probably a case of an insect living as long as a man.

phylum	**Arthropoda**
class	**Insecta**
order	**Isoptera**

Top left: 'Watch it' — a threatened male raises his pincers. Top right: Birthday suit — a freshly-peeled female rests beside her old skin.

Above left: Female earwigs are model mothers. This one is pottering anxiously round her eggs, protecting and cleaning them.

Above right: Watching over a nursery of earwig toddlers, which stay with the mother until their second moult, eating their own skins.

Earwig

*The fearsome-looking pincers of the common earwig are referred to in its scientific name — **Forficula auricularia** — since **forficula** is Latin for 'little scissors'. Curved in the male and straight in the female, they are carried at the hind end of the flattened brown body and when danger approaches they may be raised in the air and displayed as a threat. Although not as effective weapons as they look, they are nevertheless used in defence and the insect can use them to grip with some tenacity. Those of the males vary in length and fall into two more or less distinct size ranges.*

At first sight, the earwig seems to have no wings, but in fact there is a service-able pair neatly folded away beneath tiny wing cases overlapping the front part of the abdomen. These wing cases or 'elytra' like those of beetles, are the hardened front pair of wings, which in dragonflies, butterflies and other insects are still used in flight. The pincers of the earwig are said to assist in folding away the wings after use.

The tawny earwig is only half the size but otherwise much like the adult of the

common earwig. There are a few other British species, including two that have been introduced, but these are much less common.

There are some 900 species of earwigs throughout the world, differing in size from $\frac{1}{4}$ in. to $1\frac{1}{2}$ in. but otherwise similar except that some are wingless.

Rarely seen on the wing

Earwigs spend the day hidden away in dry, usually upright crevices, and are often to be found under loose bark. The common earwig is also found tucked away among the petals of dahlias. Whether or not they are doing much damage is a disputed point though they are known to eat both petals and leaves. Gardeners often provide an alternative home in the form of an up-turned flower pot, preferably stuffed with newspaper or straw. Earwigs are active at night and it is partly for this reason that they have rarely been seen flying although some — and the tawny earwig is one — often take to the wing on hot days. When earwigs are seen on clothes hanging out on a line overnight, however, it is easier to believe they have flown there than climbed.

The common earwig is widespread in Europe and has also been introduced and firmly established in the United States, becoming a nuisance in some places.

Earwigs eat plant lice

The diet includes a great variety of both animal and plant matter. To a large extent, earwigs are scavengers, but they may sometimes eat large numbers of plant lice, and have been seen to capture larger insects like bluebottles with their pincers. They will also eat fruit, leaves, flowers and fungi.

The 'broody-hen' insect

The most remarkable feature of the earwig is its family life and the 'broody-hen' behaviour of the mother. The sexes come together in September. Then, throughout much of the autumn and winter, they may be found in pairs either in chambers dug about an inch down in the earth, or sometimes just in crevices among vegetation. Late in January or towards the end of March, the male leaves — or is perhaps driven out — and the female starts to lay her oval, pearly-white eggs. Within about 2 days some 20—80 are laid, the largest females tending to produce the greatest number. At first the eggs are scattered about the floor of the chamber, but the mother soon gathers them into a pile and thereafter gives them her continual attention. One by one she picks them up in her mouth and licks them all over. At this time she is more than usually aggressive, and her only food is the occasional egg that has gone bad. The rest hatch 3—4 weeks after being laid.

The behaviour of the mothers has been subjected to scientific scrutiny. It has been found, for instance, that they recognise their eggs, when collecting up after they are laid. A female earwig will quite readily collect little wax balls or rounded stones. Later on, however, the wax balls and stones are rejected as lacking the appropriate taste or smell.

It has also been found that the eggs must be licked by the mother if they are to hatch and that the female's urge to lick them is dependent on the presence of the eggs. The urge fades in a few days if the eggs are removed, and after that it cannot be revived even if the eggs are replaced, but it will persist as long as 3 months if the eggs are continually replaced by others as they hatch.

The young earwigs are not grubs or larvae but nymphs, essentially like the parents though smaller and more dumpy, with simple straight forceps. Like domestic chicks, they stay with their mother for a while, nestling under her body. Twice they cast and eat their skins while in her care, and after the second moult they disperse, to become fully grown by about July. This cosy family picture is spoiled, however, if the mother dies, for she is then eaten by her own offspring (along with the cast skins).

The family life of the earwig represents an early stage in the evolution of a social organisation, which is developed independently and far more fully in ants, bees, wasps and termites. A relative of the earwig *(Hemimerus)* protects its eggs in a very different way. It behaves more like a mammal than a bird. Its eggs are retained within the body, where they are nourished by a sort of placenta and the young are born alive.

Do earwigs enter ears?
To some people earwigs are endearing animals, for no very clear reason. To others, through a belief that they will enter the human ear, they are objects of apprehension. This belief is reflected in the name given to the animal not only in English but in other languages, *Ohrwurm* in German and *perce-oreille* in French, to name only two. It is sometimes suggested that the English name is derived from 'ear-wing' since the extended wings are somewhat ear-shaped, but 'wig' is from the Old English 'wiggle', to wriggle, and the wings are hardly likely to be seen often enough to compete with the pincers for commemoration in a common name.

Entomologists seem to discredit the notion of earwigs entering ears, but there are authentic accounts of its having happened in medical journals and in the case-books of medical practitioners. Moreover, there is a consistent note in the descriptions of the discomfort experienced by the patients, who complain of a 'noise of thunder' in the ear.

It must be agreed with the sceptics that the earwig has no special passion for ears, but it does have an instinct to insinuate itself into cracks and crevices, under loose bark or in folds of curtains — so why not on rare occasions in the ear of an unwary camper or, more often perhaps in the past, in the ears of our ancestors who lived closer to nature? For peace of mind, when sleeping under canvas, some cotton wool in the ears is a reasonable precaution. The first aid remedy is to float the insect out with oil.

It is interesting that earwigs themselves have been used in medicine, as a cure for deafness, on the principle that like cures like, or, as it is popularly known 'a hair of the dog that bit you'. The earwig was dried, powdered and mixed with the urine of a hare.

phylum	**Arthropoda**
class	**Insecta**
order	**Dermaptera**
family	**Forficulidae**
genera & species	***Forficula auricularia*** common earwig ***Labia minor*** tawny earwig others

Below left: Earwig couple. The male can be distinguished from the female by the scimitar curve of his pincers; the female's are straight. Below: Female earwig's wing pattern. Earwigs can fly quite well, but they are rarely seen doing so because they are most active at night.

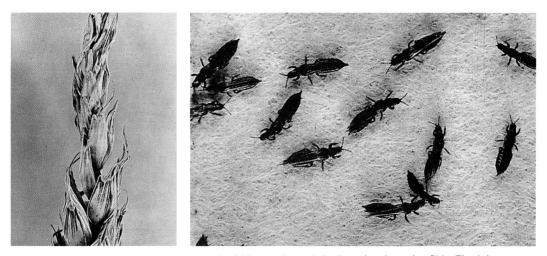

Left: Damaged corn ears: apart from direct damage, many species of thrips carry viruses and other diseases from plant to plant. Right: The culprit: **Limothrips cerealium.**

Thrips

Thrips are most unusual insects, in the structure of their wings, in their life history and, above all, because we normally neither see them nor hear them although they are frequently agricultural pests and can also annoy us in other ways. They form a small order of insects which numbers less than 2 000 species. Almost all of them are tiny, $\frac{1}{50}-\frac{1}{6}$ in. long, the giant among them being an Australian thrips which is $\frac{1}{2}$ in. long. Under the microscope they look like lice that have grown feathery wings. They have two pairs of wings, each consisting of a narrow strap fringed in front and behind with long hairs. The name of their order, the Thysanoptera, means 'fringe-wings'. On each side the wings are held together at the bases by a series of hooks, and they are folded over the back when at rest. A number of species lack wings.

There are two suborders, distinguished by the form of the ovipositor, or egg-laying organ. In the suborder Terebrantia the ovipositor is saw-like and used to insert the eggs into plant tissues. In the other suborder, the Tubulifera, the ovipositor is simple and hollow and used to lay eggs in crevices.

Force of numbers
Most of the thrips live on plants, especially on the blossoms and fruit, and feed by sucking the sap. For this they use their highly peculiar mouthparts, which form a piercing and sucking apparatus modified from the maxillae and mandibles. These are asymmetrical, the maxillae usually having a little asymmetry while only the left mandible is functional, the right-hand one being vestigial or lacking altogether.

Thrips occur in very large numbers and damage plants directly by disfiguring the flowers, spoiling the fruit and causing the tops of grasses to shrivel, a condition known as 'silvertop'. It is said that fruit, such as pears, may not even start to develop if thrips get onto the blossom in sufficient numbers. The greenhouse thrips excretes red drops that turn black and disfigure the foliage of ornamental plants. Some of the pest species have names which suggest, quite wrongly, that they live only on certain plants. The onion thrips, for example, attacks a wide variety of plants, and the honeysuckle thrips is a pest of the flowers and fruit of both blackberry and loganberry. The grain or corn thrips, is, however, well named as it attacks cereals and grasses. Besides damaging the plants directly many species of thrips carry viruses and other diseases from plant to plant. Their powers of flight are feeble, but once air-borne they may travel long distances on the wind, thus spreading the disease over a wide area.

The species that are pests of crops belong mostly to the Terebrantia. Many of the Tubulifera feed on dead leaves and fungi and some form plant galls in which they live. A few are predatory, attacking aphides, and one species is regarded in Florida as beneficial because it preys on a destructive species of whitefly.

Mixed-up metamorphosis
The thrips are as freakish in their life history as they are in their appearance and structure. In the first two stages of their larval life the young thrips resemble the adults except in size and in lacking wings. They are, however, active and feed avidly. At the third moult they cease to be active and are often enclosed in a cell or cocoon. Before

reaching the adult stage they undergo two more moults, three in the Tubulifera. The last stage before maturity is called the pupa and the one or two stages preceding this are called the prepupa. No other insects have a life history in any way resembling this unusual one.

Unseen misery
For most of their time thrips do little more than stay in one spot sucking sap with their tubes sunk in the tissues of plants. If disturbed, however, some crawl about in a leisurely manner, while others run quickly or even leap into the air. Although they do not often use it, some can fly. The smaller thrips, which are little larger than specks of dust, may get caught up in thermals. So, especially in hot weather, there may be droves of thrips circulating in the atmosphere and sometimes they land on humans. They are virtually invisible but cause an annoying tickling on the hands and face as they crawl over the skin. Some people are more susceptible to these irritations than others, and to those who do feel them they are worse than an actual pain.

phylum	**Arthropoda**
class	**Insecta**
order	**Thysanoptera**
genera & species	***Heliothrips haemorrhoidalis*** *greenhouse thrips*
	Idolothrips spectrum *Australian giant thrips*
	Limothrips cerealium *grain thrips*
	Thrips flavus *honeysuckle thrips*
	T. tabaci *onion thrips, others*

Mayfly

Mayflies make up one of the most distinct and peculiar of insect orders. They have features which are not found in any other group of insects, and all the species in the order are very much alike.

The adult has large forewings and its hindwings are small, sometimes absent altogether. Each wing has a fine network of veins, and when the insect is at rest all four wings are held close together over the back in the manner of a butterfly. The legs are small and weak and the tail ends in three, sometimes two, long filaments or cerci. The eyes are large, especially in the males. In some genera, **Cloeon,** *for example,*

the land. The compact mass of moving insects attracts the notice of females, which fly into the swarm. Each is at once seized by a male, the pair then leaving the swarm to mate. The males die almost immediately after mating and the females soon after laying their eggs, although they may have spent several years as aquatic nymphs.

The female mayfly always lays her eggs in water, but in some species she drops them from the air as she flies just above the surface. In many species the eggs are provided with fine threads which anchor them to water plants or pebbles. A few give birth to living young which have hatched from eggs retained in the mother's body. In the egg-laying species one female may lay several hundred, or several thousand, eggs.

The nymphs are always aquatic; breathing is supplemented by gills set along each side

the males have two pairs of compound eyes, one pair with small facets on the sides of the head and one pair with large facets on the top. The antennae are reduced to tiny bristles, suggesting that the insect is aware of its surroundings mainly through its sight. The jaws and other mouthparts are vestigial and functionless and adult mayflies never feed. They only gulp down air until the stomach becomes distended like a balloon. This reduces the insect's overall specific gravity and makes the mating flight easier.

About 1 000 species are known, but only those of Europe and North America have been thoroughly studied and there must be many species still undescribed.

Guiding light
The adult life of mayflies is concerned solely with reproduction. They nearly always hatch in great numbers together, and the males gather in dancing swarms over

of the abdomen. Unlike the adults, the nymphs show many differences from species to species. Some are adapted for swimming actively among water plants, others to living on the bottom, burrowing in the mud or clinging to rocks in rapidly flowing water. Nearly all are vegetable feeders, and they take from a year to as much as 4 years to reach full size. A recent discovery about free-swimming mayfly nymphs is that they orientate themselves in the water not by a sense of balance based on gravity, as had been supposed, but by the direction from which the light reaches their eyes. In an aquarium with a glass bottom, lit from below, they swim upside-down.

They mate and die on land
The event in the mayfly's life which sets the Ephemeroptera, as they are collectively called, wholly apart from all other insects is the change from a subimago to an imago. Before this happens, however, the fully grown nymph rises to the surface of the water and floats there, or crawls out onto

◁◁ *The egg patches of a mayfly **Baetis** laid under a submerged rock in a stream.*
◁ *Hatchling: the nymph of the largest British mayfly **Ephemera danica** (approx 8 × life size).*

△ *The nymph forms a subimago. The anglers' Green Drake is shown **Ephemera danica**.*
▽ *From dun to spinner: leaving behind the subimago case, an imago **Baetis rhodani**.*

a stone or reed. Its skin splits and a winged insect creeps out, resting for a time before making a short, rather laboured flight to a bush or fence or to a building near the water. Although it is winged, this insect that creeps laboriously out of the water is not the perfect insect or imago, as the final stage is called. After a few minutes or hours, varying with the species, the subimago moults again, shedding a delicate skin from the whole of its body, legs and even its wings. Then it flies away, much more buoyantly than before, but it will live at most for a few days and, in many species, only for a few hours. A subimago can be recognised by the wings which appear dark and dull due to the presence of microscopic hairs, which form a visible fringe along their hinder edges.

The fisherman's fly

Mayflies are of great interest to anglers, both on account of the part they play in supplying fish with food, and by their direct connection with the sport of fly-fishing. The hatching of a swarm of mayflies excites the fish, especially trout, and stimulates their appetites, so they take a lure more readily than at other times. The swarming is known as a 'hatch' and the fish are said to 'rise' to it. They feed both on the nymphs as they swim to the surface and on the flies, both subimagoes and adults, which touch or fall into the water.

A mayfly is far too delicate an object to be impaled on a hook like a maggot or a worm, and the flyfisherman's practice is to make replicas of the flies by binding carefully prepared scraps of feathers onto the shaft of a hook. These are then 'cast' and allowed to fall onto the surface of the water. A lure so used is called a 'dry fly', as opposed to a 'wet fly', which sinks under the surface.

The more exactly the artificial fly duplicates the species of mayfly which is hatching, the greater are the chances of success, so anglers study mayflies carefully and they have their own names for them. Any subimago is known as a 'dun' and the imagoes are called 'spinners'. Those of the species *Procloeon rufulum* are called the Pale Evening Dun and the Pale Evening Spinner respectively. *Rhithrogena semicolorata* are the Olive Upright Dun and the Olive Upright Spinner. The two stages of *Ephemera danica* have separate names, the Green Drake and the Spent Gnat.

If a well made artificial fly is swung, by means of a rod and line, into a swarm of the males whose species it represents, numbers of them will pursue it, losing interest only when actual contact reveals to them that they have been heartlessly deceived.

◁ *A short life but a gay one: having passed through all the hazards of a year or more of aquatic larval life this adult* **Ephemera vulgata** *will live only long enough to reproduce.*

class	**Insecta**
order	**Ephemeroptera**
families	**Ephemeridae**
	Caenidae (hindwings absent)
	others

Dragonfly

Colourful and powerful fliers, dragonflies are among the fastest of all insects. Most dragonflies are large insects which hold their wings stiffly extended on each side when at rest, whereas most other insects fold them over the back. The wings are capable of only simple up-and-down movement, have no coupling device joining the front and back wings, as in higher insects such as butterflies, and have a fine network of 'veins' supporting the membrane. All these characteristics show that dragonflies are primitive insects that have existed with little change for a very long time. The earliest known fossil dragonflies are from the late Carboniferous period, deposited about 300 million years ago. There were dragonflies similar to those living today in the Jurassic period, 150 million years ago, when the giant dinosaurs were roaming the earth.

The name is often used in England as an equivalent of the insect order Odonata, but the members of the suborder Zygoptera are very distinct in appearance. Living dragonflies consist of two very unequal suborders, the Anisoptera (all the familiar species) and the Anisozygoptera (only two species known, from Japan and the Himalayas respectively).

As in their relatives the damselflies, the wings of dragonflies are usually transparent and colourless, but may be tinted or patterned, and the body is often brightly coloured. They differ markedly from damselflies in having very swift, powerful flight. Estimates of their actual speed are difficult to obtain and vary from 35 up to 60 mph, but they are certainly among the fastest of all insects. The antennae are minute and the eyes enormous, occupying the greater part of the head. Each compound eye may contain as many as 30 000 facets.

Territorial instincts

Dragonflies fly a 'fighter patrol' over a fixed area. Although they are most often seen near water, which is where they breed, their powerful flight carries them far away from their breeding places, and they may be met wherever there are trees and bushes on which they can rest. One can often be seen flying back and forth over a definite 'beat', and when it lands it will do so on one or other of a small number of resting places. The beat may be an area selected as suitable for hunting prey or, especially if it is over water, it may be the territory chosen by a male dragonfly, which will then mate with any female of its own species which flies into this area. These males defend their territories strenuously against other males of the same species. After a while they begin to show signs of battle in the shape of torn wings and mutilated legs.

△ Male dragonfly **Orthetrum coerulescens**. The female of this British species is brown with black markings on the abdomen.

▽ African beauty of the family Libellelidae. The wings show the complex venation supporting the membrane which is found in all dragonflies.

Whether in hunting or fighting, the sense used most is sight; a dragonfly can detect movement 40 ft away.

Some species of dragonflies are migratory and may fly great distances over land and sea. One species *Libellula quadrimaculata* sometimes migrates in spectacular swarms. In 1862 a swarm was observed in Germany, estimated at nearly two-and-a-half thousand million strong, and in June 1900 the sky over Antwerp 'appeared black' with these dragonflies. In 1947 a huge migration of another species *Sympetrum striolatum* was seen flying overhead by observers on the south coast of Ireland.

Masked killers

Dragonflies are predatory in all their stages. The adults catch other insects on the wing, seizing them with their forwardly directed legs and chewing them with their powerful jaws. In the southeastern United States two large species *Anax junius* and *Coryphaeshna ingens* are serious predators of honey-bees.

The larvae capture their prey by what is known as a mask, a mechanism that is shared with the damselflies but is otherwise unique among insects. The labium or lower lip is greatly enlarged and armed with a pair of hooks. At rest it is folded under the head,

△ *Skimming low over the surface, a female dragonfly dips her abdomen to lay eggs.*

but it is extensible and can be shot out in front of the head, the hooks being used to seize the prey like a pair of pincers. The victim is then drawn back within reach of the jaws. Other insects, tadpoles and small fish form the prey of dragonfly larvae, and those of the larger species can make serious inroads into the numbers of young fish in a rearing pond. On the other hand, the young dragonfly larvae perform a useful service by destroying great numbers of the aquatic larvae of mosquitoes.

The 'tandem'

Mating involves the same curious process as the damselflies, in which the male transfers his sperm from the primary sexual organ near the tip of his abdomen to an accessory organ farther forward, at the base of the abdomen. He then alights on the back of a female and curls his abdomen under his own body in order to seize her head (not her thorax as in damselflies) with a pair of claspers at the end of his abdomen. He then releases the hold with his legs but retains that with his claspers. The female then curls her abdomen round in such a way that the tip of it makes contact with the male accessory organ. Both before and after mating the two may fly together, with the female held by the male claspers, in what is known as the 'tandem position'. They may even maintain this position while the eggs are being laid.

Dragonflies almost always lay their eggs in water. One of two ways is used. Some insert their eggs into the stems of water plants, as damselflies do. These include the big hawker dragonflies, *Aeshna*. Others, like the golden-ringed dragonfly *Cordulegaster boltoni* force their eggs into the sand or gravel at the margins of shallow streams. The second method is to fly close over the surface of water and repeatedly dip the tip of the body, extruding eggs at the same time, so these are washed off and sink to the bottom.

Form of jet propulsion

Most dragonflies spend their early life under water. The larvae vary in shape. Those that live in mud are short, thick-set and covered with a dense coat of hairs to which the mud clings. When such a larva is at rest, only the eyes and the tip of the abdomen are exposed, the rest being buried. The golden-ringed dragonfly has a larva of this type. Those that live among water weeds are more slender and active, but no dragonfly larvae are as slender and delicate as those of damselflies. They have gills inside the intestine a short distance from their hind opening and the larvae breathe by drawing water into the rectum and then driving it out again. This mechanism is also used for another purpose. If suddenly disturbed, the larva drives the water out forcibly, so propelling itself rapidly forward, in a simple form of jet propulsion.

When fully grown, after 2 years or more in most European species, the larva crawls up a plant growing in the water, climbs above the surface and undergoes its final moult to become an adult dragonfly.

Destruction of their habitat by pollution, drainage, dredging and infilling of ponds is the most serious threat to dragonflies and this is increasing throughout the world. As larvae, their chief natural enemies are fishes, whose own babies the well-grown dragonfly larvae prey upon. In fact dragonfly larvae probably form an important source of food for freshwater fishes. When small they are also eaten by other predatory insects, including larger dragonfly larvae, often of their own species. The adults are so swift and active that they have few natural enemies, but one small bird of prey, the hobby, feeds extensively on them.

△ *Libellula quadrimaculata* — both male and female have very similar markings on the abdomen and wings.

▽ *Dragonfly of Transvaal Lowveld, South Africa, resting. Powerful fliers, dragonflies are among the fastest of all insects.*

Biggest insects ever

The present-day Odonata are among the largest living insects. In tropical America there are damselflies with bodies 5 in. long and wings spanning 7 in. These are slender, flimsy creatures and are greatly exceeded in bulk by a Borneo dragonfly *Tetracanthagyna plagiata* whose wings also span 7 in. and whose thick body measures about 5 in.

No modern dragonflies, however, compare in size with some which lived 300 million years ago, in the forests when our coal measures were being laid down. At Commentry, in France, fossil remains of these have been found, including impressions of wings, which show that the wingspan of the biggest of them *Meganeura monyi* was as much as 27 in., about equal to that of a crow. They are by far the largest insects known to have inhabited the earth, but it is interesting that no larval remains have yet been found.

class	Insecta
order	Odonata
suborders	**Anisoptera, Anisozygoptera**

Louse

A louse is a small wingless insect which lives as a parasite on the outside of a mammal or a bird. Lice fall naturally into two distinct groups which are regarded by entomologists as separate orders.

The sucking lice (suborder Anoplura) are parasitic on mammals only and feed by sucking their blood. The biting lice (suborder Mallophaga), which exist mostly as parasites of birds although a few live on mammals, feed mainly on the feathers or hair of the host. The members of both orders have a similar appearance. They are small, pale in colour and flattened, and they have tough, leathery skins. The last two features are adaptations to protect them against scratching and other attempts by their hosts to dislodge them. Their bodies have undergone many changes linked with the parasitic way of life. Their legs are short and so are the antennae. The eyes are very small, sometimes almost non-existent. The segments of the body, so noticeable in the abdomen of a normal insect, are often not very clearly marked. There is no metamorphosis. Both types pass the whole of their lives on the body of the host, and one species of louse is often confined to one species of mammal or bird or to a group of related species.

The so-called book-louse is neither a true louse nor a parasite, but belongs to the order Psocoptera. It lives among books and furniture in damp, badly ventilated rooms.

Sucking lice

The hollow, piercing mouthparts and the way in which the claws of the legs are adapted for gripping distinguish this order of only 230 known species. The human louse can be used as a typical example. Not only is it confined to man as a host, but there are two varieties: the body louse and the head louse. The former lives on clothing next to the skin

and the latter among the hair of the head. The two varieties differ slightly in structure as well as in habits; they can be persuaded to interbreed under experimental conditions, but there is no evidence that they do so naturally. They have very similar life cycles. Their eggs, known as 'nits', are cemented on to the hair or fibres of the clothing. An adult louse lays about 10 eggs every day and in the course of its life lays about 300. At body temperature the eggs hatch in about a week, and the insects hatching from them are miniatures of the adults. They feed throughout their lives by inserting the hollow, piercing mouthparts into the skin and sucking up blood. They shed their skins three times before they are fully grown. Lice live for about 7 weeks.

The only other louse parasitic on man is the so-called crab louse which lives among the pubic hair. Its mode of feeding and life history are similar to those of the head louse.

Scratching can be fatal

In spite of its unpleasant associations, the crab louse does not convey disease, but this is very far from true of other species. By far the most serious disease carried by the human louse is epidemic typhus, which is caused by a virus-like micro-organism called *Rickettsia*. The body louse is the carrier and, rather curiously, the disease is not transmitted by its bite but by the entry of infected louse-excrement and the body fluids of crushed lice into abrasions in the skin. Scratching and seeking out lice and squashing them are therefore dangerous practices in conditions where typhus is likely to occur.

Such conditions are found in places where people are crowded together and have no opportunity to change and wash their clothes, or customarily fail to do so.

Flowers and fever

Up to quite recent times, gaols crowded with unfortunate people awaiting trial were subject to terrible epidemics of typhus. The hazard even extended to the courts of justice, because infected lice dropped out of the ragged clothing of the prisoners and transferred themselves to the court officials, witnesses and anyone else present. This risk

was recognised, though no one associated it with lice, and judges were provided with a bouquet of flowers whose scent was believed to keep away the 'evil humours' of the disease. It is still traditional in some courts for the judge to receive a nosegay of flowers. The terribly crowded conditions of the crew on ships, especially naval vessels, also led to typhus epidemics, and both 'gaol fever' and 'ship fever' were among the names by which the disease was known.

In the First World War, when conditions in the trenches were very conducive to louse infestation, a curious disease called 'trench fever' occurred. It was conveyed by lice and seems to have been a sort of mild and seldom fatal variant of typhus. After the war it completely disappeared, and so has never been investigated by modern techniques.

Our whole horror at the idea of being infected with lice is, of course, salutary, but it is quite a modern attitude. In mediaeval times the sanctity of holy men was enhanced in proportion to their lousiness. When the body of Thomas à Beckett was disrobed after his murder the lice in his hair-cloth garment, in the words of a contemporary chronicler, 'boiled over like water in a simmering cauldron'. The onlookers, far from being disgusted, were overcome with 'the joy of having found such a saint'.

Absence of lice from one's body used also to be regarded as a sign of lack of virility, and even today the religion of large numbers of people forbids them to kill a louse, though it is permitted to remove one from one's own person and deposit it unharmed on that of a neighbour. Evidently it will be some time before typhus goes the same way as trench fever.

Another quite distinct disease called relapsing fever is carried by human lice. It is easy to cure and not very prevalent.

class	**Insecta**
order	**Phthiraptera**
sub-order	**Anoplura**
genera & species	***Pediculus humanus*** human louse ***Phthirius pubis*** crab louse others

▽ *Photomicrograph of female human louse (× 20).*

▽ *Eggs or 'nits' cemented onto human hair (× 25).*

▽ *De-lousing in the fifteenth century.*

Flea

Fleas are small, wingless insects, parasites with the body flattened from side to side, making it easy for them to slip through the fur or feathers of the host. The legs are modified for rapid movement in this environment and also for powerful jumping, and the thick, hard skin is a good defence against the host's scratching.

The name 'flea' is used for any member of the insect order Siphonaptera, of which a little over a thousand species are known. The order is very distinct and isolated from other insects, but there are indications of winged ancestors and a relationship with, perhaps, the scorpion flies (Mecoptera). All fleas live, when adult, as blood-sucking parasites of mammals or birds. Their larvae live on the debris and dirt that accumulate in the lairs or nests of the animals which are the hosts of the mature insects.

The eggs are large for the size of the insect, about $\frac{1}{50}$ in. long, and white. The larvae are small whitish maggots, legless but having a pair of short antennae and biting jaws. The pupae grow in cocoons.

In a few species the female is sedentary, remaining attached and feeding in one spot. She may even burrow into the skin of the host, the tropical jigger flea **Tunga penetrans** being an example of this.

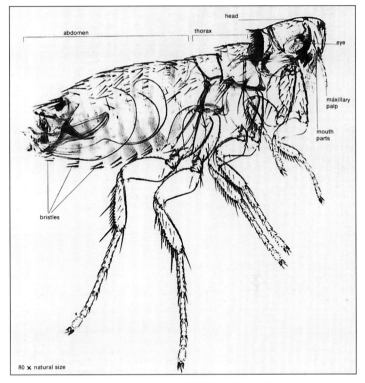

80 × natural size

△ Flea showing the tough, bristle-covered shell – a good defence against scratching hosts.
▽ A prepared specimen displays its legs which are powerful for jumping.

Choice of targets

Fleas usually parasitise only mammals and birds which have a lair or nest in which they live and breed, or which congregate in large numbers in regular roosts. The majority of known species are parasites of rodents, most of which live in nests or burrows, and insectivores and bats are also much infested. Apart from man, primates are never more than casually infested. Monkeys do not as a rule carry fleas at all. Aquatic mammals such as otters and coypus are also not attacked by fleas and among the hoofed animals, the pig is one of the few animals regularly infested.

Among birds fleas are most numerous on the species which nest in holes such as woodpeckers, tits and the sand martin, the last being perhaps the most flea-infested of all birds. The rock dove and its descendant the domestic pigeon have a special flea of their own *Ceratophyllus columbae* and this is not found on wood pigeons. Possibly it is because rock doves and domestic pigeons nest in holes and on ledges while wood pigeons make an openwork nest in trees. This underlines the basic requirement for infestation by fleas, which is a suitable environment in the host's nest for the non-parasitic debris-eating larvae.

It is unusual for fleas to be confined to one host. Both the flea of the rock dove and the sand martin's flea *Ceratophyllus styx* are restricted to the one species. Most fleas will feed and breed on a variety of hosts; the

human flea *Pulex irritans* is found also on pigs, and the hen flea *Ceratophyllus gallinae* feeds on a great number of different birds and can live on mammalian, including human, blood as well.

Carriers of disease

Fleas will also casually infest hosts with which they have no breeding association. Cat fleas, finding themselves on a human, bite readily. The incidence of the dreaded bubonic plague is mainly due to a particular flea *Xenopsylla cheopis* that normally lives on rats, leaving these bodies when they die of plague and infesting people whose hygienic standards permit rats to live in numbers in their dwellings. The bacterium *Pasteurella pestis* that causes plague affects rats and men equally severely and is conveyed from one to the other in the saliva of the fleas. In mediaeval times practically no house was free of rats and the great epidemics of plague or 'black death' killed millions of people.

In the jigger flea, the female burrows into the skin of its human host. Both sexes start their adult life as very small fleas, hopping about in the dust around human habitations. After mating the females burrow into the skin of people's feet under the toenails and grow to the size of a pea, forming a cyst. This causes a great deal of pain and is difficult to remove without causing sores or abscesses due to secondary infection. The hen stick-tight flea *Echidnophaga gallinacea*

▽ *Flea sword-fight and chariot race.*

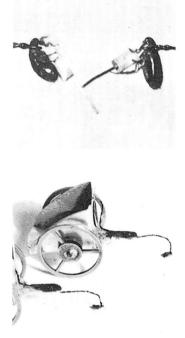

infests poultry and the females gather on the naked skin of the birds' heads and attach themselves permanently. This flea's choice of hosts is quite unusual; it infests poultry and various small mammals, clustering on their ears, and is particularly partial to hedgehogs.

Delayed hatching

The eggs of fleas are dropped into the nest of the host or may be laid among its fur or feathers, whence they are shaken out and many fall into the nest. Almost all fleas require a meal of blood before they can develop and lay their eggs. The tiny maggot-like larvae feed on dirt and debris, including dried blood, in the host's nest, or in dusty unswept corners in human habitations. When fully grown they make cocoons and pupate. The pupae often lie dormant for long periods and in some species, including the human flea, are sensitive to movement and vibration, which stimulates them to hatch. Campers, invading a deserted house that has been abandoned months before, may be greeted by hordes of fleas that hatch in response to the tramping and dumping of heavy luggage. This is an obvious adaptation to delay hatching of the pupae until a new host and source of blood appears on which newly-emerged adults can feed.

Special mouth parts

Like other blood-sucking insects fleas have special sucking mouth parts. The most important part is a narrow tube formed from three needle-like stylets, an anterior and two lateral ones. They are serrated towards the tip to increase their efficiency in piercing. An anticoagulant 'saliva' is injected before the blood sucking commences. It is this which causes the irritation associated with a flea bite, and which leads to disease organisms being passed into the blood of the host by infected fleas.

Fleas are very greedy feeders and only digest and assimilate a fraction of the blood they suck up, the rest being passed out of the intestine unchanged. It is thought that this apparently wasteful habit may have been evolved to provide a supply of dry coagulated blood for the flea larvae which are feeding in the nest of the host. If this were so it would be an example of a parent insect making provision for its larvae resembling, but far less elaborate than, that used by wasps and bees. The idea may not be as far-fetched as it appears. The larvae feed in the normal way, searching for edible particles among their surroundings and chewing them in their mandibles.

When parasite eats parasite

Fleas are regularly caught and eaten in small numbers by their hosts, usually in the course of licking, cleaning and preening. This benefits another form of parasite. The common tapeworm of dogs and cats *Dipylidium caninum* spends one phase of its life cycle in dog fleas and depends on the fleas being eaten to get from one host to another. Far more effective enemies of fleas are certain mites which live in nests and prey on the fleas in all their stages. Small beetles of the genus *Gnathoncus* are often found in birds' nests, and they also prey on fleas and their larvae.

Performing flea

At one time the flea circus was a familiar item of entertainment in country fairs. *Pulex irritans* was still an abundant and familiar insect 50 to 100 years ago when the forms of public entertainment were far less numerous and less sophisticated than they are now. At the present time the manager of a flea circus would be faced with two difficulties. He would probably have difficulty in finding an audience and he would certainly have difficulty in finding a sufficient supply of human fleas for his performers. He would therefore have to be content with dog or cat fleas, which are not easy to feed in captivity.

It was customary for the proprietor of one of these circuses to keep human fleas and feed them on his own arm. A large part of his skill lay in constructing tiny devices such as tricycles and 'chariots' which could be propelled by fleas attached to them in such a way that the crawling of the insect caused them to move. Another very delicate operation was the tethering or harnessing of the fleas with very fine gold or silver wire. There was never any question of the fleas being taught or trained in any way, though of course this was always claimed as part of his expertise by their owner. Advantage was simply taken of the natural movements of the insect when restrained in various ways. The real skill displayed by those who ran flea circuses lay in making the 'props'. One was a coach, of tiny proportions, perfect in every detail which was drawn by a team of fleas.

The relatively enormous size and rapidity of the flea's jump has puzzled naturalists since the time of Socrates. It has recently been shown that in addition to the powerful leg muscles and tendons, the flea's jumping apparatus incorporates a cap of resilin, a rubber-like protein which, when compressed and suddenly released, delivers power faster than most actively contracting muscle. Resilin is generally a component of the wing-hinge ligament of flying insects, such as dragonflies and locusts, and its presence in the thorax of fleas suggests that they have adapted and modified a flight mechanism to increase their mobility while living among fur and feathers. In other words fleas are insects which fly with their legs.

Adult fleas are remarkably long-lived. Supplied regularly with blood a human flea has survived 513 days, and a Russian bird flea is said to have lived for 1 487 days or a little over four years.

class	**Insecta**		
order	**Siphonaptera**		
genera	***Pulex, Tunga, Echidnophaga*** *others*		

Shieldbug

*Shieldbugs are also called stinkbugs—
and for good reason. They represent a
group of plant-bugs comprising four
families of the suborder Heteroptera.
All are flattened in shape and some have
an outline like that of an heraldic shield.
Most are ¼—½ in. long, but the
colourful red, black, orange and blue*
Oncomeris flavicornis *of Australia,
is 2 in. long. Shieldbugs are included in
the great order of insects called the
Hemiptera, which include the true bugs and
cicadas, all of which are characterised by
mouthparts formed for piercing and sucking.
They also grow into adults by incomplete
metamorphosis.*

    *Most shieldbugs have a superficial
resemblance to beetles, but these develop
by complete metamorphosis, involving
distinct larval and pupal stages, and
they have biting mouthparts. They also
resemble beetles in using the hindwings
for flying and the forewings as a protective
covering for the hindwings. Not all
shieldbugs can fly and most of those that
can, do so only in hot weather. In the
shieldbugs each forewing is divided into
two parts, a thick leathery basal part
and a thin membranous area towards
the tip. This results in the backs of these
insects being broken up into patterns
of triangles, which is the most
noticeable feature distinguishing them
from beetles.*

    *Shieldbugs are mainly insects of warm
climates and are most numerous nearer
the tropics. For example, less than 40
species occur in Britain, many more are
found on the continent of Europe,
especially towards the south, and, of
course, the number increases greatly in
tropical Africa.*

Useful and harmful selection

Almost all shieldbugs are found crawling
about on the foliage of trees or bushes or
in low herbage, and many of them are found
attached to particular species of plants on
whose sap or fruit they feed. The birch,
hawthorn and juniper shieldbugs take their
names from their food plants and the last
two types feed mainly on the berries. As
might be expected some of them are pests
of agriculture. One of the tortoise bugs
Eurygaster integriceps is a serious pest of
wheat in the USSR and Near East. The
green vegetable bug *Nezare viridula* has a
world-wide distribution in the warmer
countries, including southern Europe, and
does great damage to beans, tomatoes and
other vegetables. It is sometimes encountered in imported vegetables in Britain and
other northern European countries, but
does not seem to be able to establish itself
in these countries.

▷ *The bright colours of Australasian* **Cata-
canthus punctum** *warn predators; like most
shieldbugs it can emit a foul-smelling liquid.*

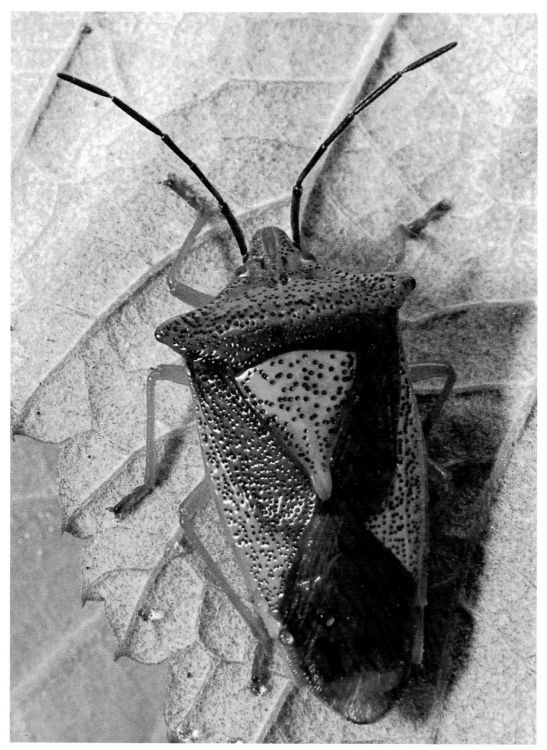

◁ *The hawthorn shieldbug **Acanthosoma haemorrhoidale** prefers the berries to the leaves; it will also feed on whitebeam and oak.*

Some of the shieldbugs are predatory and may be of service in destroying harmful insects. The North American genus *Podisus* is a useful enemy of the Colorado beetle.

Broody shieldbugs

Shieldbugs lay their eggs either on their food plant or on the ground. The eggs are laid in batches and look rather like those of butterflies and moths. They are usually developed in the insect's body 14 at a time and the batches often comprise multiples of this number. A few shieldbugs develop their eggs in dozens and lay them in two neat rows of six, lying side by side. In many species the eggs hatch by the opening of a definite lid on the top, so that under a microscope the egg cases look like little empty barrels.

The young grow by stages, changing their skins usually five times before reaching full size. Although the development is gradual there is often a startling change in colour and pattern when the adult stage is reached. *Sehirus dubius*, an interesting species quite common in continental Europe, is variable in colour. In one form of it the young are black on the forepart of the body, and red with black markings on the hinder part. After the last skin-change the adult is at first brilliant red, but it only retains this coloration for a couple of hours; its colour then darkens until it assumes its final livery of steely black.

A number of the shieldbugs are known to brood their eggs, attending and protecting them up to the time they hatch. The parent bug *Elasmucha grisea*, which lives in birch woods, goes further than this. The female lays a batch of about 40 eggs on a birch leaf, the egg-mass being diamond-shaped and compact, the right shape for her to cover with her body, and she broods the eggs rather as a hen does, for 2–3 weeks until the young hatch. The mother and small larvae stay around the empty egg shells for a few days and then move away together, in search of the birch catkins which form the main part of their diet.

Why stinkbug?

Many of the shieldbugs have glands from which they can eject an evil-smelling and ill-tasting fluid if molested. Anyone picking a berry and not noticing the shieldbug on it may get an unpleasant taste in the mouth. A bug held in one's fingers will usually resort to this same mode of defence, and the smell is so strong and offensive that 'stinkbug' is used, especially in North America, as an apt alternative name for the shieldbugs. Some kinds feed on fruits and berries and render any they touch inedible. The forest bug *Pentatoma rufipes* sometimes infests cherry orchards and spoils a great deal of the fruit in this way. It can be prevented from climbing up the trunks of the trees in spring by grease-banding the trunks.

Some species having this defence capacity are conspicuously coloured, usually black with white, yellow or red patterns. They are undoubtedly examples of warning coloration. By making themselves conspicuous to predatory enemies, especially birds, they derive protection from the fact that a bird, once it has tasted one of the bugs, will remember its distinctive appearance and avoid trying to eat others of the same species. The individual suffers but the species benefits.

Shieldbugs not protected in this way are preyed on by birds, especially tits, which seek out the hibernating bugs in winter. Far more serious enemies are the tachinid flies, whose larvae live as parasites inside the bodies of the developing bugs, killing them just before they reach maturity. These predators are in no way deterred by the bugs' repugnant fluids or lurid colours.

phylum	**Arthropoda**
class	**Insecta**
order	**Hemiptera**
suborder	**Heteroptera**
families	**Acanthosomidae**
	Cydnidae
	Scutelleridae
	Pentatomidae

*Patterns on a leaf, **Lyramorpha** and its young. The harlequin-like young grow by stages, changing their skins several times before the adult stage.*

Aphis

Aphides or 'plant lice' are a group of the Hemiptera (bugs) order of great importance to agriculture as they do considerable harm to crops, both directly, by sucking the cell-sap, and indirectly, by transmitting certain virus diseases, such as potato leaf-roll and sugar-beet yellows, from one plant to another. There are many species, some 500 in the British Isles alone, for example, but probably the best known are those referred to as greenfly and blackfly by the gardener who finds them, often in depressing numbers, on his roses and broad beans. Aphides have soft, oval bodies, small heads, compound eyes, long 6- or 7-jointed antennae, and a jointed beak or rostrum adapted for piercing plant tissues. Some have transparent wings, the first pair being much the longer. Aphides are usually about 2–3 mm long; rarely more than 5 mm.

Clouds of insects

Though most familiar as pests of cultivated plants, aphides begin their life on various wild trees and shrubs from which they migrate at intervals to other plants, both wild and in gardens. After mating in late summer or autumn, the black bean aphis *Aphis fabae* for example, lays eggs on the spindle tree or guelder rose. These hatch the following spring as winged females which fly to bean crops where they reproduce by parthenogenesis (that is, without mating). These are called 'stem mothers' as they are the beginning of a new population. Although they may reach the bean plants only singly in many cases, they breed at a tremendous rate forming large colonies, which explains the apparently quite sudden appearance of an infestation where none was visible a day or so previously.

How such a weak, delicate creature as the aphid manages to migrate so successfully from its host plant to another has been investigated thoroughly in recent years. The winged females usually leave the plants where they hatched in two main waves, one in the morning, one in the afternoon. But conditions must be favourable for the movement to take place. It never takes place at night or at temperatures below 17°C/62°F. Once airborne, the aphides are carried up on air currents, often to a great height. After several hours, descending air currents bring the aphides down and they seek out suitable plants. Sample catches taken in nets on balloons at heights up to 2,000 ft show that 30% of clouds of insects floating high up consists of aphides. They may be carried hundreds of miles over land and sea.

In preparing for flight, aphides appear to go through a kind of take-off procedure, which may be repeated several times before actual launching takes place. The centre pair of legs is raised and tucked into the hollow formed by the constriction between thorax and abdomen. Then, balancing on the remaining four legs, the aphid unfolds its wings and takes off. In spite of their apparent fragility, aphides are not easily

A winged black aphid being tended by an ant. Ants will farm large numbers of aphides, tending them carefully and milking them for the honeydew which is secreted by the aphides (approx × 12).

blown off plants.

The winged females settle on the alternative plants and produce mainly wingless offspring, but some winged individuals are produced at intervals, and these daily leave to seek out other uninfested plants.

Piercing and sucking feeders

As a family, aphides feed on many kinds of plants, but while some species may be catholic in their tastes, others can exist only on one species. The mouth-parts are modified for piercing plant tissues and sucking up the cell-sap, especially from the phloem, the main food stream of the plant. The mandibles and maxillae (mouth-parts) work together as extraordinarily fine needle-like stylets which are thrust deep

into the soft parts of the plant. The labium or tongue takes no part in the operation but has a groove in which the stylets are sheathed when not in use. Before feeding actually begins, a salivary secretion is injected into the wound made by the stylets. This prevents the sap coagulating as it flows up the stylets.

While many aphides feed externally on plants, others, far less familiar to us, form 'galls' or enclosed receptacles in which they are able to feed while hidden from the attacks of predators. Examples of aphid gall-makers may be found on trees such as poplars, elms, limes, spruce and cultivated currant bushes. Frequently, the galls form a refuge for passing the winter. In spring and summer a new generation may seek out quite different plants on which to feed without making a gall. In some species, there is simply a migration back and forth from one part of the tree, the leaves and shoots, to the roots. An example is the notorious woolly aphis or American blight of apple trees, which makes a characteristic fluffy 'wool' in which it feeds.

Oddly enough, it is their excretory habit which is undoubtedly the most striking and significant fact about aphides. In feeding, aphides take up large quantities of sap in order to get sufficient protein. The rest, the fluid rich in sugar, is given out through the anus as honeydew, often in great quantities. Being rich in sugars honeydew is much sought after by ants and some other insects.

Young without mating

For most of the year, aphid populations consist only of females which reproduce parthenogenetically at a great rate. Later in the year, winged females fly back to their primary host plants — usually trees — and lay eggs which hatch as males and females. These mate and lay eggs in crevices in the bark, which hatch in the following spring, producing only females.

A single parthenogenetic female may produce as many as 25 daughters in one day, and as these themselves are able to breed in about 8–10 days the numbers of aphides produced by just one female in a season can reach astronomical proportions. It has been estimated that if all the offspring of a single aphid were to survive, and each reproduced and multiplied, there would be in the

▽ *Greenfly bearing young actually giving birth. The offspring's body is just free of the mother* (approx × 20).

course of one year sufficient to 'equal the weight of 500,000,000 stout men'. Breeding is slowed down by adverse conditions, especially cold. If aphides are kept warm in a greenhouse, parthenogenetic females are produced continuously without a single male ever seeing the light of day.

Enemies everywhere

Many small insect-eating birds, such as tits and flycatchers, eat aphides. Ladybirds, lacewings, bugs, spiders and hover-fly larvae prey on them. In addition, certain parasitic wasps of the family Braconidae lay their eggs in aphides. The larvae consume the tissues of their hosts and eventually pupate inside the empty husk.

Some aphides have, however, evolved defensive mechanisms to guard against attack from these wasps. The aphides' blood cells secrete a capsule which envelops the parasite larva, arresting its development completely within 24 hours. Others form no capsule but appear to secrete some substance which stops the wasp larva's progress within a short period.

Aphides are also able to deter insect enemies by exuding a kind of wax from a pair of chimney-like stumps, called cornicles, on the rear end. This temporarily paralyses the attacker. Some aphides, too, are apparently so distasteful that a ladybird larva will vomit if it tries to eat one.

Ants, who rear aphides for the sake of their honeydew, also protect their charges from attack by predators. One way they do this is to eat the eggs of potential predators, such as those of ladybirds and hover-flies, which have been deliberately laid near an aphid population.

Ants' aphid farm

Long before history, man tamed and domesticated certain animals for his own uses: for pulling loads, for hunting, for companionship, but especially as food. Ants have been doing much the same thing with aphides for infinitely longer. They rear or at least closely associate with them, eating the honeydew and taking it back to the nest for the larva. Just as man is able to stimulate the production of milk in cows and goats, so too can ants encourage production of honeydew in aphides by improving conditions for their existence. This they may do by a variety of means, apart from repelling predators. They may 'herd' their charges, by forcibly confining them to the growing tips of plants which are the most nutritious, thus stimulating growth and breeding and, of course, the emission of honeydew. Where there are no ants present, the honeydew may eventually cover large areas of the plant, causing its death by wilting, by suffocation or by attracting fungi. By removing the aphides' honeydew, the ants ensure their charges' food sources.

Ants also take aphides into their nests, where they may lay eggs, or they may carry the eggs themselves from the plants on which they are laid. After emerging, the young aphides are carefully tended and 'milked' by the ants while they feed on the roots of various plants. Some aphides live only in ants' nests, and never see the light of day. For others, special shelters are built where the aphides can feed, protected from predators. Comparison with the human farmer's cattle-sheds is irresistible.

Presumably, the ants' habit of 'farming' aphides started haphazardly by attacking and killing them for food or simply by licking the drops of fluid which appeared periodically at the insects' vents. Honeydew is not produced continuously and the drop of liquid produced is in normal circumstances discarded by a flick of the aphides' hind leg. Under stimulation from an ant, however, the aphid does not discard the fluid but allows the ant to remove it, and goes on doing so, seeming to enjoy the caressings of the ant's antennae.

Under continued stimulation very large quantities of honeydew may be produced. One large aphid can produce nearly 2 cu mm in an hour, and a colony of the common ant *Lasius fuliginosus* can, it has been estimated, collect about 3–6 lb of honeydew in 100 days.

Control of aphides is something of paramount importance, but always difficult, and it is depressing for the gardener to know that the presence of ants in an aphid colony contributes directly to the increase of the problem. It has been calculated that in accelerating growth and reproduction in aphides and protecting them from predators, ants can indirectly double the loss in the yield of bean plants as compared with when aphides alone are present.

class	Insecta
order	Hemiptera
sub-order	Homoptera
family	Aphididae

Doodle bug

Doodle bug is the name given to insects of the family Myrmeleontidae, grouped in the order Neuroptera which includes the alderflies and which bear some resemblance to dragonflies, and more particularly to the lacewing flies, which they resemble in appearance and habits, in both larval and adult stages. The adults have long thin bodies and two pairs of slender wings of about equal size. Their heads are small with short, thread-like antennae, knobbed at the tips. The largest are little more than 3 in. The larva has a short, thick, fleshy body and dispro-portionately large calliper-like jaws which are armed with strong spines and bristles that help to grasp its prey, mainly ants. This habit of preying on ants has led to the English name ant-lion, a translation of the French name, which is 'fourmi-lion'. The name is also thought to be derived from the habits of the larva. There are several species of doodle bug in the United States, especially in the south and south-west. The student of etymology may be interested to know that this name was applied independently to the flying bomb in 1944. There are more than 600 species of doodle bugs. The typical European species is **Myrmeleon formicarius**, *the adult of which is about 1 in. long with a wing span of 2 in.*

Habits

Doodle bugs are found in woods, forests and plantations wherever there is a sandy soil. The larvae of many species burrow in the sand, the entrance of the burrow being at the bottom of a conical pit, 2 in. deep and 3 in. in diameter at the top, which is also dug by the larva. Groups of these pits can be readily seen in places in southern Europe where the soil is fine and quite dry, and sheltered from the weather, for a shower of rain would destroy the pits and smother the doodle bugs. Likely places are the entrances to dry caves, beneath over-hanging rocks and trees, below the eaves of houses, and in similar sheltered sites.

The adults are active from June to August, usually at dusk or during the night. Their flight is somewhat feeble and awk-ward. One reason why this type of insect is named after its larva is because the adults are very inconspicuous even in strong day-light, flying only when the light is failing or has gone, seldom being seen except when attracted to lights.

Pit-trapped victims

Adult doodle bugs have been relatively little studied. They are reported to feed on fruit and on small flies, and they may possibly feed on the honey-dew produced by aphids, as do the lacewings. The larva sets and springs one of the most spectacular traps

△ *Doodle bug gripping an ant in its vice-like jaws.*
◁ *The delicate beauty of the harmless adult doodle bug is in vivid contrast with its vicious hunting larva.*

▽ *The gigantic calliper-like jaws or mandibles of the doodle bug larva which firmly seize its victim. Together with the secondary jaws or maxillae, two tubes are formed down which flows a paralysing fluid.*

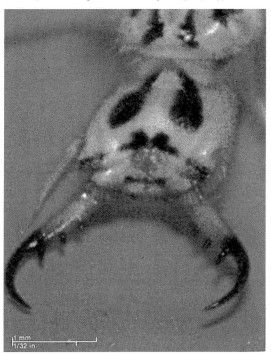

in the animal kingdom. Buried at the bottom of its pit, with only camouflaged head and strong jaws exposed, it waits for grains of sand disturbed by a passing ant or spider to fall and provide a trigger to spring its trap. Immediately sand is scooped on to the head by the jaws and the larva then jerks its head forwards and upwards, catapulting a stream of sand with great force and accuracy at its intended victim. This barrage, the steep sides of the pit, and the sand being undermined by the doodle bug's digging, together cause the victim to slide down to within reach of the doodle bug's jaws where it is immediately seized.

Sometimes the doodle bug gets only an unsatisfactory grip on its prey. In this event it may toss its victim rapidly against the sides of the pit until it gets a firm hold. It may even temporarily release its victim and again hurl sand at it if it shows signs of escaping. But once firmly held, the prey is drawn partially beneath the sand and then the second function of the calliper-like jaws comes into effect. These jaws are deeply grooved underneath. When the maxillae or secondary mouth parts are pressed against them, together they form two tubes down which a paralysing fluid flows, to be injected into the victim's body. When its struggles have ceased digestive juices are then injected in much the same way. These dissolve the tissues which the doodle bug then sucks up and swallows. Finally, the empty case of the insect's body is tossed up and over the edge of the pit by the doodle bug using the same technique as when catapulting sand grains.

Although the eyes of the larva are well-developed they seem to play no part in detecting the presence of food. If a few grains of sand at the edge of the pit are dislodged so they roll down the side and strike the doodle bug larva in wait at the bottom, it will immediately begin hurling sand upwards. Since it will react in this way when no prey is visible it is a fair assumption that the eyes play little part.

Occasionally doodle bug pits are grouped so close together that there is little chance of the occupants all getting sufficient food. This is offset by the larvae being able to fast without harm for up to 8 months.

Not all species of doodle bug dig pits. Some capture their prey by speed, others do so by stealth or ambush, perhaps lurking beneath stones and rubbish. It is interesting to note that while the highly specialised and somewhat sedentary pit-making species can only walk backwards, the more active species are able to do so in any direction.

Three-year life cycle

After mating, the female doodle bug lays her eggs singly in the sand. These are white and oval, and being sticky on the surface, immediately become encrusted with a layer of sand, which serves as a protective camouflage. Within a day of hatching, the young doodle bug has already dug a pit, of a size proportionate to itself. Thenceforth, the larva goes through three stages known as instars. At the end of each of these, the larva leaves its pit temporarily and hides beneath the sand for about a week to ten days. During this period it casts its old skin,

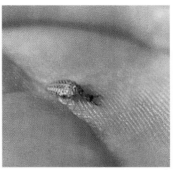

Doodle bug larvae although very vicious are quite small. Here a larva is held in the palm, clearly showing its size.

and then digs a new pit and begins to feed again. Probably the length of time spent as a larva depends to a large extent on the food available. But even with plenty of food it is estimated that the life-cycle from egg to adult takes from 1–3 years, and far longer under unfavourable circumstances. Once fully grown the larva pupates beneath the soil at the bottom of the pit, within a spherical silken cocoon. As in all insects of the order Neuroptera, the silk is produced by the Malpighian tubules; these structures are named after Malpighi, the 17th-century Italian microscopist who first described them. The silk is given out through the anus. This contrasts with caterpillars of butterflies and moths, for example, whose silk is produced by glands in the head. Almost as soon as the silk makes contact with the air, it hardens and, like the eggs, the cocoon is further protected by sand which sticks to its outer surface, although the innermost layers of silk never become sanded. Only when the cocoon is completed does the doodle bug larva shed its skin for the last time, revealing the cream-coloured pupa. The period of pupation to emergence of the perfect winged insect is usually about a month. Just prior to emergence, the doodle bug pupa cuts a hole in the cocoon with its pupal mandibles, and, using its 'free' pupal legs, crawls part way out of the cocoon before emerging as the perfect insect. At this stage, the pupal skin splits, and the adult works its way to the surface of the soil where it then climbs up a plant or tree from which it can hang while the body hardens and the wings expand and dry.

Innate abilities

Before man settled down to agriculture he lived by hunting and capturing wild animals. No doubt one of the first things he learnt to do was to build a pit in which to trap his quarry. Whether he merely stumbled on the idea or thought it out carefully in the first place is something we shall never know. Whichever way it was, however, he devised various methods of using the pit. He would camouflage it with branches of trees so that the animal passing that way did not suspect a trap. He would plant pointed stakes in the bottom of the pit or lurk nearby ready with a spear to make a kill. These and many variations have been used

for thousands of years and are still in use in various parts of the world even today. All the methods bear some resemblance to the tactics used by the doodle bug. Indeed, some of the things the doodle bug does seem to be an improvement on human techniques and therefore have the appearance of intelligence. We can be fairly sure that man started using pits because his better brain capacity enabled him to see the advantages and also to improve on method. Here is the essential difference between the things that insects do and the things we do. The insect merely follows an inherent behaviour pattern. We would find if we examined the pits and the behaviour of thousands of doodle bug of a given species that each individual trapped its prey in exactly the same way as every other individual of its species. Each doodle bug larva would start with the same method and would continue to use this method throughout its lifetime as a larva, without any improvement on it. Everything it does is therefore inborn or innate.

Nevertheless, those who study insects find themselves being forced to admit that there are times when even insects appear to depart slightly from the inborn pattern of behaviour, to adjust their actions to the varying needs of the moment or to the

Doodle bug trapping pits. Should an ant or spider walk too near this steep-sided pit, it is doomed. The doodle bug disturbs the sand so the victim slides down to be gripped by its waiting jaws.

changing circumstances, in a way which suggests that some sort of thought or some sort of intelligence, no matter how rudimentary, is being brought to bear on it. As a result, scientists now tend to talk about insects having plastic, that is, flexible behaviour.

class	**Insecta**
order	**Neuroptera**
family	**Myrmeleontidae**
genera	*Myrmeleon, Palpares, Hesperoleon, and others*

Caddis-fly

Caddis-fly is the common name given to the insect order *Trichoptera*, of which between 4 000 and 5 000 species are known throughout the world. Their nearest relatives are the *Lepidoptera* (butterflies and moths). The antennae are long and many-jointed. The adult insects look rather like moths and fly mainly at night, often coming to artificial lights.

Most of the larvae are aquatic, living in freshwater and breathing by external gills on the sides of the abdominal segments. These are the well-known caddis-worms, which build tubular cases to protect their bodies, although not all caddis-fly larvae do this. All of them spin silk.

Underwater builders

By far the most interesting feature of the caddis-flies is the life of the aquatic larvae, which varies in the different families and genera. They can be divided into two types, those which build portable cases, and are almost all vegetarians, and those which live free and are at least partly carnivorous. The case-builders use many materials in various ways to build their tubes. Members of the genus *Phryganea*, which includes the largest caddis-flies, cut pieces of leaves and stick them together with silk. The most familiar cases are probably those of *philus*, which are made of small stones, and pieces of plant stems or empty snail shells. If removed from their cases and given beads or similar objects, some of these caddis-flies will use the artificial material to make new ones. *Stenophylax* and *Heliopsyche* use fine sand grains to make their cases, the one a straight cylinder, the other a spiral tube that looks remarkably like a small snail shell. Cases made of stones or sand often have their weight reduced by a bubble of air trapped inside. *Heliopsyche* is American, all the others mentioned are found in Britain.

All the cases are tubular and open at the one end, where the larva pushes out its head and thorax to move about or feed. The rear end is closed with a silken mesh so that a current of water can flow through and aerate the gills. All caddis-larvae have a pair of hooked limbs at the back, used to hold onto the case – so tightly that attempts to pull the larva out invariably injure it. It can easily be made to leave its case, however, by pushing the head of a fairly large pin through the mesh of the rear opening.

Most of the larvae with non-portable cases live in silken tubes, in flowing water, some living under stones in swift upland streams. In the genus *Plectronemia* the larva is nearly 1 in. long and makes a silk tunnel with the open end facing upstream widely flared to form a trumpet-shaped net. Any small animal or piece of plant material carried into this trap by the current is seized and eaten by the larva, which thus gets its food in very much the same way as a web-spinning spider. A number of other stream-dwelling caddis-larvae make nets of various shapes to gather food. When they are damaged, or choked with inedible material, the larvae clean and repair them.

△ Protective tubular cases, open at one end, are built by caddis-fly larvae from pieces of plant stems and leaves, and small stones and shells, bound together with silk (3 × natural size).
▽ The caddis-worm **Lepidostoma hirtum** partly emerges from its tubular case to feed (×16).

△ Adult caddis-fly **Stenophylax permistus** has large wings and flies mainly at night. The adult is short-lived, for only a fraction of the annual life cycle (3 × natural size).
▽ Caddis-fly head magnified about 20 times. The compound eye's many facets can be clearly seen.

Adult feeds on nectar

The mouth-parts of adult caddis-flies are vestigial, and if they feed at all as adults, they can probably take in only liquid food. In the wild they probably feed from flowers with exposed nectaries, but will take sugar and water in captivity. Fed in this way they can be kept alive for 2 or 3 months, but given only water they live for less than 2 weeks. The case-bearing larvae eat mainly the leaves and stems of live plants and may be a nuisance when one is trying to establish water lilies in a pond. A cabbage leaf tied to a string, thrown into a pond and left for a few hours, will often be covered with case-bearing caddis-larvae if it is taken out carefully. The large case-bearing larvae of *Phryganea* catch and eat water insects as well as plant food. Most of the tube-dwelling or free-living larvae have a mixed diet.

Life history

The eggs are laid by the females in spring and summer. Some kinds drop them on the surface as they are flying over, others crawl underwater and stick them to stones or plants in a jelly-like mass. Some of the larvae do not make cases or tubes until they have moulted their skins several times, others make tiny cases as soon as they hatch. When the larva is fully grown, nearly a year later, it pupates, inside the case if it belongs to a case-bearing species, otherwise in a silken cocoon. When the time comes for the adult insect to emerge, the pupa bites its way out of the case, being equipped for the purpose with strong mandibles, and swims to the surface of the water. There it splits open, releasing the adult caddis-fly, which can fly almost immediately on emergence. The life history usually takes a year to complete, of which the adult life is only a small fraction.

Anglers and caddis-flies

These insects are of interest to anglers for two reasons. The larvae, taken out of their cases, make excellent bait for the man who watches a float. The adults, when they hatch in quantity, cause a 'rise' of trout, that is to say the fish are stimulated to come to the surface and feed, and this is of prime interest to the fly fishermen.

Entomologists always speak of caddis-flies by their Latin names, but anglers use an English terminology that is hardly ever heard except in the context of fly fishing. They are known collectively as sedge flies, the large *Phryganea grandis* being the great red sedge or murragh. There is a group of species called silverhorns, and some have names of their own such as Grannom, Caperer and Halford's Welshman's Button.

Artificial flies are made in imitation of caddis-flies. To make a murragh a piece of dark grey-black or black-claret mohair or seal's fur is used for the body, a dark brown-speckled feather from a fowl's wing is used for the wings and two dark red cock hackles (the feathers from the neck) complete the job; only the soft fibres near the base of the feather being used.

class	**Insecta**
order	**Trichoptera**
genus	***Limnephilus, Phryganea***

Colorado beetle

*Familiar to many people from the pictures displayed in police stations and elsewhere, the Colorado beetle is a dreaded potato pest. It is $\frac{3}{10}$ in. long, a little bigger than a ladybird. The convex, shiny back is longitudinally striped black and yellow, and the thorax, the region just behind the head, is spotted black and yellow. The specific name **decemlineata** means ten-striped, as there are five black stripes on each wing-cover. The larva is equally conspicuous, orange-yellow with black markings on the head, black legs and three rows of black spots along each side. It has a characteristic hump-backed appearance.*

Potato pests

The Colorado beetle is a serious pest, feeding on potato leaves both as larva and adult, though it may occasionally resort to other plants of the potato family.

It passes the winter as a mature beetle, hibernating underground at a depth of 10–12 in. In late spring it comes out and, if it does not find itself surrounded by potato plants, flies in search of them, often for a distance of many miles. The female lays her eggs on the leaves, usually on the underside; they are yellow in colour and laid in batches. The larvae hatch in a few days, feed voraciously on the leaves and are fully grown in about 3 weeks. They then burrow into the soil to pupate, and a new generation of beetles emerges in 10–15 days. In Britain this second brood appears in late July or August, and if the weather stays warm a third generation may be produced. As soon as bad weather sets in, the beetles burrow into the soil and hibernate until the following spring.

The damage is done to the haulm, or above-ground part of the plant, which may be completely stripped of its leaves, so that the tubers cannot develop. The large number of eggs produced by each female and the rapid succession of generations are factors which make the Colorado beetle such a formidable pest. A single individual emerging in the spring may have thousands of descendants by the autumn.

33 insect enemies

The Colorado beetle seems to have no natural enemies that are effective in reducing its numbers. There are at least 33 different kinds of insects that prey on it, including bugs, beetles, wasps and flies, and one fly lays its eggs in the larvae of the Colorado beetle. Yet these account for only $\frac{1}{5}$ of the total. Spraying the potato foliage with a modern insecticide is the usual method of control. The important thing is obviously to spot any infestation as early as possible and exterminate local populations before they have a chance to spread. Anyone who finds a Colorado beetle, either in a potato field or casually, should immediately report the matter at the nearest police station. The specimen *must* be taken along for its identity to be checked. This surveillance has so far proved effective.

△ *In late spring a female Colorado beetle will lay a batch of yellow eggs on the potato leaf, which hatch in a few days.*

▽ *Fully-grown larva, about 3 weeks old. It is ready to burrow into the soil and pupate for about 15 days before emerging as an adult.*

An entomological curiosity

Like many insects which have become pests, the Colorado beetle is especially interesting. Almost all species of insects are conditioned to live in some particular type of climate. If the climate differs from that of their natural environment they will fail and die out at some stage in the life cycle. The Colorado beetle is a conspicuous exception to this rule. It can live the year round out of doors in Canada, where the winters are arctic in severity, in the hot deserts of Texas and Mexico and in the British cool wet climate. The beetle's habit of hibernating deep underground as an adult is probably the most important factor in promoting this quite unusual ability to adapt itself to any climate in which men can grow potatoes.

A potato bridge

Among the discoveries made in the Rocky Mountains by the American explorer Stephen Harriman Long, in the early 1820's, was a pretty black-and-yellow-striped beetle feeding on a sort of nightshade called buffalo burr *Solanum rostratum*. Neither it nor its food plant were particularly abundant, and it was simply an attractive insect living in a state of balance with its environment.

The buffalo burr is a member of the potato family. The potato is native to Peru and Ecuador, in South America. It was brought to Europe by the Spaniards and later found its way to the new colony of Virginia in North America. How this happened is not known. Neither Sir Walter Raleigh nor Sir Francis Drake, both of whom are credited with discovering it, took it there. In the course of the opening up and settlement of western America in the 1850's, potatoes were introduced and cultivated by the pioneers, and in Nebraska in 1859 it was found that the 'buffalo burr beetle' was turning its attention to the potato. Its numbers increased rapidly and it began to spread. No control measures were known at that time and the beetle spread from potato field to potato field, frequently destroying the whole crop. From Nebraska in 1859 it appeared in Illinois in 1864, in Ohio in 1869, and it reached the Atlantic coast in 1874. This indicates an average rate of travel of 85 miles a year. The potato fields of the United States had formed a bridge from west to east along which the beetle could travel. It also spread 400 miles northwards into Canada. The Atlantic formed a barrier, however, until 1922.

Then it was found in the Gironde region of France and from there it has extended its range all over continental Europe. It appeared in Tilbury in 1901, but the next outbreak in Britain was in Essex in 1933, where prompt control measures exterminated it. It has appeared from time to time in Britain since then, but has always been prevented from establishing itself. In 1946 there was a real danger it might become established. In 1947 infestations were discovered at 57 centres. In 1948 there were 11, and in 1949 not one was found. Prompt control measures had proved effective, much to the relief of the many British potato farmers.

class	**Insecta**
order	**Coleoptera**
family	**Chrysomelidae**
genus & species	*Leptinotarsa decemlineata*

Adults and larvae of the brightly-coloured Colorado beetle often live together on the same plant. Scourge of potato crops the world over, the Colorado beetle is an insect with an international price on its head, but if outbreaks are reported early, prompt control measures usually prove effective.

Glowworm

The glowworm is a beetle belonging to the family Lampyridae which also includes the fireflies. Many centuries ago anything that was long and crawling was called a worm. The female glowworm lacks wings and it was this and her general appearance that was responsible for the name.

Male and female of the common European glowworm **Lampyris noctiluca** are yellowish grey-brown. The male has large eyes and two very tiny light-producing organs at the tip of the abdomen. He also has wings covered by the usual wing cases of beetles, and his length is about $\frac{1}{2}$ in. The female, slightly longer than the male, differs little in shape from the larva and the last three segments of the body, on the underside, are yellowish and strongly luminescent.

A second species of glowworm **Phosphaenus hemipterus** is widespread over continental Europe.

△ Fickle flasher: having attracted three males to her powerful light, a female glowworm mates with one, ignored by her disappointed suitors.

▽ Incandescent cousin: female African beetle of the closely related family Phengodidae waiting in the grass for response to her light.

The lure of the lights

Adult glowworms are most active in June and July. Preferring slightly damp places, they may be found on hedgerow banks, hillsides and in rough meadows, especially where there is a plentiful supply of snails. By day they hide in cracks and crevices. After nightfall the female climbs onto a prominent piece of foliage and takes up a position head down so her luminous end is prominently displayed. The female glowworm's method of light-production is the same as in the firefly. Beneath the light-producing bands is a whitish, opaque layer which not only prevents absorption of the light into the body, but reflects it back, making full use of all the light. The winged male homes on the female's light for mating. The light may be visible to us over 100 yd or so under suitable conditions, but may be 'doused' as we approach and switched on again after an interval. By contrast, the larvae light up as a result of being disturbed, which suggests that in them the luminescence may serve as a defence, frightening away some enemies. The larvae's light also is slightly different from that of the adults, being more intensely green.

Short-lived adults

The pale yellow eggs are $\frac{1}{20}$ in. diameter. Usually they are laid in ones and twos over a period of a couple of days on grass stems or moss, or in or on the soil. They hatch in a fortnight, the larvae being almost exact miniatures of the adult females except for the simpler structure of the legs and a series of paler spots at the front corners of each body segment. Growing by a series of moults, the larvae reach the adult stage in three years. The pupa of the male differs from that of the female, reflecting the different appearance of the adults. Emerging from the pupae after about 8 or 9 days, usually in April or May, the adults live for only a short while after mating and egg-laying. During mating neither sex glows.

Making the most of youth: doomed to starvation as an adult, a glowworm larva gorges itself on a tiny garden snail (12 × life size).

Larvae feed, parents starve

Adult glowworms take no food, although it is often asserted that they do. The larvae feed on snails which they discover by following their slime trails. They drive their hollow, curved mandibles into the mollusc and inject a dark fluid, partly paralysing and partly digestive. This rapidly reduces the snail's tissues to a pre-digested soup-like liquid which the glowworm then sucks up. Newly-hatched glowworms are only ⅓ in. long. They feed on the smaller snails. Sometimes the larvae feed communally, crowding round the lip of the shell and feeding side by side. After a meal the glowworm pushes out a white sponge-like device from its anus. With this it can clean away from its head and back any remains of slime resulting from its meal.

Lucky to survive

Glowworms fall victim to any insect-eating animal, despite the glowing lights on their bodies, but especially to toads and hedgehogs, both of which feed at night. Some are eaten by frogs and spiders, and there are mites which penetrate the soft joints between the body segments of the larvae and feed on their body fluids. The larvae are particularly vulnerable to mites when they have shed their skins at the periodic moults, making them fair game for these parasites.

On the decline

The twinkling lights of a modern city are an irresistible attraction to the eye of young and old alike. It is doubtful, however, whether any of the artificial illumination produced by man has the same aesthetic quality as that from a well-stocked colony of glowworms seen on a moonless night. It is not surprising that poets have made so much of this. Unfortunately, the chances of seeing it today are on the whole much smaller than in times past. Glowworms, useful and attractive insects, have died out from many areas where they were once common. The reasons for this are not easy to see, but it almost certainly springs from the pressure on land for housing, factories, intensive farming, combined with more efficient draining of the land. No doubt the use of insecticides is also partly to blame. What is quite certain is that it is not natural enemies that have brought about this fall in numbers, because toads and hedgehogs are all less numerous than they used to be.

Ironically, there may be another reason. Many insects are irresistibly attracted to artificial light, and in this the male glowworm is no exception, in spite of the fact that it has its own, highly individual 'bright light' to go to—that emitted by the female. Even the weak, flickering light of a candle-flame will attract a glowworm, as Gilbert

White, one of the first naturalists, records. In many areas, it seems, modern artificial lighting systems have become a serious threat to glowworm survival, in that the male glowworms are finding them far more alluring than the more modest glow produced by the females, which as a result may languish in vain and even die 'old maids'! Once attracted to the lights of large buildings the male insects may damage themselves in hitting 'or being burnt by them, and then fall to the ground stunned or dazzled, to be subsequently eaten by a variety of small animals; or the attraction may simply disrupt the delicate balance of nocturnal flight activity. Fortunately there are still many areas where such hazards are less pronounced, as is indicated by the fact that the greatest numbers of glowworms are found in areas which are comparatively less developed industrially.

phylum	**Arthropoda**
class	**Insecta**
order	**Coleoptera**
family	**Lampyridae**
genus & species	***Lampyris noctiluca***

Ladybird

Small, brightly coloured beetles, oval or almost circular in outline, ladybirds were regarded with affection long before it was realised they are useful as well as pretty. The name ladybird (sometimes ladybug or lady beetle) dates from the Middle Ages when the beetles were associated with the Virgin Mary and called 'beetles of Our Lady'. Their coloration is generally red or yellow with black spots and the pattern tends to be variable, extremely so in some species. A few, like that known as **Coccidula rufa**, are brown without conspicuous markings, and are not usually recognised as ladybirds. The colourful species have a strong and unpleasant smell and they taste equally bad. Their bright colours doubtless serve as a warning to predators not to try to eat them. Both ladybird adults and their larvae prey on aphids, destroying them in great numbers.

The four commonest species in Europe are the two-spot, ten-spot, seven-spot and twenty-two-spot ladybirds. The first is red with a single black spot on each wingcase but black specimens with four red spots are common, and the beetle is sometimes yellow with black spots. The underside and legs are black. The second is reddish or yellow, usually with five black spots on each wingcase, but the ground colour may be black as in the last species. The underside is brown and the legs yellowish. The seven-spot is larger than the first two species and its colours hardly vary at all. It is orange-red with a black spot on the line dividing the wingcases and three others farther back on each side. The last is much smaller with 11 black spots on each side on a bright yellow ground. One of the largest and most handsome species is the eyed ladybird **Anatis ocellata**, which has black spots on a red ground, each spot being

▷ △ △ The lunate ladybird of the South African high veld **Chilomenes lunata** laying a batch of eggs. There are 5–50 in a batch, but the beetle lays several batches, usually to a total of about 150 eggs, though 1 000 has been recorded. To provide for the young, the female lays them in an aphid-infested place. They hatch in about 3 weeks.

▷ △ Eggs of the lunate ladybird. The larvae will start their aphid massacre, made easy by the mother's consideration and the soft, defenceless prey, straight away. The massacre continues even after pupation. Some idea of the extent of aphid and scale insect control by ladybirds can be had from the record of a single larva's eating 90 adult and 3 000 larval scale insects. This appetite, and the high rate of reproduction, make it a very beneficial beetle.

▷ Scourge of the aphids: larvae of the S. African ladybird **Cryptolaemus** hunting. Protected by a waxy secretion, then by warning colours, and a vile taste as adults—an easy life at all stages.

surrounded by a halo of yellow. It may be ⅖ in. long and lives among pine foliage.

The first four of these have been given the scientific names **Adalia bipunctata, A. decempunctata, Coccinella septempunctata** and **Thea vigintiduo-punctata** respectively. Even scientists sometimes jib at long names so these four ladybirds are usually referred to as **2-punctata, 10-punctata, 7-punctata** and **22-punctata**.

Winter hibernation

In summer ladybirds fly actively about among foliage. In winter they hibernate as adults, often in large groups. Sometimes 50 or 100 of them can be found crowded together under a piece of loose bark, on a post or in a porch. They often congregate in houses and usually go unnoticed until they come out in spring. In California crevices and caves on certain hilltops are well known as hibernation resorts where ladybirds gather in their thousands.

Hordes of ladybirds

Ladybirds usually lay their orange-coloured eggs on the undersides of leaves, in batches of 3–50. Several batches are laid by one female, totalling 100–200 eggs, sometimes more. Because the beetles themselves feed on aphids or greenfly they tend to choose places where these are abundant in which to lay, so the larvae find food handy from the start. The eggs hatch in from 5 to 8 days, turning grey shortly before they do so. The larvae are active, bristly and variously coloured in patterns of black, orange, blue and red. Like the adult beetles they feed on aphids, but since they are growing rapidly they are far more voracious. The larval stage lasts 3 weeks or so, during which time several hundreds of aphids are eaten.

When thousands of aphid-eating ladybirds are each laying hundreds of eggs and every larva is consuming hundreds of aphids, it can be imagined that very large numbers of greenfly are destroyed, and the benefit to plants, both wild and cultivated, is enormous. The pupa is usually attached to

◁ △△ *A pupa, the ladybird's only lull in feeding.*

◁ △ *Full circle: adult lunate ladybirds feeding on a liberal supply of aphids.*
Even man, for hundreds of years, has contributed to the ladybirds' mollycoddled existence by recognising the need to keep them alive. They have even taken their place in English folklore with the rhyme 'Ladybird, ladybird, fly away home, your house is on fire, your children alone', a reference to the custom of burning hop vines at the end of the season, no doubt with many larvae on them. The second stanza, 'Except little Nan, who sits in a pan, weaving gold laces as fast as she can' concerns the colourful larva weaving a pupal case. These lines, spoken when a ladybird landed nearby, must have saved many an extremely useful insect's life.

◁ *The black sheep: one of the few vegetarian ladybirds* **Epilachna dregei** *which spoil the group's fine reputation by feeding on potato leaves.*

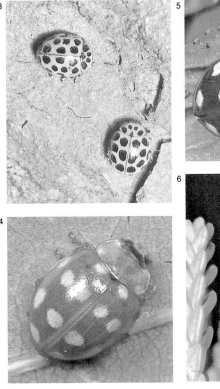

a leaf. The whole life cycle takes from 4 to 7 weeks, so several generations of ladybirds may be produced in a summer.

One small group of ladybirds are not predatory but feed as larvae on plant food. For example, there is a species, the twenty-four-spot ladybird *Subcoccinella vigintiquatuorpunctata* (certainly better written *24-punctata*), which eats clover.

Ladybird farms

The principle of using one species of insect to control the numbers of another is now well known, and is often advocated as being preferable to the use of poisonous insecticides. An early example of an operation of this kind concerns the use of a ladybird. Towards the end of the last century the Californian citrus orchards were devastated by the cottony-cushion scale insect, which was accidentally introduced from Australia. A brightly coloured ladybird *Rhodalia cardinalis* was found to be a natural enemy of the scale insect in Australia, and in 1889 some of these ladybirds were brought to California and released in the orchards. They effectively controlled the scale insect there and they have since been introduced to South Africa.

The Californian citrus growers were also troubled by aphids and other plant bugs, and use was made of a native ladybird, a species of *Hippodamia,* that hibernates, as mentioned earlier, in caves in the hills. These were collected and sold to the citrus

farmers by the litre (8 000 to 10 000 beetles in each litre) and later by the gallon. This control was started in 1910, neglected, then revived during the Second World War.

Even this is not the end of the story of useful ladybirds in California. In the 1920s the orchards were attacked by another scale insect *Pseudococcus*. Again a ladybird was brought from Australia, by the name of *Cryptolaemus montrouzieri*. This failed to breed under natural conditions in Western America, so huge ladybird factories were maintained where they were bred, with careful control of temperature and other conditions, on potato shoots infested with *Pseudococcus*. In 1928 alone 48 million ladybirds of this species were set free in the Californian orange orchards.

(1) *Searching every nook and cranny of a rock face for prey* **Propylea 14-punctata**.
(2) *The writing on the wings: the unusual markings of* **Coccinella hieroglyphica**.
(3) *Beauty as well as usefulness: the black and yellow* **Thea 22-punctata**.
(4) *The lighter colour variation of* **Calvia 14-guttata**.
(5) *Mopping up the plant parasites on a leaf, a dark colour variety of* **Calvia 14-guttata**.
(6) *Not all ladybirds have spots: a striped ladybird* **Paramysia oblongoguttata**.
(7) *One of the best-known ladybirds, the two spot* **Adalia bipunctata**.

class	**Insecta**
order	**Coleoptera**
family	**Coccinellidae**

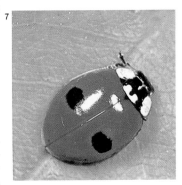

The beautiful apollo butterfly, **Parnassius phoebus,** *resting with wings outstretched.*

Apollo showing its bright spot markings.

Apollo butterfly

One of the family of butterflies known as the swallowtails, not unlike them in shape, but lacking the tail-like appendages on the hind wing which give the family its name. The apollo and its relatives are not brightly coloured, most of them being white, with spots and eye-like markings of black and red. They are nevertheless elegant and beautiful.

Range and habitat

The common apollo is found in mountainous regions of Europe, from Scandinavia to the Alps and Pyrenees. It flies at fairly low altitudes. There is, however, a related species, the alpine apollo, which occurs at higher altitudes. About 30 species of apollo butterflies are known, ranging through Europe and Asia to North America. Many are mountain butterflies and some species range up to 20,000 ft in the Himalayas. Owing to their inaccessible habitat some of the Central Asiatic species are extremely rare and highly prized by collectors.

Life history

The caterpillar of the common apollo feeds on orpine, a kind of stonecrop. The caterpillar is black with red spots and, when fully grown, spins a cocoon in which to pupate. Growth is slow and it takes 2 years to complete the life-history. So far as they are known the early stages of all the species are similar, and the larvae feed on stonecrops and saxifrages. The habit, very unusual among butterflies, of spinning a cocoon is no doubt correlated with the need for protection from frost at high altitudes.

Only the common apollo habitually flies at low altitudes, and there are indications that some of the bodily structures of apollos as a whole may serve as an alpine kit. The body is covered with hairs, like a fur coat. It is dark in colour, which may help to absorb heat from the sun. The wings, white with black spots, are proportionately larger than in other butterflies, so exposing a greater surface to the sun's rays, and also assisting the butterfly in its unusual soaring habit. Moreover, they are so thinly covered with scales as to be almost translucent, which probably assists the absorption of the sun's heat.

God-like butterflies

Apollo butterflies have been seen in the Alps soaring above hillsides on uprising wind currents with wings outstretched and motionless. Soaring flight, common in birds, is rare among insects. Apollo was a Greek god of the mountains and the vegetation and later the sun god. All this makes the choice of name for these butterflies singularly apt. The god-like character is, however, marred by a North American species, *Parnassius autocrator*. The caterpillar, brilliant orange in colour, gives off a most unpleasant odour from just behind its head whenever danger threatens. All apollo larvae (and swallowtail too) have an organ (the osmeterium) behind the head that gives off an odour, but this is usually faint and at any rate not unpleasant to the human nose.

class	**Insecta**
order	**Lepidoptera**
family	**Papilionidae**
genus	*Parnassius*

Pyrenees mountains where the alpine apollo can be found at high altitudes. The common apollo lives at much lower altitudes in mountainous regions from Scandinavia to the Alps and Pyrenees.

Caterpillar of European apollo **Parnassius apollo,** *which takes nearly 2 years to grow.*

△ *Male birdwing,* **Ornithoptera priamus,** *feeding. Only the male birdwings have the attractive iridescent markings on their wings. The unfortunate females have to make do with less spectacular markings.*

Birdwing

Imagine a butterfly with a wingspan that is sometimes more than 10 in. and you have some idea of the size of the birdwing butterfly. This amazing wingspan of some of the genera was what provoked naturalists to dub them 'Ornithoptera' (bird-winged). The males are somewhat smaller than the females. Their wings are large and velvety and usually of a black or purplish shade. These wings are made even more attractive by their beautiful iridescent markings in blue, green, pink, orange or gold. That is the male. The unfortunate female has to make do with less spectacular markings. Her wings are speckled with a uniform white instead of the fluctuating colour ranges that make the male so irresistible.

The birdwing's width and size comes from its long, graceful forewings. The hindwings, by comparison, are small. One characteristic of the swallowtail family, to which they belong, is the long tail on each of the hindwings. These tails can only be seen in the birdwings on the tailed birdwing **Ornithoptera paradisea** *and on one or two others. Butterfly collectors named several birdwings after*

their current heroes. One was named after Queen Victoria: Queen Victoria's birdwing **Ornithoptera victoriae** *; and one of the White Rajahs in Sarawak, Rajah Brooke, had the pleasure of seeing his name immortalised in butterfly-collecting circles by having perhaps the most beautiful of all the birdwings,* **Troides brookiana,** *called after him. Birdwings live in open woodland or forest, from southern India and Sri Lanka across to northern Australia, New Guinea and the Solomon Islands.*

Birdwings fool the entomologists

Very little is known about some of the species. It is only recently, for example, that the life cycle of Rajah Brooke's birdwing has been described. No one has ever succeeded in finding its caterpillars in the wild, but an entomologist in Sumatra has finally succeeded in breeding them in captivity.

For a long time, entomologists listed, as one of the unusual 'features of Rajah Brooke's birdwing, the fact that the female was rarely seen. They even put the ratio of males to females at as much as 1 000 : 1. They based their statistics on data they got from collections made at places where the birdwings congregate, such as river banks or seepages and other damp places.

Then it dawned upon somebody that the reason they were getting these extraordinary figures was because it was only the males of the species who congregated at these spots. This explained the unusual figure of 1 000 : 1, which was quite unlike the statistics they had obtained on other species, showing the males and the females to be almost 50 : 50. Enquiries in other sources revealed, as a matter of fact, that females of the common birdwing *Troides helena* are somewhat more numerous than the males.

Birdwings live in the trees, especially in the canopy of foliage at the tops of the taller trees. When the entomologists realised this they had the answer to the mystery of the 'elusive butterfly'. They were not rare at all.

It was just that the female of Rajah Brooke's birdwing and both sexes of other species did not come down to seepages and damp places and remained totally unattracted by the bait, such as carrion, which was put out for them. This made collecting them rather tricky. The collectors found that they had to resort to shooting the birdwings with 'dust shot' as if they were birds. However, when birdwings do fly low they are easy to catch because their flight is slow, direct and unsuspecting. It makes a welcome change for the collector who is constantly being frustrated by the bouncing, weaving flight of many other butterflies.

Above: Rajah Brooke's birdwing. It was thought that the males outnumbered the females by 1 000 : 1, as only the males were usually seen. Females were then found in the treetops, making numbers equal (life size). Right: Wonderful action shot of birdwing, **Troides rhadamantus**, *alighting on a flowerhead. Its long thin feeding tube, the proboscis, is already extended so it can suck the flower's nectar.*

What they eat

Birdwing caterpillars feed on plants of the Aristolochiaceae family and on betel leaves. The adults feed on flowers. Some of the closely related swallowtail butterflies also feed on plants of the same family. These are known to be distasteful because of a chemical in the plant but it is not known whether the birdwings are also distasteful to their predators.

Life cycle of a birdwing

The eggs of the common birdwing are laid singly on the upper sides of leaves. From the eggs hatch caterpillars bearing six rows of fleshy tubercles which run the whole length of the body. The caterpillars also have a curious Y-shaped organ, called an osmeterium, on the head. This is connected with glands in the body. When a caterpillar is alarmed the osmeterium is worked in and out, exuding an unpleasant smell.

After the caterpillars have fed for a month, they turn into chrysalises on the vertical stem of the plant where they have been living. The chrysalis has the typical form of the swallowtail family. The lower end is anchored to the plant stem by a silken pad. The body and upper end is supported by a silk thread which passes around the stem of the plant, in very much the same way that a lumberjack is secured to a tree with a safety-belt. After three weeks the adult butterfly emerges from the pupa.

The cost of rarity and beauty

Lots of people collect butterflies, from schoolboys with their little collections of the more common kind to professional entomologists with neat rows of specimens in glass-topped boxes marked 'Do Not Touch'. It is a hobby that can be taken to great lengths, like anything else. We are now all familiar with those tense scenes in auction rooms when paintings or postage stamps fall under the hammer for thousands, or even hundreds of thousands, of pounds. Many a non-collector has found it hard to understand why a painting suddenly becomes so amazingly valuable after being ignored by everyone for years and years.

How does one put a price on a painting or a stamp, which intrinsically is only worth the price of the materials it is made of? Two of the main criteria must obviously be its rarity or its beauty. Add to these the fanaticism of some buyers and the tension and competition in an auction room and you have some of the reasons why people pay such inflated prices.

Butterflies are just like paintings and stamps. Serious collectors have always been willing to pay for unusual specimens that they have been unable to catch themselves and the price is arrived at through a combination of beauty and rarity. If a butterfly is spectacularly beautiful and rare it can be valuable. By contrast, a small, dull one, even if it is very rare, is usually not worth much. There has always been a trade in butterflies and they are even bred especially for the purpose. Not surprisingly birdwings have always been in demand. Many 'part-time collectors' supply them from New Guinea, the Solomons and Northern Australia. Good specimens of the common species are available at a pound or two, although rarer ones might cost £25 ($60) to £30 ($70).

In 1966 a large collection of butterflies was auctioned in Paris and a collector paid £750 ($1 785) for a specimen of the very rare birdwing *Troides allotei* from the Solomon Islands. It was an amazingly high price to pay for a specimen.

It should be very interesting to see, in years to come, whether this butterfly maintains its value or whether other collectors decide that even a very pretty butterfly is not worth that much and spend their money on a motor car instead.

class	**Insecta**
order	**Lepidoptera**
family	**Papilionidae**
genera	*Troides*
	Trogonoptera
	Ornithoptera

Burnet moth

The bright colours of the burnet moths make them very conspicuous. They are small with thick bodies, long forewings and short hindwings; the antennae are thickened near the tip and then pointed. Most are brightly coloured, the forewings dark metallic blue or green with scarlet markings and usually separate spots, the hindwings with a black border. This applies to all the British species, but in southern Europe white and yellow-spotted ones occur. In the beautiful **Zygaena carniolica**, of central and southern Europe and western Asia, the red spots are surrounded by white rings. Occasionally yellow-spotted forms occur as rare varieties of the normally red-spotted species.

Burnets from around the coasts of the Mediterranean occur in immense numbers and great variety. They extend in small numbers to temperate Asia and southern Africa and also into northern Europe. They belong to the family Zygaenidae which has many species with very metallic-looking colours and often bizarre-shaped wings. One subfamily of Zygaenidae has species where the hind wing, instead of the normal rather rounded shape, is thin and forms long trailing streamers behind the forewings.

Many of the brightly coloured species are day fliers, their colours warning predators that they are distasteful. In Europe some of the species are of very local distribution and many are confined to limestone districts where the soil is suitable for their food-plants to grow.

Moths in a meadow

Burnets usually live in colonies, often occupying only part of a hillside or a single meadow, and the colonies may persist for a few years and then die out. In a flourishing colony, the moths are often abundant, sometimes half-a-dozen or more being seen on a single flower-head.

The burnets are all day-flying moths and are most active when the sun is shining. The flight is slow and buzzing, and when at rest the moths are sluggish and can easily be captured without a butterfly net. They are on the wing at various times from June to August.

Tubular tongues for nectar

The adult moths feed on the nectar of flowers, sitting on the flower-heads and probing the nectaries with their long tubular tongues. The caterpillars feed on the leaves of low-growing plants. The food-plants of the three common British species are trefoils and clover. The mountain burnet feeds on crowberry, and one of the other northern species on thyme.

Annual life cycle

Normally the burnets have an annual life cycle, the caterpillars feeding during the late summer, hibernating through the winter and completing their growth during the

△ Burnet moth, **Zygaena trigonellae**, drying its wings (5 × life size).

▽ The beautiful **Zygaena carniolica** is found in central and southern Europe and western Asia.

spring and early summer of the following year. The mountain burnet is exceptional in taking more than one and possibly as much as four years to complete its life-cycle. Only a short time is spent as a pupa and the adult moths probably live only two or three weeks.

The caterpillars are thick and slug-shaped, green or yellow with a regular pattern of black spots. The pupa is enclosed in a characteristic spindle-like cocoon of parchment-like silk, shining yellow or white in colour. The cocoons are usually attached to a stem of grass or some other plant, those of the commoner species being conspicuous and easy to find. After the moth has hatched the black empty pupa shell always sticks out.

Safety in nastiness

Their habits would seem to make the burnets an easy prey for birds and other insect-eating animals, since they are slow-flying, conspicuous, and make no attempt to hide, and little to evade capture. They are all very ill-tasting, however, and to some degree poisonous, so that a bird which has pecked one of them is never likely to attack another. Their conspicuous appearance is associated with this, as it is to their advantage to be easily recognisable so that predators have no difficulty in learning to avoid them. Another day-flying moth, the cinnabar *Callimorpha jacobaeae*, of Europe and western Asia, quite unrelated to the burnets, has a

Burnet moth caterpillar, magnified 8 times, feeding on trefoil, one of its food-plants.

but this did not last for a very long time.

Within seconds it was almost literally running round in circles, stopping every so often to bite at cool grass blades or to rub its beak on the grass, the bare earth, or any stick or stone it came across, while saliva dripped from its beak. From time to time it spread its wings in the manner that has come to be associated with birds that have something acrid or pungent in the mouth.

Clearly the rook was agitated and going through an unpleasant experience, one it was unlikely to forget. The bill-cleaning and

agitated movement went on for some minutes. Moreover, during that time it repeatedly attacked its companion, with whom it had just been feeding harmoniously, chasing it with vicious stabs of the beak.

phylum	**Arthropoda**
class	**Insecta**
order	**Lepidoptera**
family	**Zygaenidae**
genus	**Zygaena**

Six-spot burnet, a common European species.

Five-spot burnet moths mating on an empty cocoon that has an empty pupa shell sticking out of it.

similar red and black pattern and is also protected by having a nasty taste.

The poison of the burnet moths is discharged in the form of a yellow fluid from the region of the neck, and it contains histamine and hydrogen cyanide.

Bad taste

A rook living in an aviary with a magpie as a companion was offered a burnet moth, experimentally, to see whether it would accept or reject it. It picked up the moth, dismembered it in rook fashion, by severing the wings and biting off the head. Then it took the body of the moth into its mouth –

Previous page: Turquoise Forester moth,
Procris statices.

Copper butterfly

The wings of these butterflies have the colour and lustre of polished copper and are marked with dark spots and bands, sometimes with blue or purple as well. They are a group of small butterflies in the family Lycaenidae, and are thus allied to the blues and hairstreaks. They are widely distributed in the temperate and cold regions of the northern hemisphere, both in the Old and the New World. There are, however, three species in temperate New Zealand. Presumably their ancestors arose from the same stock as those in the northern hemisphere and in time became separated.

The caterpillars are slug-shaped and, in the majority of species, feed on various kinds of dock or sorrel. Like those of many of the blues group, the larvae of some species are attended by ants for the sake of a sweet secretion which they produce. In the case of the coppers this exudes all over the body, unlike many others of the family, which have a single orifice connected with a special gland.

There are nearly a dozen species known in Europe and North Africa, but only two were known to reach Britain; one is a familiar butterfly of open country in general, the other is an insect which unhappily became extinct. They are known respectively as the small copper and the large copper.

Small copper

This is a pretty, lively and even rather aggressive little butterfly. The males establish territories and try to chase all other butterflies away, flying out and attacking individuals of their own species and other, larger ones as well. They have no weapons and are quite incapable of injuring each other.

The small copper has an enormous range extending from Europe right across Asia to Japan, over a large part of North America and northward to beyond the Arctic Circle. It is divided into distinct subspecies in different parts of its range but they are all very similar in appearance. Some of these subspecies range into Africa. Another ranges almost as far north as any butterfly, into Ellesmere Land, and is one of the five butterflies found in Greenland.

Three generations a year

The larva feeds on dock and sorrel and the life cycle is passed through so quickly that there may be three generations in a good summer. The caterpillar is green with a brown line along the back and clothed with short greyish hairs. It is not attended by ants. The pupa is pale brown or greenish and attached to a leaf or stem of the food plant. The species overwinters as a larva but not (as in most larval hibernators) at any particular stage of its growth. The butterfly is on the wing continuously from May to October.

▷ *Small copper at rest. These far-ranging butterflies often breed three times a year.*

△ A small copper shows its wing pattern while taking a meal off a sprig of heather.

▽ One of the Dutch large coppers introduced to Wood Walton Fen on great water dock plant.

Small copper larvae feed on dock and sorrel.

not unlike those of the small copper.

The large copper was discovered in Britain a little before 1800, in the fens of East Anglia, a habitat that was rapidly shrinking due to artificial drainage. Butterfly collecting was already a popular pastime, and the coppers were persecuted without restraint. Not only did collectors visit their haunts, but dealers encouraged the local people to capture them in all their stages for sale at prices ranging from a few pence to a shilling, rich rewards for the poor of those days. The butterfly held out for half a century, the last specimens being taken in 1847 or 1848. The British large copper could probably have been saved if a reserve had been created where it could have been secure from the greed of collectors and from destruction of its habitat, but at that time the idea had not occurred to anyone that active measures might be taken to preserve rare animals from extinction.

The large copper is still found in many parts of Europe and Asia, but the British subspecies was larger and finer than any of the Continental forms. About a thousand preserved specimens of it exist, but as a living animal it has gone for ever. The great water dock is the food plant of the large copper. The caterpillar, which is attended by ants, is green and looks like a much flattened slug. It hibernates when young, feeds in the following spring, and the butterflies appear in July and August.

Two other species, the scarce copper and the purple-edged copper, were included as British by early entomologists. It is not impossible that they once lived in Britain and became extinct before collecting became methodical and widespread.

Butterfly naturalisation

In 1915 a subspecies of the large copper was discovered in the province of Friesland, Holland, and named *Lycaena dispar batavus*. It resembles the extinct English race more closely than any other and the idea occurred to some British naturalists to try introducing it to the fenland nature reserves in East Anglia. It is rare in its native haunts, and some difficulty was experienced in obtaining living specimens. This was overcome, however, and the first butterflies were released by the Society for the Promotion of Nature Reserves in Wood Walton Fen, Huntingdonshire, in 1927. The experiment was successful and later was repeated at Wicken Fen, owned by the National Trust, in Cambridgeshire. The Dutch large copper is still maintained at Wood Walton and is bred artificially and released every year to supplement wild stock and to ensure against any accident to the small wild population.

The small copper is exceedingly variable, and its more extreme varieties or 'aberrations' are eagerly sought by collectors. Reduction or modification of the pattern of black bands and spots produces most of the varieties, but in one of the rarest and most highly prized the copper ground colour is replaced by silvery white.

Large copper

In this species the wing span is about $1\frac{7}{10}$ in. and the male and female are very different. In the male all four wings on the upper side are brilliant burnished copper with only narrow dark borders and small central dots. The female has dark markings

phylum	**Arthropoda**
class	**Insecta**
order	**Lepidoptera**
family	**Lycaenidae**
genus & species	*Lycaena dispar* large copper
	L. hippothoe purple-edged copper
	L. phlaeas small copper
	L. virgauteae scarce copper

Purple emperor

A large, showy and sometimes rare butterfly, the purple emperor is named after the purple iridescence on the wings of the male, which can only be seen when viewed from a particular angle. Otherwise they are dark-brown, almost black, with a line of white patches and an inconspicuous eyespot on each hind wing. The white patches are very occasionally missing and such purple emperors are known as the variety **iole**, *much sought after by collectors. The underside of the wing has an intricate pattern of brown and grey with bands of white. The female is very much like the male but lacks the iridescence and is slightly larger. Her wingspan is 3 in. compared with $2\frac{1}{2} - 2\frac{3}{4}$ in. of the males.*

Purple emperors are found locally in many parts of Europe and Asia.

Two plants needed
Purple emperors' preference for oak woods is one factor which limits their distribution since these woods become scarcer year by year due to man's activities. Purple emperors do, however, survive in woodlands that have been stripped of all tall trees. They are on the wing in July and the first half of August but even in bright weather and in places where they are known to live they are not easy to see. They are not attracted to flowers like so many other butterflies and spend most of their time around the tops of oak trees. The dull coloured females are easier to find because they descend to lay their eggs in sallow bushes. The males spend their time perching on leaves and periodically flying high across a clearing or soaring up almost out of sight on their powerful wings. Sometimes several males may be seen chasing each other in circles.

Slug-like caterpillar
Purple emperors lay their eggs on the upper surfaces of sallow leaves. Each female ranges over a considerable area, laying one egg on each leaf, although she may revisit a bush later and so lay another egg on a leaf already bearing one. Other females may also use that leaf, so it is quite possible to find several eggs on one leaf. The egg is like a minute blancmange, $\frac{1}{25}$ in. high, almost hemispherical with about 14 radially arranged ridges. At first it is green, then the base becomes purple, and just before hatching it turns black. The caterpillar emerges about a fortnight after the egg is laid. It is yellow with a black head and measures just a little over $\frac{1}{10}$ in.

After 10 days of eating the sallow leaf on which the egg was laid the caterpillar sheds its skin. It is now green, the same colour as the sallow leaf, and it looks very much like a slug, with a pair of horns projecting from the head and a body tapering to a point at the rear end.

The caterpillar continues to feed through the summer and into autumn. It grows to $\frac{1}{2}$ in. and changes to brown, so matching the autumn leaves. When not feeding it lies

along the midrib of the leaf so that it is very inconspicuous. In October the caterpillar retires to a twig or a fork between two twigs, and spins a mat of fine silk on which it rests for the winter. In the following April the caterpillar changes colour back to green, and starts feeding on the fresh leaves, growing to $1\frac{3}{4}$ in. before pupating in June. Pupation takes place on the underside of the sallow leaf where it lays a mat of silk and runs more silk up the leaf stem to the twig, presumably to act as an anchor. The chrysalis hangs from the silk mat by a number of small hooks. Just before pupating the caterpillar changes to a very pale green, matching the underside of the sallow leaf, and making the chrysalis very difficult to find. The adult butterfly emerges in about 3 weeks.

Lured to the ground
Although male purple emperors spend most of their short lives in the tops of the trees, they do sometimes come down, feeding on the sap that oozes from wounded trees and sometimes on the honeydew of aphides (page 110). They also descend to the ground to drink at puddles or to feed on animal carcases or horse droppings. At one time purple emperors were caught by placing the rotting corpse of a rabbit or other animal in a woodland ride, but this method is not successful now, probably because the

Brilliant beauty – a purple emperor sunning itself on a sprig of oak leaves. This attractive butterfly is, unfortunately, not very common and is seen even more rarely than one would expect as it spends most of its time at the tops of oak trees. Although it can survive in young oak plantations, mature oak woods are becoming fewer and fewer.

The butterfly's purple colouring, possessed by the male only, is normally seen only on one wing, as in this picture. In some lights both wings are iridescent, the purple scales changing colour with the incidence of the light. There are also dark scales caused by melanic pigment.

purple emperor has become so rare. They can also be attracted by bright objects and there are several stories of male purple emperors coming down to settle on car radiators, and even flying headlong into cars as they are being driven along.

phylum	**Arthropoda**
class	**Insecta**
order	**Lepidoptera**
family	**Nymphalidae**
genus & species	***Apatura iris***

Vanessids

*The Vanessids include some of the most colourful butterflies in the northern hemisphere, and some of these have a wide distribution. The scientific name, **Vanessa**, is now restricted to the Red Admiral, although this species, and all the others here included in the popular name Vanessids, are in the same family (Nymphalidae). Vanessids have the front pair of legs reduced in size, only the rear two pairs being used for walking. They are fairly large butterflies, with a powerful flight. Most of the species resident in northern Europe pass the winter hibernating as butterflies, others are continuously brooded in the subtropics and migrate northwards in summer. Their caterpillars bear an armature of branched spines and the pupae, or chrysalises, which are suspended by the tail, are ornamental with shining metallic spots. It was the ornamentation of these pupae which led the early butterfly collectors to call them 'aurelians', from the Latin **aureus**, golden. 'Chrysalis' has a similar derivation from the Greek chrysos also meaning golden.*

Species of Vanessid are found on all continents. Generally, they are large powerful fliers. Many of the tropical species feed on ripe fruit or even on the rotting carcass of a dead animal.

Peacock

This beautiful butterfly ranges from Britain eastwards to Japan. It is resident in Britain and spends the winter hibernating in dark sheltered places, often in attics and out-houses. It is quite easy to breed peacock butterflies, by keeping them in a cage in a cool, dark room for the winter. They can then be 'tamed' before releasing them in the spring, so they will remain in the garden and will come to be fed on sugar-water. They have only one generation a year, and the habit of hibernation results in the butterfly having an unusually long life in the winged state. A peacock butterfly in captivity lived for 11 months. Its food plant is nettles.

Red Admiral

The red admiral is the popular name for a butterfly which has several subspecies. One found in Europe, Asia and the Canaries, is the familiar European one. Formerly it was believed to occur in the United States but a distinct subspecies occurs there. This is found from Canada to Mexico and on some West Indian Islands and has been introduced to Hawaii. There is even one distinct species of Red Admiral which is known only from Hawaii. Other species of Red Admiral are found in India and the Far East.

Map butterfly

There are many species of Nymphalids known as Map butterflies from the appearance of the pattern on the wings. The European Map butterfly is widespread in France and elsewhere in Europe. Attempts to introduce it to Britain have failed. It is remarkable in being represented by two distinct seasonal forms. Unlike most vanessids it overwinters as a pupa, and the butterflies which hatch in May are chequered tawny and black and look rather like fritillaries. The larvae from the eggs of these spring butterflies feed and grow rapidly,

pupate and produce in July a generation of black-and-white butterflies totally unlike their parents. The length of day during the larval stage determines which form the mature butterfly shall assume. By exposing the caterpillars to long or short 'days', using artificial light, successive generations of either form can be bred. Its food plant is entirely nettles.

Camberwell Beauty

This butterfly is known as the mourning cloak in North America. It is, like the red admiral, distributed all over the northern hemisphere, and it also goes down the Andes, in South America. In spite of its wide distribution it is a great rarity in Britain. It appears to need the severe continental winter to induce proper hibernation. It feeds on willow, poplar and birch.

Small tortoiseshell

This gay little butterfly ranges right across the Eurasian continent to Japan. It is one of the commonest species in Britain and can be seen in gardens throughout most of the spring and summer as it goes through two generations in a year. The butterflies of the second generation hibernate and reappear in spring. Its food plant is nettles.

Large tortoiseshell

Up to the first two decades of this century this butterfly was not uncommon in southern England, but it has suffered a decline and is now by far the rarest of the resident vanessids in Britain. It is still occasionally seen in Essex and Suffolk and is common in central and southern Europe. Its food consists of elm foliage.

△ *Mourning cloak – a vanessid that hibernates as an adult, feeding on the sugar-rich sap from trees when it emerges in early spring.*
△ ▷ *Bird's eye view of a small tortoiseshell.*
▷ *The most widespread butterfly in the world – the painted lady. In the spring it migrates in vast numbers from North Africa to Europe.*
◁ *The rich-hued vanessid of European summer – each year the red admiral flies north from the Mediterranean to lay its eggs.*
▽ ◁ *Peacock butterflies on a spray of* **Buddleia,** *a favourite food plant of adult butterflies.*
▽ *The tattered look of the comma provides excellent camouflage when the wings are folded.*

They taste with their toes

As already mentioned, all the nymphalid butterflies (vanessas, fritillaries, emperors and others) are 'quadrupeds', the forelegs being stunted and not used for walking. Those of the males have only two terminal joints and are brush-like. In the females these legs are more slender with four terminal joints and are only sparsely haired. They are used as sense organs, the end joints serving as organs of taste. A red admiral can distinguish, by touching with its forefeet, between pure water and a sugar solution $\frac{1}{200}$ of the strength required to be detected by the human tongue.

Spare the nettles

Farmers and people obsessed with the idea of 'tidiness' wage a relentless war on nettles, spraying them ruthlessly wherever they grow. But nettles should be allowed to grow in places that are not needed for cultivation or pasture. Five of the vanessid butterflies described here depend on nettles for their larval food. If those who aim to exterminate this plant had their way we should see much fewer gaily coloured butterflies.

Comma butterfly

The recent history in Britain of this very attractive butterfly is in curious contrast to that of the large tortoiseshell. Up to about 1920 it was confined to a small area in South Wales, but about that time it began to spread over southern England and the Midlands and has maintained this wider distribution. Like the other resident British vanessids it hibernates as a butterfly, but remains in the open in woods and hedges, sheltering under leaves instead of seeking shelter in natural hollows or buildings. When its wings are closed the coloration and irregular outline make the butterfly look like a withered leaf. Without this the butterfly would never survive the hunting of winter-hungry birds. It goes through two generations in the summer and the larva feeds on nettles and elm.

Painted Lady

This is known as the thistle butterfly in North America. It has the distinction of being the only butterfly with a world-wide distribution, without the formation of any well defined races or subspecies. The reason for this is that the urge to migrate is so powerful and persistent in this butterfly that its populations are subject to constant mixing, which of course prevents the formation of local races. In Britain and northern Europe the painted lady is a summer migrant of the same type as the red admiral. The main breeding ground of the European painted ladies is North Africa, and travellers there have witnessed the hatching of thousands of pupae among the sand dunes and the start of the butterflies' massed flight towards the Mediterranean. Its food plant is thistles.

phylum	**Arthropoda**
class	**Insecta**
order	**Lepidoptera**
family	**Nymphalidae**
genera & species	*Aglais urticae* small tortoiseshell *Araschnia levana* map butterfly *Nymphalis antiopa* Camberwell beauty, or mourning cloak *N. io* peacock butterfly *N. polychloros* large tortoiseshell *Polygonia c-album* comma *Vanessa atalanta* red admiral *V. cardui* painted lady or thistle butterfly, others

Mosquito

There are 2 000 species of mosquito living everywhere from the Tropics to Arctic latitudes, often in enormous numbers. While not all are troublesome to man, some species are notorious bloodsucking pests which transmit distressing diseases such as malaria, yellow fever, elephantiasis and filariasis.

Mosquitoes are slender-bodied insects, about ¼ in. long, with a single pair of narrow wings and long slender legs. In most of them the wing veins and the rear edge of each wing are decorated with small scales. The antennae are hairy in the female and copiously feathered in the male, except in members of the subfamily Dixinae. In most species the female has a sharp tubular proboscis adapted for piercing and sucking fluids, usually blood. Exceptions to this are again found in the Dixinae, which are also unusual in having transparent larvae, known quite appropriately as phantom larvae.

Basically 'mosquito' and 'gnat' have the same meaning, the first being Spanish, the second Old English. Today many people speak of small insects that 'bite' as mosquitoes, and similar but equally small, harmless insects, especially those seen in dancing swarms, as gnats. The confusion is the same among scientists—judging from popular books on the subject—who speak of **Culex pipiens,** the commonest mosquito in Europe, as the common gnat, but otherwise restrict the use of the word 'gnat' to the Dixinae.

There are two main groups of mosquitoes, the culicines and the anophelines, represented by the genera **Culex** and **Anopheles** respectively. The wings of culicines are transparent or slightly tinted, while the wings of anophelines are usually marked with dark and light spots or patches. Another difference is that the female culicine has a pair of very short palpi beside the long proboscis while the palpi of the anopheline female are as long as the proboscis. The best way of distinguishing the two is that when resting the culicine holds its body horizontal to the surface on which it is standing and the anopheline tilts its body upwards.

Eggs in any water

Mosquitoes lay their floating eggs in water, which may be fresh, brackish or salt, according to the species. With few exceptions each species chooses a particular kind of

▷△ Blood transfusion. An adult mosquito **Culex pipiens** sucks up blood through its tubular proboscis. Most of them are specialised in their habitat also at this stage, each species usually preferring a particular type of host. (14 × life size)
▷▽ Bloated with blood. A female mosquito **Culex pipiens** has just taken her last blood meal before she lays her eggs.

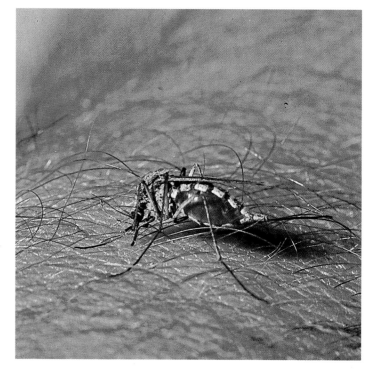

△ *The feathery antennae of the male (×60) are sensitive to sound vibrations, but only when the long hairs are erect. Some species keep them permanently erect so are always ready to mate while others erect them only at certain times of the day.* △ *Impending doom? A swarm of mosquitoes.*

watery situation, which may be the margins of ponds or lakes, in ditches, seepages, waterfilled cart ruts or hoofprints, polluted waters, water collected in holes in trees – usually at the top of a bole where branches fork – in aerial plants growing on trees or in pitcher plants. Water butts are often homes for mosquito larvae, but the eggs have even been seen in the water bowl put down for a pet dog. *Anopheles* lays single eggs, while *Culex* lays its eggs in compact masses or egg-rafts.

Each larva has a broad thorax in which all three segments are fused and an abdomen of 9 segments. The head bears the simple larval eyes and a pair of developing compound eyes. Brushes of bristles either side of it sweep fine particles of animal or plant food into the mouth, except in those larvae that extract dissolved food from the water, or prey on other insect larvae, usually other mosquito larvae. The thorax and abdomen are also decorated with long bristles. At the tip of the abdomen are four gills and a breathing siphon which can be pushed through the surface film of water to take in air. Some larvae feed on the bottom, others nearer the surface. They swim with twisting movements of the body, coiling and uncoiling spasmodically. Mosquitoes rest just beneath the surface hanging down more or less vertically. At the slightest disturbance of the water they quickly swim down but, after a while, they must return to hang from the surface film in order to breathe.

Lively pupae
Larval life lasts about a week in most species, depending on temperature, but in those feeding on other insects it is prolonged, with usually only one generation a

year. The pupae are active but do not feed, and the pupal life is short, at the most a few days. Pupae are typically bulky, having a large rounded head and thorax combined, with a pair of breeding siphons on top, and the abdomen more or less curled around it. In the last stages of development the pupa rises to the surface of the water, its hard outer skin splits, and the adult mosquito pulls itself out of the pupal husk and takes to the air.

The love call
Soon after leaving their pupal skins, the adults mate, after which the males die. The females must take a meal for their eggs to develop, either of blood or, in some species, nectar or sap. A few can manage on food stored during the larval stage. Some species of mosquitoes take the blood of mammals, others the blood of birds or even of amphibians. Sometimes a female will take another drink of blood after laying.

In the interval between leaving the pupal skin and mating the mosquitoes must rest. If a male takes to the wing too soon, his wings do not beat fast enough to proclaim him a male and other males will try to mate with him. He may lose some of his legs in the process. If a female takes off too soon, her wingbeats will be so slow the males will not recognize her until she has been in the air for a while and the pace of her wingbeats has quickened.

Surviving hard times
In temperate latitudes the females of some species pass the winter in sheltered places, such as caves, hollow trees or houses, especially in cellars. A few species lay their eggs in dry places which will be flooded in late winter or spring. These eggs can withstand

dry and cold conditions, and in some instances will not hatch successfully without them. When the female of *Anopheles gambiae*, a malaria-carrier, lives in desert areas, she gorges herself with blood and then shelters in huts, cracks in rocks or in rodent burrows, until the rains come. The dryness delays her egg-laying. Other species of desert mosquitoes lay thick-shelled eggs able to hatch even after 1–2 years, and in some cases up to 10 years later.

War on mosquitoes
Mosquitoes have many enemies. Airborne mosquitoes are eaten by birds such as swallows and flycatchers hunting on the wing. The larvae and pupae are eaten by small fish. The guppy, called the millions fish because of its large numbers in its native home, is used to control mosquito larvae and has been introduced into rivers in infested areas to keep down their numbers. Another control is to spray oil on waters of ponds and swamps. A small amount of oil will spread to cover a wide area with a thin film which prevents the larval mosquito from breathing at the surface of the water.

Homing on victims
When a female mosquito takes blood from a malarial patient, she will pass the malaria parasite by her saliva on to the next victim whose blood she sucks. It is the same with yellow fever, although a different species of mosquito is involved, and with elephantiasis, filariasis, and other mosquito-borne diseases. There are several defensive measures which can be taken to keep the mosquitoes away. This is usually achieved by netting or by deterrents, or by killing the larvae or the mosquitoes, or changing the habitat and

reducing the number of people carrying the disease who act as a reservoir for further infection. The use of deterrents depends on the behaviour of a mosquito in homing on its victim. An increase in the carbon dioxide in the air, as from human breathing, makes a female mosquito take off and fly upwind. As she draws near her victim the slight increase in temperature and humidity directs her more certainly towards her target until she can see where she needs to land. In these later stages the concentration of carbon dioxide is also greater, but certain chemicals (deterrents) will confuse her and make her swerve away.

Mysterious outbreaks

The ague was once prevalent in Europe but was stamped out largely by the draining of the marshes. When soldiers serving in the tropics during the First World War returned home after contracting malaria, it was feared they might act as a reservoir for malaria (or ague). With the air traffic of today there once again is the fear that infected mosquitoes may be introduced into countries at present free from their diseases, and steps must be taken against them. Thirty years ago an African mosquito *Anopheles gambiae* found its way to Brazil, and 60 000 people died before the malaria was brought under control. In the Second World War, in Colombia, yellow fever suddenly struck villages where it had been unknown. In due course it was traced to the monkeys living high in trees which formed a reservoir, the carrier being a mosquito whose larvae lived in water in aerial plants growing in the tree tops. Woodmen felling some of these trees were attacked by mosquitoes from pupae in the aerial plants. The disease was then spread by a species of mosquito living at ground level.

Odd behaviour

Not all mosquitoes are troublesome; some are highly interesting. The larvae of *Mansonia* do not need to swim to the surface of the water to breathe. They have a saw-like apparatus for piercing water plant roots and drawing off the air contained in them. The females of another species *Leicesteria* lay their eggs onto their hindlegs which they then push through small holes in bamboo stems where water has collected. The eggs fall into the water and later hatch. A New Zealand mosquito *Opifex* has unusual mating behaviour. The males fly over water waiting for pupae to come to the surface to release the females within. They then mate with the females before they can get out. A mosquito *Harpagomyia* of Africa and southern Asia settles on tree trunks waiting for ants to pass. It then flies over to an ant, holds the ant's body with its front pair of legs and does not let the ant go until it has brought up a drop of food from its crop. The oddest story of all is, however, of a tropical American carrier of yellow fever which seems to prefer laying its eggs in water in flower vases, even those in hospital wards. In dealing with an outbreak of yellow fever in New Orleans it was found that the mosquitoes were breeding in the water in flower vases placed on the graves of the unfortunate yellow fever victims.

△△ *Life afloat. Compact rafts of the eggs of the common gnat* **Culex** *beside a duckweed plant. Between them mosquitoes lay their eggs in almost every type of water, although the majority live in fresh water. Each individual species is, however, very limited in its habitat.*
△ *Living down under? A mosquito larva hangs from the surface in still water. It breathes through the respiratory tubes which reach up to the surface. The head, thorax and abdomen are clearly visible as are the mouth brushes which hang like a drooping moustache and sweep particles into the mouth. (7 × life size)*
▷ *Bulky but active. Mosquitoes spend only a few days in this pupal stage, whether the life cycle lasts a year or 10 days. (13 × life size)*

phylum	**Arthropoda**
class	**Insecta**
order	**Diptera**
family	**Culicidae**

138

A housefly cleans itself by rubbing its first pair of legs together. This common fly spreads disease mainly as a result of its indiscriminate feeding habits. Bacteria may be carried on the legs or body, or in the proboscis and so be exuded onto food with the next flow of saliva.

Housefly

Many different kinds of flies come into houses. Some are accidental intruders that buzz on the window panes trying to get out into the open air again. Others enter houses in the autumn to hibernate in attics and roof-spaces. But there are two kinds that make our houses their home. One is the housefly, the other is the lesser housefly. The first is stoutly built and in both sexes the abdomen is yellowish or buff. Lesser houseflies are smaller and more slender, the females dull greyish, the males similar but with a pair of semi-transparent yellow patches at the base of the abdomen. The two are also distinguished by a difference in the veins of the wings which can easily be seen with a lens. This difference separates the two species regardless of sex.

Both have a wide distribution, the housefly being found throughout the tropics as well as in almost all inhabited temperate regions.

Kiss-in-the-ring flight

Houseflies pass their adult lives in houses, flying about the rooms and crawling over food that is left exposed. Both species breed in the sort of refuse that accumulates around the dwellings of people who live unhygienically, but their habits differ in detail. Lesser houseflies appear earlier in the season than houseflies, which build up their numbers rather slowly after the winter and are not usually abundant until July. The males of lesser houseflies fly in a very distinctive way. They choose a spot in a room, often beneath a hanging lamp or similar 'landmark', and fly as if they were following the sides of a triangle or quadrilateral, hovering momentarily at the corners and turning sharply at them; a single fly will continue to follow the same course for long periods. If, as often happens, more than one fly is patrolling in the same area, one of them will intercept the other and the two whirl together for an instant and then part again. The expression 'playing kiss-in-the-ring' aptly describes this activity, but they are in fact all males, and always lesser houseflies.

Flies in summer—and winter

The breeding habits of the two species are similar but the larva of the lesser housefly prefers food rich in nitrogenous compounds, such as urine or bird droppings. These flies are nearly always abundant where chickens are kept. The larvae of the housefly are less particular. Manure and compost heaps, the night soil from old-fashioned privies and house refuse of any kind all provide them with breeding-grounds.

The eggs are laid on the larval food, and the adult flies also feed in places of this kind. The eggs are white, about $\frac{1}{25}$ in. long and a female housefly may lay as many as 900 in batches of 150. They hatch in as little as 8 hours if it is very warm, otherwise in 1–3 days. The white legless maggots feed rapidly and may reach full size in under 2 days, but can live for 8 weeks in colder and less favourable conditions. At 15°C/60°F houseflies will breed continuously throughout the year, taking about 3 weeks from egg to adult, but in the tropics the cycle is completed in a week. The pupa is formed in an oval brown capsule called the puparium, which consists of the last larval skin; instead of being shed at pupation this is retained and plays the same part as the moth cocoon.

The lesser housefly has a similar life cycle, but its larva is very different in appearance, being flattened and beset with rows of short branched tentacle-like processes on the upper surface of the body.

Flies disappear in winter time, and the question where they go is often asked—and it once formed the theme of a popular song. There seems no simple answer to it. Houseflies may hibernate as adults or continue breeding slowly in warm places, especially in buildings where cattle are kept. Probably the fly has different adaptations for wintering in different parts of its range. In warm regions it breeds all the year round.

Sucking up their food

Adults of both species feed by settling on moist organic matter of almost any kind and sucking up nutrient liquid from it. If the material is dry the fly regurgitates a drop of liquid on to it and sucks up the resultant solution. Crude sewage and a bowl of sugar are equally attractive and the insect may fly straight from one to the other. The feeding apparatus consists of a short sucking proboscis expanded at the end into a sponge-like organ with which the fly mops up its liquid food. Flies that have overfilled their stomachs will often regurgitate on any surface on which they happen to be resting, leaving little dirty spots.

People will sometimes assure you that they have been bitten by a housefly. The mistake is excusable because the stable fly *Stomoxys calcitrans* looks almost exactly like a housefly. Its mouthparts are, however, very different, consisting of a stiff piercing organ, and they feed, as horseflies do, by sucking blood. Their bite is quite painful and they can penetrate one's skin through a thick sock. The stable fly breeds in dung mixed with straw and is far less common now than when horses were kept in large numbers.

Bearers of disease

The most important disease-carrying insects are those which feed on our blood, taking micro-organisms from infected people and injecting them into the blood of healthy ones. Examples are the tsetse fly and some mosquitoes. Houseflies do not feed in this way, but by feeding on excrement and exposed foodstuffs they are potential carriers of gastro-intestinal diseases such as dysentery. Houseflies taken from a slum district have been found to carry on average over $3\frac{1}{2}$ million bacteria per fly, and over a million in clean districts. These are not all disease bacteria, but some of them are very likely to be. Infants and small children seem to suffer most from fly-borne disease. In a tropical village infant mortality dropped in one year from 22·7 to 11·5 per cent when flies were controlled by an insecticide.

It is not difficult to kill flies in vast numbers by spraying such substances as DDT and chlordane on the places where they feed and breed but they have a remarkable capacity for developing resistance to specific poisons. No individual fly develops resistance during its lifetime, but some will almost always survive a spraying and these will include individuals having, by an accident of nature, some degree of immunity to the pesticide being used. This immunity is inherited by their offspring, in varying degrees, and the most resistant of these will again survive and breed. Selection of this kind continues with every generation until the insecticide is useless in any concentration at which it is safe to use. The process is exactly the same as the natural selection through which evolution has taken its course. These examples of acquired resistance in insects are in fact examples of very rapid evolutionary change, and they form one of the most compelling arguments against relying too much upon pesticides in our efforts to control harmful insects.

Control of houseflies is best achieved by depriving them of breeding places. The modern civilised way of life has already gone a long way towards doing this with water-borne sanitation, the use of covered dustbins and the decline of the horse as a means of transport.

class	**Insecta**
order	**Diptera**
family	**Muscidae**
genera & species	**Musca domestica** *housefly* **Fannia canicularis** *lesser housefly*

Top right: Photomicrograph of a leg. The last segment has a pair of claws and two suction pads which help the fly to walk on smooth surfaces (× 60).
Bottom right: Housefly just about to land.
▽ Wings of housefly (top) and lesser housefly (bottom). The differences in venation can be used to distinguish the two types of fly.

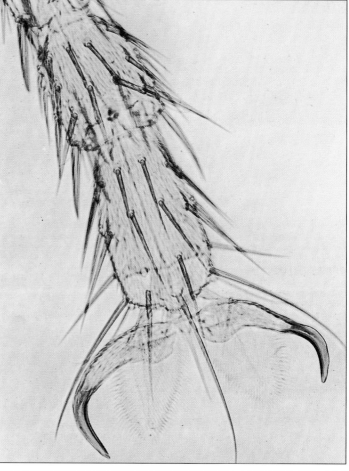

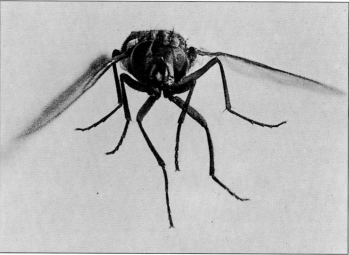

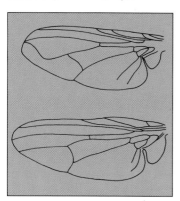

140

Bumble-bee

Bumble-bees are rather like honeybees (see page 143) except that they have a larger body which is covered with stiff yellow, orange or red hairs. The bumble-bee also has a sting which it can use to inject venom into the body of an enemy. The sting is a modified ovipositor—a tube-like organ used by other insects to deposit their eggs.

Bumble-bees are also known as 'humble-bees'. Both names come from the lazy humming sound made by the bee as it flies from one flower to another.

The bumble-bee is found all over the world. Most species live in the tropical or sub-tropical zones but they can also be found in places as far apart as Arctic Canada and Tierra del Fuego, and the equivalent of this range in the Old World. They are not native to Australasia, but were introduced there when settlers found that none of the local bees would pollinate the red clover plant which they had introduced. So the bumble-bee was brought in to do the job.

Buzzing around from flower to flower

Under a microscope the hindleg of a bumble-bee is an interesting sight. The outer face of the 'shin' is flat and polished but along each side there is a row of stiff bristles. These bristles make up what is called the pollen basket. If you watch a bumble-bee flying from one flower to another it is quite easy to see the large yellow balls of pollen attached to its hindlegs. When the bee forces its way into a flower the pollen is rubbed off onto its body hairs. The bee then brushes the pollen from its body, moistens it with a little nectar and sticks it onto the pollen basket. When it gets back to the nest it uses its forelegs to remove the balls of pollen from this basket and put them into the egg-cell.

The bumble-bee is attracted to the flower by the nectar, which it sucks up through a special extendible tube. The nectar is then stored away in the crop or honey stomach.

Flowers and bees depend upon each other for their existence. The bee benefits from the pollen and the flowers benefit by being 'cross-pollinated'. This cross-pollination occurs when some of the pollen from one flower is rubbed off onto another flower, thus fertilising it.

It is for this reason, to attract bees rather than people, that flowers have evolved their attractive colours and scents.

The life cycle of a queen bee

Usually it is a pure accident if an insect meets one of her offspring. This is because most insects lay their eggs and then leave them to hatch out by themselves.

Some insects, however, are different. They are called social insects. This kind of insect stays with her offspring and they, in turn, stay with her and help look after her next brood. Wasps, honeybees and ants are all well-known examples of social insects. In their case thousands of individuals live in one nest. Most of them are sexless or, rather, under-developed females. These workers care for the breeding female, the queen, and for her eggs and larvae. Bumble-bees are social insects too, but their communal life is not as well developed as the others. There are fewer workers in the colony and they all die before the winter.

The life of a bumble-bee colony begins in autumn. A young female bumble-bee leaves the nest, mates and finds a sheltered spot where she can spend the winter hibernating. When spring comes—the actual date depends upon the species—the young queen emerges and suns herself until she is fully active. Then off she flies in search of pollen and nectar from the spring flowers. The queen needs pollen because it contains large amounts of protein which is used to build up in her ovaries the eggs to be laid later.

Soon the queen starts looking for a suitable place to build her nest. She might take over the abandoned nest of a fieldmouse, a vole, or a hedgehog. Or she might pick somewhere else: a disused bird's nest, a thatched roof, a bale of hay or even a discarded mattress. Her favourite sites are along hedgerows and banks or in old, neglected corners of fields and gardens. Nowadays it is not easy for the queen bee to find this kind of place. Modern intensive and mechanised farming demands that these unproductive corners be ploughed up so that every square foot of ground pays its way. The result is that bumble-bees, which are in a sense vital to the pollination of crops, are themselves becoming scarcer.

The queen usually builds her nest at the end of a tunnel. The tunnel may be several feet long, if she has used an old mouse nest, but some species prefer tunnels only a few inches long, so they build their nests in thatch or similar places. Some kinds of bumble-bees, known as carder-bees, even manage to build their nests on the surface. They do this by combing grass and other material into a tight, closely-woven ball.

If the queen has taken over the nest from a former occupant there is always plenty of nest material readily available. She fashions this into a small inner chamber lined with only the finest grass and roots. She stays in here for a day or two drying it out with her body heat. Insects are cold-blooded, but the larger ones generate enough heat, especially with their flight muscles, to keep their bodies a few degrees above air temperature outside the nest.

Food in a 'honey pot'

By now the eggs are developing inside the queen bee. She begins to make an egg-cell out of wax. The wax is secreted from between the plates on the underside of her abdomen. She goes out to collect pollen which she stores in the egg-cell, in which 8–14 eggs are laid. The cell is then covered

*Male mating with queen bee **Bombus agrorum**. Young males are produced at the end of the season. After mating the queen finds a sheltered spot where she can spend the winter hibernating until the spring.*

*Bumble-bee queen, **B. hortorum**, incubating her first batch of brood which have reached the pupal stage. She stores surplus nectar in a wax 'honey pot' near the entrance of the nest to provide food in bad weather.*

with a cap of wax. The queen spends some of her time settled on top of the eggs to keep them warm. She also goes out feeding and brings home any surplus nectar which she stores in a 'honey pot' near the entrance to the nest. The 'honey pot' is made of wax and is about ¾ in. high and ½ in. across. It provides a source of food when the weather is too bad for the queen to go out foraging.

When the larvae begin to hatch out of the eggs they are just helpless maggots with very little in the way of legs or sense organs. They do nothing except feed on the pollen which has been stored in the egg-cell and on the mixture of nectar and pollen which their mother regurgitates to them. But they grow amazingly quickly on this diet. They shed their skins several times and then spin a cocoon and pupate.

At this point the queen carefully removes the wax from around the cocoons and makes it into new egg-cells. She puts these on top of the cocoons and lays the next batch of eggs in them. Eventually the first brood emerge from their cocoons as fully developed workers. They spend a day or two drying out while their wings expand and harden. Then they are ready to go out collecting food and to tend the next batch of larvae.

Before long a whole colony of several hundred workers has been built up. The queen, however, never becomes a helpless egg-laying machine as happens with ants and termites. She can still make egg-cells and feed larvae although she hardly ever leaves the nest to forage.

Towards the end of the summer, some of the eggs produce males and fertile females. The males develop by parthenogenesis—that is to say, from unfertilised eggs. The females, the next generation of queens, appear at first to be exactly the same as the sterile female workers but they grow much larger and eventually leave the nest to mate with the males. The males differ from other bumble-bees by having larger antennae,

which they use to locate the females. They do not have a sting.

Once the old queen has produced the males and the new queens she stops laying worker eggs. Gradually the whole colony dies out. After mating the males also die. It is winter again and only the young queens are left to survive through to spring.

Bumble-bees fighting for their lives

Bumble-bees have many enemies, large and small. The worst ones are insect-eating birds like the bee-eater, but there are plenty of others. Badgers or skunks and other mammals will dig up bees' nests both for the honey and for the bees themselves.

Naturalists once observed a skunk scratching at a nest until the irate inhabitants flew out. The skunk caught each one in its forepaws and killed it by rubbing it against the ground.

Fieldmice and shrews also attack bumble-bee nests, and among the smaller animals that are enemies of the bees are robber flies. They grapple the bees with their legs and suck their blood. Then there are the 'mites' which live in the air-sacs or 'lungs' of the bees and also suck their juices. Another enemy is the wax moth. It lays its eggs in bumble-bee nests and its caterpillars ruin the egg-cells by burrowing through them.

The cuckoo-bee is a close relative of the bumble-bee and in its own way another enemy. Cuckoo-bees do not have pollen baskets with which to collect stores of pollen. So instead they invade the nests of bumble-bees and lay their eggs there. The eggs develop into males and females, but not workers, and they have to be tended by the bumble-bee workers.

In a fight the bumble-bee will defend itself by biting and stinging. It rolls onto its back, with its jaws open and sting protruding, and sometimes squirts venom into the air. Its sting is not barbed, like the sting of a honeybee, so it can be withdrawn from the corpse of an enemy and used again.

Economic importance

Charles Darwin began many controversies with his famous book *On the Origin of Species*. One of the things he mentioned in the book was that only bumble-bees visit the flowers of the red clover. This is because the red clover has a long, narrow flower and other bees do not have long enough tongues to reach the nectar which lies at the base of the flowers.

Darwin pointed out that if bumble-bees became rare or extinct the red clover would also die out. This would have serious economic effects, he said, because cattle are fed on red clover.

He went on to quote a Mr H Newman who said that more than two-thirds of bumble-bee nests in England are destroyed by mice. He claimed that bumble-bee nests were more common near villages and towns, where cats were plentiful. Therefore a large number of cats would mean a larger crop of clover because the cats would eat the mice who killed the bees.

Later a German scientist intervened to remark that a large number of cats would be good for England's economy because he considered England's wealth to be based on her cattle.

In a true Darwinian spirit, TH Huxley then stepped in to supply the final link. He suggested that, since old-maids were very fond of cats, the sensible way to strengthen the economy of the country would be to increase the number of old-maids. Less weddings and more spinsters was the short answer, according to Huxley.

class	**Insecta**
order	**Hymenoptera**
family	**Bombidae**
genus	***Bombus***

A batch of cocoons, two of which have been cut open to show the pupae inside. These will emerge as fully developed workers and will then spend a day or two drying out while their wings expand and harden (8 × lifesize).

*When the temperature of their nests becomes too high some of the workers fan currents of air with their wings to cool the nests (**B. ogrorum**).*

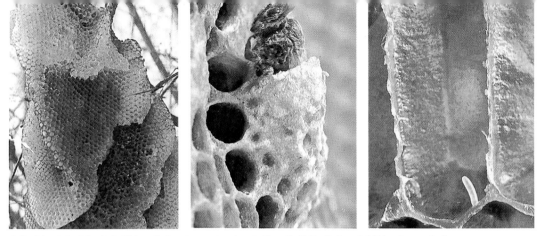

Left: A tree-suspended nest of wild bees. Centre: A queen struggles out of her cell. Right: Each egg is laid in a hexagonal cell.

Honeybee

*Any of the four species of social bees belonging to the genus **Apis** can be called honeybees but the name is most usually associated with the European domestic bee **Apis mellifera,** sometimes called the western honeybee. This differs from all other social bees and social wasps of temperate climates in forming colonies that survive the winter by living on reserve stores of food, so a particular dwelling site or nest may be occupied for an indefinite length of time. In social wasps and bumble bees all the members of the colony die at the end of the summer except the fertilised females or queens, which hibernate and found new colonies in the following spring.*

In the colonies of social bees, wasps and ants there are two kinds of females. The fertile females are called 'queens' and the sterile females are the 'workers', the latter doing all the work of maintaining the economy of the colony. In the wasps, most bees and some ants, the egg-laying organ or ovipositor of both types of female is transformed into a sting, connected with a poison gland. In the queens the eggs are extruded from an opening at the base of the sting.

Bees have been kept for their honey by man for many hundreds of years. Throughout most of history this has been mainly a matter of inducing them to make colonies in hollow receptacles of various kinds, such as earthenware pots, logs and straw baskets or 'skeps', and then robbing them of their honey. Until recently their breeding has been entirely uncontrolled and even now they are not domesticated in the same way as dogs, cattle, or even silkworms.

Household chores

The great majority of European honeybees are now living in hives although wild colonies may be found, almost always in hollow trees. In midsummer a strong colony normally contains one queen, 50 000 to 60 000 workers and a few hundred males or drones. The expectation of life of a worker bee at this time is only 4–6 weeks and her span is divided into two periods. For just under 3 weeks after emerging from the pupa the worker's duties lie within the hive, where she is fed at first by older bees, but later feeds herself from the stores of honey and pollen. Her first spell of work is as nursemaid to the developing larvae, to whom she passes on a great deal of the food she eats, partly by direct regurgitation and partly by giving them a jelly-like secretion from certain salivary glands in her head. By the time she is about 12 days old her wax glands have developed and she turns to building and repairing the comb of geometrically arranged cells in which the larvae are reared and food is stored. At this time she also goes out for short flights around the hive, learning the landmarks by which to guide herself home when she ventures farther afield.

From about 12 days to 3 weeks old she takes over the nectar and pollen brought in by returning foragers, converting the former to honey and storing it away. At the same time she helps to keep the hive tidy, carrying outside dead bees and other debris. At 3 weeks old she is ready to go out foraging herself for nectar, pollen, water and resin, which are the four substances needed for the hive's economy. The last is used to make a sort of varnish-like cement called 'propolis' with which crevices and any small openings in the hive are sealed up.

Searching for nectar

In searching for nectar-yielding flowers the worker bee is guided by her senses of smell and sight. Bees have good colour vision but it differs from our own. They cannot see red at all but can see ultraviolet 'colour', invisible to us but revealed by photography by ultraviolet light. Bees guide themselves to and from the hive by reference to the angle of the sun, or of polarised light from the sky, and have a time sense which enables them to compensate for the continuous change in the sun's position.

Foraging is very hard work and after 2–3 weeks of it the worker is worn out and dies. Workers hatched in the autumn have a much longer life before them, as they build up food reserves in their bodies and their activity is reduced through the winter. They keep warm by huddling together in a mass and feeding on the honey that they have stored.

The queen rules her great horde of daughters, not by example or wise counsel, but by secreting from her body a substance whose presence or absence controls their behaviour. Her chief role, however, is egg-laying, and at midsummer she may be laying 1 500 eggs a day, totalling more than the weight of her own body. This enormous fecundity is needed to compensate for the shortness of the workers' lives.

The idle drones

Mating with and fertilising the queens is the only useful part played in honeybee economy by the drones. During summer they usually live 4–5 weeks and are fed by the workers, not even seeking their own food among the flowers. In autumn the drones remaining in the colony are turned outside to die of starvation or chill.

New colonies are founded by what is known as swarming. As a preliminary to this extra queens are produced in the hive and then large numbers of workers, accompanied by some drones and usually one queen, leave the hive and fly together for some distance. Then they settle in a large cluster and search for a suitable place, where a new colony is made by some of the workers. At this stage they can easily be persuaded to settle down in artificial quarters of any kind merely by shaking the swarm, with its attendant queen, into a suitable receptacle, such as a beehive.

Natural and artificial breeding

Queens may be produced in a hive in response to ageing of the mother queen or to the urge to swarm. In either case they fly out to seek mates when they are about a week old. A drone that mates with a queen condemns himself to death. The reason for this is that his genital organs become so firmly fixed in the queen's body that they are torn out when the two bees part, and he dies almost immediately. The sperm is stored by the queen in an internal sac called the spermatheca, and sperms are released to fertilise the eggs as she lays them. Here there is a strange departure from the condition normally found in animals. All eggs that are fertilised produce females, either workers or queens; drones are only produced from eggs that develop without being fertilised.

The larva and pupa stages of honeybees (collectively known as the 'brood') are passed in the wax cells into which the eggs are laid, one in each cell. The larvae are entirely helpless and are fed by the workers. The development of a worker bee takes 21 days, 3 as an egg, 6 as a larva and 12 as a pupa.

The natural mating behaviour of queen and drone bees makes any control of pairing and breeding impossible, but in recent years a technique for artificially inseminating chosen queens with sperm from chosen drones has been developed. It is a difficult process requiring delicate manipulation under a microscope, but by this means selected strains of bees can now be bred.

'Common' and 'royal' food

The natural food of bees consists of nectar and pollen, the nectar supplying the energy-producing sugar and the pollen being a source of protein. The bees also make honey from nectar and store it for food. It is untrue to say that bees suck honey from flowers; nectar and honey are chemically distinct and the latter is much more concentrated. The larvae are fed partly on a mixture of nectar or honey and pollen and partly on a secretion from various glands of the young workers, the substance that is often called 'royal jelly'. When a fertilised egg is laid in a normal sized cell the larva is fed at first on jelly and later on pollen and honey, and it develops into a worker. When production of queens is needed the workers make larger cells into which the reigning queen lays ordinary fertilised eggs. The larvae from these, however, are fed until they are fully grown on royal jelly alone and they develop into queens. Drone larvae are fed similarly to those of workers but for 2 more days, 8 instead of 6.

Bees will readily drink a solution of sugar in water and are often fed on this during the winter by bee keepers who take most of their stored honey but are also concerned to keep their bees alive.

Enemies and disease

In spite of their stings bees are preyed upon by birds, dragonflies and some kinds of wasps. Certain moths called wax moths lay their eggs in the hives and the larvae live on wax, pollen and general comb debris, doing serious damage if they are at all numerous. The big death's-head hawk moth is said to invade colonies and steal the honey, piercing the wax comb with its short, stiff proboscis. It was called the 'Bee Tyger' by the early entomologists.

The greatest menace to honeybees, however, is disease and starvation.

Fierce relatives

Only four species of the genus *Apis* are known, and one of them, the eastern honeybee *Apis indica*, is so similar to *Apis mellifera* it is sometimes regarded as a subspecies. It is domesticated in tropical Asia.

Both the other species inhabit the eastern tropics. The giant honeybee *Apis dorsata* is a large bee which makes enormous hanging combs in the open. An overhanging surface is chosen at a considerable height from the ground. Large branches overhanging cliffs and buildings, especially water towers are favourite sites for colonies. These bees may be dangerous if molested and there are records of people being attacked and stung to death. Nevertheless the Dyaks of Borneo climb by night with smoking torches, throw down the combs and gather the honey.

The little honeybee *Apis florea* is by contrast an inoffensive little insect, reluctant to use its sting. A colony consists of a single comb the size of the palm of a man's hand, which contains only 1 or 2 oz. of honey.

In tropical America stingless bees of the genus *Trigona* (not closely related to the Old World honeybees) make large colonies in hollow logs and similar places and they used to be domesticated for their honey by the Maya Indians of Mexico.

phylum	**Arthropoda**
class	**Insecta**
order	**Hymenoptera**
family	**Apidae**

A drone makes landfall beside the queen, who is surrounded by workers. From her body the queen secretes a substance whose presence or absence controls the behaviour of the great horde of her daughter-workers, who supply the hive or colony.

Method in their madness: this is a workers' conference, carried out in dance language. To tell each other where flower-nectar is to be found, worker bees have evolved two sorts of dance: a round dance for nearby nectar and a tail-wagging dance for distant nectar.

Wasp

To most people a wasp recalls the black-and-yellow insect often abundant enough in summer to be a nuisance, but in its broader sense the term 'wasp' includes any of the stinging Hymenoptera that is not a bee or an ant.

The common wasp *Vespula vulgaris* and the German wasp *V. germanica* are equally common in Europe, and so alike that the workers are difficult to distinguish, though the queens can be separated by the pattern of their yellow and black markings. Except to entomologists these two are just 'wasps', without any thought of there being more than one species. Almost all that is said here jointly concerns both.

The nearest European relative to the wasp is the hornet **Vespa crabro**, and they are more distantly related to the paper wasps **Polistes**. Their American equivalents, with similar habits, are known colloquially as 'yellowjackets'.

Four other species of **Vespula** are found in Europe, all very similar in appearance to the two common kinds. The red wasp *Vespula rufa* also nests underground, but the tree wasp *V. sylvestris* and the Norwegian wasp *V. norvegica* hang their nests in trees and bushes. Finally there is the cuckoo wasp *V. austriaca* whose queen enters the nest of a red wasp, kills some of the workers and supplants the queen. The parasitic invader's brood is reared by the red wasp workers, the offspring of the parasite consisting entirely of fertile males and females.

▽ *Lover of liquids – a wasp feeding. Adult wasps feed on nectar, fruit and tree sap.*

Fear-inflicting German wasp. Wasps usually sting only when annoyed or if their nest is approached.

Elaborate paper building

The history of a wasps' nest really begins in the autumn of the year previous to its construction, when the big queen wasps leave the nests where they were hatched, mate and then hide themselves, to pass the winter in hollow trees, sheds and attics. The queen finds a rough beam or piece of sacking, clamps her jaws onto a fibre and hangs dormant for six or seven months. She emerges in late spring and seeks a crack in the ground or an old mouse's hole running under a tree root. Just below this she digs out a chamber, removing the earth in her jaws. Then she flies repeatedly to and from a fence post or dead tree, each time bringing home a little pellet of paste made by rasping away the wood and moistening the resultant material with saliva. This substance is plastered on to the underside of the root, where it hardens to form a kind of cardboard or paper. A little curved canopy is fixed onto this foundation and a paper stalk is made, pointing down from the centre of the canopy. A cluster of hexagonal cells, also of paper, is then made round the stalk, with their open ends downward. The queen lays an egg in each then encloses this first comb in a bag of paper about as big as a golf ball, with a hole at its lower end.

Building a city

All this time the queen has been feeding on nectar. When the eggs hatch into small white larvae she divides her time between feeding them on the juices of chewed-up insects—they are growing and so require a protein diet—and adding more cells to the comb, enlarging the enclosing bag as she does so. By the time the larvae from the earliest eggs have passed through the pupal stage to produce the first workers, she may have added a storey to her house, built below the first and hanging by little stalks of paper. To make room for the growing nest the queen may have to excavate more earth and carry it away.

When the worker wasps, which are non-reproductive females, appear in quantity, they take over from the queen the job of extending and enlarging their home. New storeys are added, one below the other,

increasing to the maximum diameter of the nest and then decreasing again to give it a roughly spherical shape. Quantities of earth are removed by the workers and wood pulp is brought back for construction. The anchorage to the root is strengthened as the bulk and weight of the nest increases, and struts and stays are made between it and the surrounding earth. The queen stays at home, fed by her sexless daughters, who must also bring home animal food for all the growing larvae. As each cell is completed she places an egg in it until a population of as many as 5 000 wasps, or more in very big nests, is built up and maintained. The total number of the queen's offspring that hatch, live and die in the service of the nest throughout a summer may be five times this number.

Make do and mend

When complete the nest is a hollow sphere 8–9 in. wide, containing 6–10 horizontal combs which extend more or less right across it. The nest is comparable to a house built of bricks and mortar, yet there is a difference: although the nest has a basic external form, the inside is continually being nibbled away and repulped to be added, together with fresh pulp, to the outside and to the expanding combs, so the whole structure is constantly changing.

At the end of the summer a generation of males and functional females is produced. The latter are the queen wasps, similar to workers but larger; the males are about the same size as the workers but have much longer antennae. Eggs which produce workers and queens are always fertilised by spermatozoa from the store which the queen acquired at mating and keeps in her body. Males are produced from unfertilised eggs, from which the queen withholds sperm as she lays them. After mating the males soon die and the queens hibernate. At the end of the summer the workers become lazy and cease to maintain the economy of the nest, and they and the old queen die with the first frosts of autumn.

The workers feed on nectar and fruit juices and also accept drops of liquid exuded by the larvae. The larvae and queen are fed

by the workers on the juices of captured insects; wasps destroy great numbers of bluebottle flies.

The larva is a white legless grub and it maintains its position in the upside-down cell by pressing its body against the sides. When fully grown it closes the cell by spinning a papery cover across the mouth. During its life its excrement accumulates at the end of the intestine and is voided all at once in the last larval skin when it changes into a soft white pupa. The wasp emerges 3–4 weeks after the eggs were laid.

Guests and parasites

A hoverfly *Volucella* enters wasps' nests and lays its eggs without any interference from the wasps. Its curious prickly larvae play a useful part in the nest as scavengers, living in the midden below the nest, where dirt and dead bodies accumulate, and also entering vacated cells and cleaning out the deposits of excrement. This helps in making the cells available for re-use. The larvae of the moth *Aphomia sociella* also live as scavengers in wasps' nests. Late in the season, when the nest is 'running down', these invade the combs and devour the grubs and pupae. The larva of a rare beetle *Metoecus paradoxus* lives parasitically on the grubs of wasps in underground nests. It is at first an internal parasite (like the larva of an ichneumon or a tachina fly), however, it later emerges and devours its host. It is a remarkable fact that *Metoecus* apparently invades the nests of only the common wasp, never those of the German wasp, although to our eyes the two species look exactly the same.

The wasp's sting

This formidable weapon is really an ovipositor or egg-laying organ that has become transformed into a tiny hypodermic needle connected with a poison gland. The eggs are extruded from an opening at the base of it. Wasps sting if they are squeezed or restrained, as when they accidentally crawl inside someone's clothing. They also attack and sting if the nest is interfered with or even simply approached. The inhabitants of large, well-populated nests are more aggressive than those of small ones. The two main constituents of the venom are histamine and apitoxin. Old-fashioned remedies such as washing soda and ammonia were based on the mistaken idea that the venom is an acid of some kind, and they are ineffective except in giving reassurance. Genuine relief is given by the application of antihistamine to the site of the sting and by taking antihistamine tablets.

phylum	**Arthropoda**
class	**Insecta**
order	**Hymenoptera**
family	**Vespidae**

Barnacle

TH Huxley once described barnacles as animals that 'stood on their heads and kicked food into their mouths'. No description could better fit the basic features of barnacles.

They are common sea creatures which encrust rocks and the piles of piers, or foul the bottoms of ships. They are often mistaken for molluscs, as they bear a resemblance to limpets or mussels, and until the early part of the 19th century this was the general opinion of zoologists. Then, in 1829, a surgeon by the name of Vaughan Thompson, discovered that barnacles had free-swimming larvae that had the characters of crustaceans, so they were, in fact, related to amphipods, shrimps and lobsters.

The barnacle's head is firmly cemented to rock or timber by secretions from the first pair of antennae, or antennules. The body is enclosed in five limy plates that give the barnacle its superficially mollusc-like character, and within the cavity formed by these plates and the body lie the six pairs of forked limbs that are fringed with stiff hairs, or setae. These limbs, or cirri, equivalent to the limbs used for walking or swimming by other crustaceans, beat in unison, flicking out through a gap between the plates then withdrawing again, in a grasping action. Food is collected on the setae or is drawn in by the current set up by the beating of the cirri. This also circulates water with dissolved oxygen around the gills for respiration.

One million on every yard of shore

Acorn barnacles are the most numerous animals on the shore, clustering in groups on rocks and seaweeds. Their numbers on a shore on the Isle of Man have been estimated as being one thousand million in a stretch of about 1 000 yd, and figures of 30 000/sq yd are often quoted.

There are two major types of barnacle. The acorn barnacle at first sight resembles a small limpet but the shell is made up of several plates. The common barnacle of British shores *Balanus balanoides* attains a diameter of nearly $\frac{1}{2}$ in. while the American *Balanus nubilis* reaches a diameter of nearly 1 ft. Acorn barnacles extend well up the shore, as well as living on ships, and may be exposed to the air for a considerable time each tide. A muscle running across the body contracts to pull the plates together preventing the barnacle from losing water when the tide is out, and this is why there is the impression of the barnacle having a solid shell. When the tide floods back, the plates are swung open and the feathery limbs commence their continuous clutching of food. While the barnacles are exposed, however, they are not completely shut. There is a small hole left through which air can percolate. Oxygen then dissolves into the water in the cavity between the plates and is absorbed into the body.

△ *Acorn barnacles, **Balanus**, thrust their feathery feet through the mantle opening and withdraw them. in a grasping motion into their mouths. A shell of overlapping plates protects their bodies. (14 × life size).*

△ *Goose barnacles, **Lepas anatifera**, are arthropods which hang upside down on tough long stalks.*

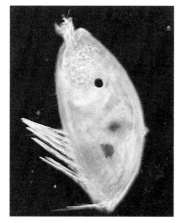

△ **Balanus** *nauplii and diatoms in plankton. After several moults it passes into the cypris stage. (100 × life size).*
▽ *Cypris, enclosed in bivalve shell, will soon attach itself by antennal discs on top of head. (100 × life size).*

The other type, the goose barnacles, hang from a tough stalk that is formed from the front part of the head. They are occasionally found thrown up on the beach but normally live on floating timbers, buoys and ships' bottoms. They are also found on flotsam such as bottles, lumps of oil etc. Some species form a mucous bubble that hardens to act as a float from which several individuals may hang.

Both acorn and goose barnacles may live on other animals such as turtles and whales. One acorn barnacle, *Coronula*, is commonly found on whale skin. It reaches a diameter of 3 in., and may in turn have several goose barnacles attached to it.

The habit of settling on metal plates and timbers makes barnacles a considerable pest as a layer of barnacles on a ship's bottom severely reduces its speed. From early times it has been the practice to ground ships and careen them, scraping the encrustations from below the waterline. A foul-bottomed ship is at a tactical disadvantage in action, while shipment of cargo becomes more expensive as the time of the voyage is increased. Nowadays fouling by barnacles is reduced by special paints that deter the larvae from settling.

Filter feeders

Like other sedentary animals, barnacles can do little more than wait for food to come to them. They generally settle where there is likely to be a current of water passing over them which will carry fresh food for the cirri to sweep up as it passes. As the cirri sweep back into the shell they fold over rather like a clutching hand so any prey they have is firmly trapped in their meshes. The food is then swept down towards the mouth where it is wiped off the cirri by the appendages surrounding the mouth. These also sort out edible from inedible particles. Edible matter is pushed into the mouth and the rest is pushed away.

Small creatures up to 1 mm long can be caught in the net of the cirri. These include the larvae of other crustacea and of other marine organisms. Small organisms such as single-celled planktonic plants are also caught and eaten, as are bacteria which are only 1/500 mm long. The bacteria are too small to be caught by the beating cirri but are swept into the cavity by the current they set up. Here they are trapped in the net formed by two more pairs of stationary cirri which lie by the mouth. These cirri have an extremely fine net of setae with meshes only one micron across.

Remarkable fertilisation

Barnacles are hermaphrodite, each individual having both male and female organs. Fertilisation takes place within the cavity formed by the plates and the body. The eggs are fertilised by sperm cells of a neighbouring individual which unrolls a 1½in. long penis through the opening of its own shell and protrudes it into one of its neighbours. Normally barnacles are found in dense groups and there would be no difficulty in finding a mate. Occasionally individual barnacles are found by themselves and in some cases they produce young, presumably by self-fertilisation.

Development of the egg takes about four months, but the larvae are not released from the parent until conditions are favourable for their growth, when the adults secrete a so-called 'hatching substance'. This is secreted when the adults are well fed, so that larvae will be released when there is an adequate supply of food for them too. In British waters this is in early

spring, at the time when the food source of minute planktonic plants is most abundant.

The newly-hatched larva is a minute creature called a nauplius. It has a round head tapering to a spiny tail and three pairs of limbs with which it rows itself around in a characteristically jerky fashion. The nauplius larva feeds and grows, moulting several times and eventually changing into a cypris larva, resembling a minute two-shelled shellfish like a mussel. The cypris larva has six pairs of limbs. It does not feed but drifts in with the incoming tide, feeling around with the first pair of limbs, or antennules, for a suitable place to settle. It searches around a rock or piece of timber, turning this way and that. As it reaches more suitable conditions it turns more frequently. This keeps it in the suitable place until it is almost turning in circles in the best place. Then it anchors itself by its antennules and rapidly changes into the adult form. The limy plates are secreted and the limbs change from walking legs to waving cirri.

Young barnacles feel for their future homes

Choosing a place to settle is very important, for once adult, a barnacle is unable to move for the rest of its life, which may be several years. It must find, therefore, a place with a rough surface in the shade and where there is a suitable current to bring it food. Some American species have been shown to need a current from ½–1 knot.

Experiments have shown that barnacles are stimulated to settle when they come into contact with other barnacles, or even with surfaces where other barnacles were once attached. Further research showed that the barnacles were secreting a protein called arthropodin. This is a substance secreted through the skins of crustaceans, such as crabs, and of insects. On reaching the surface of the skin the protein hardens. Some protein is left behind in a thin film on the attached surface when the barnacle dies, and it is for this film that the cypris searches with its antennules. Although the film may be too fine to see with a microscope, the cypris feels it rather than smells it. Somehow, it is able to detect the shape of the molecules of the protein.

This behaviour is important because if it can find some arthropodin, and barnacles can distinguish between arthropodin of their own and other species, the barnacle larva can settle in a place that is almost guaranteed to be a suitable environment because other barnacles have successfully settled there before. Moreover, it will mean that other barnacles will settle there, so ensuring cross-fertilisation.

phylum	**Arthropoda**
class	**Crustacea**
subclass	**Cirripedia**
order	**Thoracica**
genera & species	***Balanus balanoides*** *common British barnacle*
	B. nubilis *American barnacle*
	Lepas anatifera *goose barnacle*

Crayfish

The crayfish is a freshwater crustacean. It looks like a small lobster, 4 in. or more long, and coloured sandy yellow, green or dark brown. The head and thorax are covered with a single shell, or carapace, which ends in front in a sharp-pointed rostrum. Its eyes are compound and stalked. On its head is a pair of small antennules which are richly supplied with sense-organs, and a pair of long antennae, which are organs of touch. These have excretory organs at the base. The crayfish has a pair of strong jaws and two pairs of smaller accessory jaws, the maxillae. The second pair of maxillae drives water over 20 pairs of feathery gills on the bases of the thoracic limbs.

On the thorax there are three pairs of appendages, which are used to pass food to the jaws, a pair of stout pincers and four pairs of legs, which the crayfish uses to walk forward. The abdomen is divided into segments and has five pairs of limbs on its underside. The first pair are grooved in the males and are used to introduce sperm onto the female. The other four are swimmerets. The crayfish can swim speedily backwards with forward flicks of its abdomen, which ends in a fan-shaped tail. It does this to escape.

Crayfish in cooler waters

The two families of crayfish are confined almost entirely to temperate regions: the Astacidae in the northern hemisphere, the Parastacidae in the southern hemisphere. There are no crayfish in Africa, but they are present in Madagascar. There is none in the greater part of Asia, but they are found in Korea and the northern islands of Japan. The largest crayfish *Astacopsis franklinii* lives in Tasmania and may weigh up to 9 lb. Another large crayfish related to it is sold as Murray River Lobster in southeastern Australia. One of the Tasmanian crayfish, known as a land crab, habitually leaves the water and burrows in damp earth in forests. In the Mammoth Cave in Kentucky, in the United States, there are several crayfish living in the underground waters. They are colourless and blind; the eyes are gone, leaving only the stalks.

Naturalized aliens

Only one crayfish *Potamobius pallipes* is native to Britain. It is known as the white claw. A larger European crayfish *Astacus fluviatilis*, reared on farms especially in France, has been introduced into the Thames, and is known as the red claw. An American species, introduced into Germany, has become established there. The three species have similar habits. They live in rivers and lakes, especially those with hard water which contains the lime needed for their shell. They feed mainly at night, resting by day in burrows in the mud or under stones, but can sometimes be seen moving about by day.

They eat smaller aquatic animals such as insect larvae, snails, worms and tadpoles, and a small amount of plant food. In the Mississippi Valley they graze on rice during the night. This infuriates the local farmers who regard them as pests.

Unusual breeding habits

Crayfish mate in the autumn. The male turns the female over and sheds milt through the first pair of abdominal appendages onto her abdomen, where it sticks. The female then goes into a burrow to lay her hundred or so eggs. These become attached to bristles on her swimmerets where they are fertilised by contact with the milt. The eggs hatch the following spring. Unusual for a crustacean there is no larval stage. The newly-hatched crayfish are transparent, and tiny replicas of the adults. They remain attached for some time to the female's swimmerets, which they grasp with their claws.

Life and death in crayfish

In many parts of the world, crayfish are considered a delicacy. Sometimes they are eaten raw although this can prove to be hazardous, because crayfish carry a fluke larva. If this is swallowed with a crayfish it will migrate through the wall of the gut to the lungs, where it matures to the adult parasite. In time the adult lays eggs which are ejected with the sputum. From the eggs hatch first stage larvae which infest snails. The cycle of parasitic infection is completed if a snail is eaten by a crayfish.

One interesting aspect of the life of a crayfish is that it grows by periodic moults. This is common knowledge and is often stated in books on natural history. Most crustaceans and insects grow like this. But although it is always stated simply, the process itself is complex. In crayfish it takes place in four stages. First the calcium salts, the chalky matter in the old shell, are taken back into the blood, ready to be laid again in the new shell being formed beneath the old one. Then the old shell, or such as remains of it, now merely a tough cuticle, is shed and the body takes up water and swells. Then the calcium salts are laid down in the new cuticle and this takes time to harden.

The moult of a crayfish takes 6 hours. During this time the crayfish fasts and stays in hiding. It is a very dangerous period for it; not only is it vulnerable especially to enemies, but it is also in danger from the many attendant difficulties of the process itself. It has only recently been realized, in fact, that many crayfish die during this complicated moulting process.

Preparing to carve: a freshwater crayfish about to feed off a male stickleback.

phylum	**Arthropoda**
class	**Crustacea**
order	**Decapoda**
families	**Astacidae**
	Parastacidae
genera	*Astacus fluviatilis*
& species	*Potamobius pallipes*
	others

Hermit crab

Hermit crabs live in abandoned sea snail shells, and in all of them the form of the body is modified accordingly. The banana-shaped abdomen, protected in its 'hermitage', is soft and curves to the right to fit the inside of the snail shell. The front end of the body has the hard covering typical of crabs and lobsters and the right claw, larger than the left, is used to close the entrance of the shell. The two pairs of legs behind the claw are used in walking, but the next two pairs are small and are used to grip the shell. The last pair of limbs on the abdomen, which in a lobster form part of the tail fan, are sickle-shaped and used for holding onto the central column of the shell. There are swimmerets

on the left side of the abdomen only.

*The robber or coconut crab **Birgus latro** of the South Sea Islands, is a land-living hermit crab several pounds in weight and 6 in. across. The adult has lost the shell-dwelling habit and although the abdomen is still twisted it has a hard covering and is kept tucked under the thorax. The stone crabs **Lithodes,** found off the coasts of Britain, although looking like true crabs, show their hermit crab ancestry in their small asymmetrical abdomen.*

Strange houses

The common hermit crab of European seas is the soldier crab *Pagurus bernhardus*. Normally only the young are found on the shore, their red and yellow front ends projecting from winkle, topshell or dog whelk shells.

They are nimble despite their burdens and are well-protected from the pounding of waves and from drying up when the tide is out. The older ones reach a length of 5 in., live in deeper water and occupy the larger shells of common and hard whelks. On tropical coasts live semi-terrestrial hermit crabs of the genus *Coenobita*. These usually occupy ordinary snail shells, but East Indian coenobites have been seen wearing such odd substitutes as joints of bamboo, coconut shells and even a broken oil lamp chimney. *C. diogenes* of Bermuda lives in shells that are in fact fossil or subfossil, since they be-

*The face of a squatter: hermit crab **Pagurus megistos.** The massive right claw acts as a 'door' when the crab retreats into its shell. The legs are adapted to the crab's home-changing habits. Only the two pairs behind the claws are used for walking; the rest grip the shell.*

longed to a snail *Livona pica* now extinct in Bermuda. *Pylopagurus* is a hermit crab whose shell becomes encrusted with a bryozoan (moss animal). The shell is said to be dissolved leaving only the moss animal's chalky skeleton, which cloaks the crab and grows with it.

Another hermit crab *Pylocheles*, found in deep water in the Indian Ocean, lives in pieces of bamboo. Its abdomen is straight. *Xylopargus* of the West Indies lives at 600–1200 ft in hollow cylinders of wood. The rear end of its body is shaped to make a kind of stopper. Some marine hermit crabs have less mobile homes. They live in holes in coral or sponge. This is a habit to some extent shared by lobsters and perhaps indicates the origin of the hermit crab's way of life. The coconut crab makes burrows at the bases of coconut trees and lines them with coconut husks.

Feeding on sago and coconut

Hermit crabs are mainly omnivorous scavengers, tearing up food with their smaller left claws and transferring it to their mouths. *P. bernhardus* also feeds on tiny animals and plants, tossed with sand and debris between its mouth parts with its left claw. Some other hermit crabs can filter particles from the water with bristles on the antennae. Every so often they wipe the antennae across the mouth to take the food collected. The land-living coenobites often climb bushes for plant food and may even attack young birds. The robber crab is said to hammer in the eye-holes of coconuts, but probably feeds mainly on coconuts already cracked open in falling from the tree. It also eats carrion, fruit and sago pith. It, too, is a climber, and can scale the trunks of sago palms and other trees. A local belief is that when the robber is up a tree it can be caught by tying a girdle of grass high up round the trunk. When the crab comes down and its body touches this it lets go, under the impression it has reached the ground, and falls and is stunned. In fact, it takes more than a fall of this kind to stun the crab.

Breeding and growth

P. bernhardus breeds through much of the year and females with 10 000–15 000 dark violet eggs attached to the swimmerets on their abdomen are to be found at most times. Such crabs, in berry as they are called when laden with eggs, come partially out of their shell from time to time and fan their swimmerets to aerate the eggs. As the larvae hatch, moulting at the same time to become zoea larvae, the mother crab sits partly out of her shell and gently wipes the swimmerets with a brush of bristles on her small fourth pair of legs. The tiny shrimp-like zoea larvae shed their skins four times, growing each time, but at the fourth moult the young hermit crab first seeks a snail shell for a home. This stage lasts 4–5 days. Sexual maturity is not reached for a year or more. The sexes differ externally only in the form of the swimmerets which have differing functions, but in many species the male is larger than the female.

Periodically, the growing hermit crab sheds its external skeleton. A split appears on the abdomen and the crab wriggles out of its old skin. As the hermit crab outgrows

△ *Free food and transport in exchange for what? Hermit crabs often pick and 'plant' anemones on their backs. It has recently been shown that this gives protection from octopuses, their main enemy.*

its 'home', this must be replaced with a larger one. The crab examines the new shell all over for several minutes with its claws, then, if it seems good enough and the coast seems clear, it hurriedly transfers its abdomen from the old shell to the new. Sometimes one hermit crab may try to drive another from its shell.

The 'terrestrial' hermit crabs *Coenobita* and the coconut crab *Birgus* must visit the sea to hatch their eggs, for their larvae are marine. Though the adult coconut crab does not carry a shell, the young stages coming ashore do so.

Strange partnerships

Like any hard object lying on the sea bed, the shell of a hermit crab tends to become encrusted with weed, sponges, barnacles and hydroids. Certain sea anemones, however, regularly associate with hermit crabs and form close partnerships with them. Large specimens of the common *P. bernhardus* often carry the anemone *Calliactis parasitica* on their shells, sometimes several of them. As the hermit crab feeds, the anemone sweeps the ground with its outstretched tentacles and gathers fragments left by the crab. The hermit crab may sometimes benefit from bits of food caught by the anemone. Another hermit crab, Prideaux's hermit crab *Pagurus prideauxi*, light reddish-brown in colour and 2 in. long, regularly carries the anemone *Adamsia palliata* which, unlike *Calliactis*, is to be found on hermit crab shells and nowhere else. The basal disc of the anemone wraps tightly around the shell,

completely enclosing it. As the crustacean grows, so does the anemone, adding to the effective capacity of the shell. Thus the shell does not have to be replaced. The mouth of the anemone, in this case, lies just behind that of the hermit crab. Anemones are armed with stinging cells and these help protect the hermit crab, discouraging, for instance, the attacks of octopus and squid. *P. prideauxi* is immune to the poisons of the stinging cells which can be fatal to other hermit crabs. *Paguropsis typica* goes a stage farther than *Pagurus prideauxi* in carrying *Anemonia mammilifera* without a snail shell. Another species of hermit crab *Parapagurus pilosi-manus* has large eyes in spite of the fact that it lives in water too deep for light to penetrate: it has been suggested that it finds its way about by light from the phosphorescent anemone which cloaks it.

phylum	**Arthropoda**
class	**Crustacea**
subclass	**Malacostraca**
order	**Decapoda**
family	**Paguridae**
genus & species	***Pagurus bernhardus*** ***P. prideauxi***
family	**Coenobitidae**
genera & species	***Coenobita*** ***Birgus latro***

Peripatus

Peripatus is one of the most extraordinary animals living today. A relic from the past, it was once thought of as a link between the soft-bodied ringed worms, such as the earthworm, and the hard-bodied arthropods, which include insects, spiders and crustaceans.

Its body is rather worm-like, tapering towards the hind end. It is 1 – 3 in. long but can be extended or contracted, and is sinuous in movement. The colour of peripatus is very variable, ranging from dark slate to reddish-brown in the various species, and there is usually a dark stripe down the back. The skin is dry and velvety to the touch and there are 20 or so pairs of short baggy legs each ending in a pair of hooks and ringed like the body. There is a pair of flexible antennae on the head with an eye at the base of each. The eyes are simple although each has a lens. They are directed outwards and upwards and probably do no more than distinguish between light and darkness. The sensory hairs clothing the antennae and most of the body are organs of touch and taste.

*Going for a stroll: a peripatus from New Zealand **Peripatoides novaezealandiae**.*

Must live in damp places

Peripatus is dependent on moist conditions, being found only in damp forests in South Africa, Australasia and South America. It lives under stones, rotting wood, the bark of fallen trees and similar damp places, being unable to withstand drying. In a dry atmosphere it will lose a third of its weight in less than 4 hours and will dry up twice as fast as an earthworm, and 40 times as fast as a smooth-skinned caterpillar its own size. The cause lies in its breathing system. An insect breathes through branching tubes or tracheae. Because the openings are few there is little loss of water and, moreover, there is an efficient mechanism for closing the openings when necessary. Peripatus has unbranched breathing tubes so it needs far more of them, with an opening to each tube, which means a rapid loss of water from the body when the surroundings are dry. As a result peripatus is found in 'islands', damp localities separated from other colonies by dry country.

Sticky threads for defence

The moment peripatus is disturbed it throws out one or two jets of a milky-white fluid from little nozzles or oral papillae, on the head, one either side of the mouth. On contact with the air the fluid solidifies immediately into sticky beaded threads of slime 3 – 12 in. long. The fluid is in reservoirs, one each side of the head, shaped like the rubber teat of an eye-dropper. Although the threads stick to one's fingers they do not stick to the velvety skin of peripatus itself, but insects and other small animals become entangled in them.

This entangling seems to be accidental because the threads serve more as a defence. Their food is mainly small insects such as termites and they also eat other small animals such as woodlice.

Haphazard mating

The mating of peripatus can only be described as casual. The male places capsules containing sperms on the female, apparently at random since he will place them even on her legs. He may place them at times on another male. For a long time it was not known how the sperms reached the ova. Then it was found that white blood corpuscles in the female body migrate to the skin immediately beneath a capsule and break through it by digesting the cells of the skin. At the same time the lower wall of the capsule breaks and the sperms enter the female's blood stream and find their way to an ovary. There in large numbers they force their way through the wall of the ovary. If an immature female receives sperms the young egg cells feed on them and grow for a year before they are ready to be fertilised by a second mating. Except in a few species which lay eggs the embryos develop in the uterus taking in nourishment from the mother through its walls. In one South American species special tissues are formed, making a kind of placenta, to pass food from the mother's body to the growing embryos. Development takes 13 months and as young are born each year there is one month in each year when a female is carrying two sets of embryos, one just beginning to develop, the other nearly ready to be born.

Evolutionary bridge?

The theory of evolution, in which it is assumed life began in water, requires two main invasions of the land. One, by the vertebrates, meant a change from gill-breathing to lung-breathing and indications of how this may have taken place are seen, for example, in the lungfishes, the coelacanth and the various newts and salamanders. Among the fossils, also, there is an almost complete series showing how this came about. The other invasion is that which brought the invertebrates on land, and the most important change was that from the aquatic ringed worms, such as the fanworm, and the crustaceans, leading to insects and spiders. If one were asked to draw a hypothetical animal to bridge the gap between the ringed worms and the insects, one could not fail to draw something very like peripatus. Moreover, in its internal structure as well as its outward appearance, this animal looks like the forerunner of both millipedes and centipedes, and they in turn look like forerunners of modern insects. We know from fossils that insects, millipedes and centipedes, in the form we know them today, were already in existence 400 million years ago, so any ancestors linking the two must have been in existence even earlier. It is of interest therefore to find there is a fossil *Xenusion* in the rocks of over 500 million years ago that looks almost the same as peripatus. It is little more than a rusty coloured stain in a piece of limestone rock, yet its shape and the structure of its body and legs can be seen clearly enough to leave little doubt that the peripatus living today and the *Xenusion* of 500 million or more years ago could be closely related. From it or from animals very like *Xenusion* began the line which, through numerous changes, led to the millipedes, centipedes and insects, while another line of descent was continued, almost unchanged, in peripatus.

Theory devastated

This represents the views held a few years ago. It reads almost like a scientist's dream, for everything falls so neatly into place. Then two things happened. First, fresh fossils have come to light from Australia, southwest Africa and England, which are clearly related to *Xenusion* but are much more complete. Together, this fresh evidence leaves little doubt that this supposed missing link between worms and insects was, in fact, a near relative of the sea pens, of the phylum Cnidaria, that are related to corals and jellyfishes.

The second event was hardly less devastating to the cherished idea that peripatus is a worm-insect, a bridge between the Annelida, and the Arthropoda (insects, spiders, crustaceans, millipedes and centipedes). Dr. Sidney Manton, the leading authority on the Onychophora, leaves us in no doubt that in its structure, mode of development from egg to adult and in its movements, peripatus is wholly arthropodan. Although it is undoubtedly primitive in many of its features, such as the simple head, the long series of similar limbs and, in certain features of its internal anatomy, peripatus is utterly unconnected with the ringed worms.

phylum	**Arthropoda**
class	**Onychophora**
genus & species	***Peripatus capensis*** **P. moseleyi**, *others*

Index

Note: page numbers in italics *denote illustrations*

Acknowledgements

This book is adapted from *Purnell's Encyclopedia of Animal Life*, published in the United States under the title of *International Wild Life*.

AFA: F.G.H. Allen; E.H. Herbert, Geoffrey Kinns, A.C. Wheeler; J. Allan Cash; Heather Angel; Toni Angermayer; R. Apfelbach; Atlas: Drogesco; Australian News and Inflormation Bureau; M.E. Bacchus; Barnabys; Bavaria: Sune Berkeman, W. Harstrick, Helmut Heinpel, B. Leidmann, W. Rohdich, H.W. Silvester, A. Sycholt; S. Beaufoy; S. Bisserot; R. Boardman; K. Boldt; Michael Boorer; British Antarctic Survey; British Museum, Natural History; Alice Brown; Fred Bruemmer; Ralph Buchsbaum; Kent Burgess; Jane Burton; Robert Burton; H.R. Bustard; Colin Butler; N.A. Callow; Camera Press; Carolina Biological Supply Co; James Carr; Centre de Documentation du CNRS; A. Christiansen; John Clegg; F. Collet; Dolly Connelly; J.A.L. Cooke; Gene Cox; Micro-colour Int.; Ben Cropp; Gerald Cubitt; Cyr Colour Agency; Peter David; W.T. Davidson; R.B. Davies; T. Dennett; Colin Doeg; G.T. Dunger; Herman Eisenbeiss; Andre Fatras; Douglas Faulkner; Forestry, Fish & Game Commission, USA; Harry & Claudy Frauca; J.B. Free; Carl Gans; G.S. Giacomelli; John Goddard; E. Grave; Hans Gundel; W.D. Haacke; H. Hansen; R.A. Harris & K. R. Duff; Bruce Hayward; Robert C. Hermes; Peter Hill; M.J. Hirons; E.S. Hobson; W. Hoflinger; E.O. Hoppe; Eric Hosking; Chris Howell-Jones; David Hughes; G.E. Hyde; Jacana: Brosset, A.R. Devez, J. & M. Fievel, Gerard, P. Summ, B. Tollu, J.P. Varin, P. & C. Vasselet, J. Vasserot, Bel G. Vienne, A. Visage; Roy Jarris; Michael Johns; Palle Johnsen; Peter Johnson; Keystone; G.E. Kirkpatrick; E.F. Kilian; H. Klingel; A.B. Klots; A. Kress; H.V. Lacey; Yves Lanceau; Leonard Lee Rue III; Henning Lender; D.B. Lewis; E. Lindsey; H.A.E Lucas; Wolfgang Lummer; Michael Lyster; Kendall McDonald; Malcolm McGregor; Steve McGutcheon; Mansell; Aldo Margiocco; Marineland, Florida, USA; John Markham; Meston; Walter Miles; Carl Mills; Lorus & Margery Milne; G. Mundey; N. Myers; Natural History Museum; K.B. Newman; NHPA: Andrew Anderson, F. Baillie, Anthony Bannister, F. Blackburn, Joe Blossom, N.A. Callow, J.M. Clayton, Stephen Dalton, E. Elkan, C. McDermot, W.J.C. Murray, Hugh Newman, Brian O'Donnell, Graham Pizzey, Gordon F. Woods; Okapia; Oxford Scientific Films; Ram Panjabi; Klaus Paysan; B. Pengilley; Photographic Library of Australia; Photo Library Inc; Photo Res: Des Bartlett, Jane Burton, Bob Campbell, C. Ciapanna, Jack Dermid, Peter Jackson, Russ Kinne, N. Myers, R.T. Peterson, D.C. Pike, Masood Quarishy, Dick Robinson, H.W. Silvester, Vincent Serventy, James Simon, Tomanek, Simon Trevor, Howard E. Uible, Joe Van Wormer; Graham Pizzey; Joyce Pope; Popperfoto; Roebild; Root/Okapia; G. Puppell; Walter Scheilhauer; Friedel Schox; Philippa Scott; Gunter Senfft; M. Severn; Shell Photograph; H. Shrempp; E. Slater; M.F. Soper; South African Tourist Corporation: A.J. Southward; Helmut Stellrucht; W.M. Stephens; John Tashjian at Arizona Sonard Desert Museum, Fort Worth Zoo, San Diego Zoo, Steinhart Aquarium, Tacoma Aquarium, Vancouver Aquarium; Ron Taylor; Ronald Thompson; Sally Anne Thompson; Time Life Inc; William Vandivert; John Visser; J.J. Ward; P. Ward; John Warham; Constance P. Warner; A.N. Warren; Birgit Webb; We-Ha; Alison Wilson; D.P. Wilson; M.A. Wilson; Gene Wolfsheimer; John Norris Wood; Zoological Society, London.